The Price of Federalism

A TWENTIETH CENTURY FUND BOOK

The Price of Federalism

Paul E. Peterson

THE BROOKINGS INSTITUTION
Washington, D.C.

About Brookings

The Brookings Institution is a private nonprofit organization devoted to research, education, and publication on important issues of domestic and foreign policy. Its principal purpose is to bring knowledge to bear on current and emerging policy problems. The Institution was founded on December 8, 1927, to merge the activities of the Institute for Government Research, founded in 1916, the Institute of Economics, founded in 1922, and the Robert Brookings Graduate School of Economics, founded in 1924.

The Institution maintains a position of neutrality on issues of public policy. Interpretations or conclusions in Brookings publications should be understood to be solely those of the authors.

Copyright © 1995

THE TWENTIETH CENTURY FUND, INC.

41 East 70th Street, New York, N.Y. 10021

Library of Congress Cataloging-in-Publication data:

Peterson, Paul E.
The price of federalism / Paul E. Peterson
    p.   cm.
Includes bibliographical references and index.
ISBN 0-8157-7024-3 (cl : alk. paper). — ISBN 0-8157-7023-5 (pa : alk. paper)
    1. Federalism—United States.   2. Federalism.   I. Title.
JK325.P477   1995
321.02'0973—dc20   95-13773
                                                      CIP

9 8 7 6 5 4

The paper used in this publication meets the minimum requirements of the American National Standard for Information Sciences—Permanence of paper for Printed Library Materials, ANSI Z39.48-1984

Set in Garamond Book

Composition by Harlowe Typography Inc.,
Cottage City, Maryland

Printed by R. R. Donnelley & Sons Co.
Harrisonburg, Virginia

To
John and Sarah

The Twentieth Century Fund sponsors and supervises timely analyses of economic policy, foreign affairs, and domestic political issues. Not-for-profit and nonpartisan, the Fund was founded in 1919 and endowed by Edward A. Filene.

Foreword

Seen in the perspective of 220 years of American history, the balance between the federal government and the states appears to involve the relentless accretion of power, resources, and responsibility to the national level. For any given generation of policymakers, however, this sense of inevitability evaporates in the heat of their immediate struggles over who does what and, perhaps even more importantly, which level of government pays the bills. The phenomenon is particularly apparent now as a noisy, populist-like reaction to the trend toward a larger federal presence dominates domestic politics. But sadly, the poetry appropriate for a constitutional debate is being swamped by the rough political prose of the mid-1990s.

The United States has the lowest total tax burden in the industrialized world; it is lower still if one focuses on revenues collected by the national government. It also has, among the modernized nations, the most decentralized government structure. America still lacks the extensive national social welfare structure that is the normal pattern, for example, throughout Western Europe. By Old World standards, we also have limited old age, retirement, health, and unemployment benefits. But a man from Mars arriving in the midst of the current debate in Washington might well imagine that a great revolution was necessary to reverse the excesses of some uniquely powerful and oppressive central state mechanism. The charge in Washington is to roll back just about every area of public activity. Even moderates fret that unless we do so the nation will be bankrupt at some point early in the next century.

Understanding why our politics has this special character is not easy, although the continuation of race and economic inequality as central domestic issues no doubt is at the heart of the explanation. Still, the ongoing debate would be immeasurably clarified if we shared a common comprehension of the facts of our governmental division of responsibility and financing. Perhaps the most important contribution of the pages that follow is that they provide significant elements of that factual context.

Paul Peterson, Henry Lee Shattuck Professor of Government at Harvard University, demonstrates that the lion's share of the federal government's domestic resources is directed toward redistribution— caring for sick, poor, and needy Americans—rather than education, infrastructure, and other investments intended to enhance the nation's economy. Conversely, the states devote greater effort toward economic development as opposed to redistribution. Peterson views these circumstances as benign, asserting that both the federal and state governments are concentrating their efforts on what they do best. Although some may argue that there are compelling reasons why federal efforts to enhance economic growth are at least as valuable as redistributive activities in enhancing living standards for all Americans, Peterson brings fresh insight and information to the debate over federalism.

Unfortunately, the political debate over these issues seems unlikely to follow any rational pattern. As this book went to press, the U.S. House of Representatives was voting for huge cuts in federal spending on both redistributive and economic development activities. Few legislators were discussing the relative merits of, say, Amtrak as opposed to the Supplemental Nutrition Program for Women, Infants, and Children. At the same time, the Food Stamps program won a reprieve not because of its proven success but because farm state representatives were unwilling to incur the wrath of constituents who profit from the sale of their agricultural products to bearers of federal food vouchers. Today, political prose is devolving into simple-minded doggerel.

The Fund has published many works over the years that address the division of responsibilities between the federal and state governments, especially with regard to specific policy issues, most recently *Turning Promises Into Peformance: The Management Challenge of Implementing Workfare* by Richard P. Nathan. Currently, the Fund is supporting a series of essays, "The New Federalist Papers," that address the fundamental structure of our representative democracy in an era of substantial constitutional debate.

Like all arguments about whether the contemporary mix of government is appropriate, there are sure to be disagreements about Professor Peterson's conclusions. If, however, this work helps to elevate the substantive quality of the debate, it will do a great deal of good. America, regrettably, is particularly ill served by the superficial and ultimately corrosive character of the assault on government and public officials at all levels. Let us at least try to disagree about reality and not fight our politics in a world of shadows.

Richard C. Leone, *President*
THE TWENTIETH CENTURY FUND
March 1995

Author's Preface

Partisan debate and ideological formulations have clouded public understanding of the role to be played by federalism in American government. Many conservatives predisposed against governmental action think the national government should all but abdicate responsibility for domestic policy. Many liberals in favor of a more active government think almost all tasks can be better performed by the national government.

These differences have been accentuated by the surprise Republican victories in the congressional elections of 1994. Since the elections, Republican leaders have called for the devolution of a broad range of governmental activities to state and local governments. They have proposed drastic cuts in the national government's involvement in education, transportation, manpower training, housing, energy, and crime control. Under their tutelage, Congress has passed a law forbidding the imposition of additional unfunded mandates on state and local governments. In a particularly controversial decision, the House of Representatives has voted to transform a long-standing welfare entitlement program into a block grant over which state and local governments would have great discretion. This decision to decentralize welfare policy is politically enticing at a time when those in need of welfare assistance are widely perceived as undeserving. Politicians in Washington can avoid blame for the welfare mess by handing over to lower tiers of government the obligation to clean it up.

The stance taken by Republican policymakers in 1995 is almost the mirror image of the one taken a generation ago by Democratic Presidents John Kennedy and Lyndon Johnson and, ironically enough, by Republican Richard Nixon. At that time almost every problem in society was deemed worthy of attention by the national government. The biggest changes occurred in social welfare policy. Congress expanded social security, enacted the medicare and medicaid programs, instituted food stamps, created a plethora of housing programs, mandated the education of the disabled, and extended a wide variety of new social services to the poor. But the changes were hardly confined to welfare policy. The national government also became heavily involved in policy arenas long thought to be the exclusive prerogative of local officials, including mass transit, road construction, metric learning, sewage treatment, police training, summer recreation programs, and historic preservation. Federal funding of local infrastructure was particularly attractive to a professionalized Congress increasingly filled with members eager to gain reelection by claiming credit for bringing home some bacon. It was difficult to find a problem for which policymakers did not have a Washington-based solution.

In the study that follows, I will show that each of the two political parties has been half right. Republican leaders are correct in attempting to give back to states and localities custody over basic public services and other programs that foster economic development. When control over these policies is decentralized to state and local governments, the country enjoys a more efficient and productive public sector. But Democratic leaders who defend national direction of social programs are correct in concluding that redistributive policy is the job of the national government. In a society in which businesses and workers are highly mobile, state and local governments cannot finance welfare and other redistributive policies. The very competition among states and localities that enhances local capacity to facilitate economic development destroys their ability to fund high-quality social programs. Any state that provides effective programs for the needy becomes a welfare magnet that attracts more poor people from other parts of the country. To avoid becoming a magnet, each state is forced to cut its welfare benefits, inducing among the states a race to the bottom.

Pessimists might think that the federal system is becoming increasingly misaligned. Since members of Congress have an incentive to take credit for pork barrel projects, one might expect inappropriate national funding of developmental projects to increase. Conversely, members have every reason to duck responsibility for welfare spending and strong political incentives to ask lower levels of government to bear the cost of other social programs. But the findings reported in the pages that follow suggest that the opposite has happened. Despite the fact that each party is only half right in its understanding of the nature of the federal system, the overall direction of public policy has been moving in a quite sensible direction. With national power divided between the two parties over much of the past twenty years, bargains have had to be struck. More often than not, the compromises have made sense, and the price of American federalism has fallen.

Signs are abundant that this era may be coming to an end. The price of American federalism, never trivial, may once again be on the increase. This book is written in the hope that a better understanding of the logic of the federal system will help keep social costs to a minimum.

I am grateful to the Twentieth Century Fund for encouraging me to try to address these issues by providing the bulk of the support for the research reported below. The project also received support from the Ford Foundation, the La Follette Institute of Public Affairs at the University of Wisconsin, and the Henry Grossman Fund of the Center for American Political Studies at Harvard University.

Jerome Maddox is coauthor of chapter 6. He, Frederick M. Hess, Don S. Lee, Chad Noyes, John Peterson, and Kira Sanbonmatsu assisted with data collection, entry, verification, and statistical analyses. D. Stephen Voss assisted and provided technical expertise in conjunction with the out-of-sample prediction reported in chapter 5. Alison Kommer and Sarah Peterson provided valuable staff assistance.

Derek Bok, Thomas R. Dye, Morris Fiorina, David C. King, Harding C. Noblitt, Barry G. Rabe, Martin Shefter, Michael Wiseman, the staff of the Twentieth Century Fund, and several anonymous readers commented on all or portions of earlier versions of the manuscript. Their suggestions have improved the manuscript. Any remaining errors are my own.

Contents

Tables

Figures

The Price of
Federalism

1

The Evolution of Modern Federalism

*All Americans have long been agreed that the only possible
form of government for their country is a Federal one. . . . But
regarding the nature of the Federal tie that ought to exist there
have been keen and frequent controversies. . . .*
Lord James Bryce, *The American Commonwealth*

"Turn your face to the great West," said Horace Greeley, "and there
build up a home and fortune."[1] Accepting his advice, generations of
restless and ambitious Americans moved westward hoping to find a
chance for a better life. Many found in California an "El Dorado with
its beaches and mountains, its sunshine, its majestic forests, its fountain
of eternal economic opportunity."[2] They built a state that became the
envy of its neighbors and the near equivalent of a nation.

The state's economy was nearly recession proof. Its bond rating was
as golden as the early afternoon sun. In 1987 the state of California
even gave taxpayers a rebate: so much excess money had accumulated
in the treasury that it seemed best to give it back to the voters. Proud
of their land and the bountiful world erected thereon, Californians
exhibited an open self-confidence not quite duplicated elsewhere. "Californians are a race of people," O. Henry said. "They are not merely
inhabitants of a state."[3]

Hardly anything in the state's history could have prepared its residents for the economic and fiscal disasters that would befall them in
the latter part of 1990. "California had not gone through many economic downturns before," said one local businessman. "We had assumed we were on the cutting edge and were always dabbling with the

new. . . . When everything is going well, you do not challenge your assumptions."[4] Only the oldest of residents, together with readers of John Steinbeck's *Grapes of Wrath*, could recall a California unable to pay its bills.

The 1991 Fiscal Crisis

Yet that is what happened on July 1, 1992, when the once Golden State asked vendors to accept registered warrants in lieu of dollar bills.[5] The flirt with bankruptcy had come quickly. The budgetary shortfall doubled from an estimated $7 billion in January 1991 to more than $14 billion by May 1992. With the deficit constituting as much as 25 percent of the state's operating budget,[6] the state's AAA bond rating slipped to a level no higher than that of the state of Arkansas.

The immediate cause was a concatenation of simultaneous, mostly unanticipated economic reverses. Few expected the national recession to persist into the first half of 1992. Few realized that a sudden end to the cold war would decimate the California defense industry, which accounted for 20 percent of the nation's military procurement. Few understood that the housing and office boom of the 1980s, driven by tax shelters and Japanese investments, invited a real estate bust when the shelters disappeared and Japanese financiers returned home.

If the California debt crisis was precipitated by fast-moving changes in the California economy, the reverses brought to light underlying rigidities in the state's governmental structure. Some of the difficulties were peculiar to California. The state's regulatory climate was more restrictive—and more bureaucratized—than most other states'. Its workmen's compensation program was poorly designed. Local governments were restricted from raising property taxes by the infamous Proposition 13 approved by California voters in 1978. Without needed monies, local investments in schools and public infrastructure fell.

But as the state's fiscal crisis deepened, many saw in California a metaphor for more general problems in American federalism. It was one thing for New York City to lurch toward bankruptcy in 1974. New York was regarded as little more than a cross between Sodom and Gomorrah, a city only Batman could rescue. Conventional wisdom declared its fiscal policies wanton, its taxes excessive, its politics corrupt, its workers overly protected by politically powerful unions, its administrators caught in a hopeless bureaucratic web, and its social service delivery system lavish to a fault. When New York asked for a federal bailout, President Gerald Ford did not tell the city to "Drop Dead," as a *New York Daily News* headline implied. But few of those who had not taken a bite of the Apple would have cared if the president had.

California was another matter. If New York was the past, California was the future. If fiscal disaster could overtake California, it might happen anywhere.

Signs that California's problems were endemic to American federalism soon surfaced. Local government in California (and most other states) had suffered steep cuts in federal and state aid. California's medicaid program was growing at double-digit rates, in part because the national government was asking California (and other states) to expand the number of services covered by the program. In 1993 Governor Pete Wilson asked the national government for $1.7 billion to fund services to immigrants that Congress had imposed upon California (and other states) by passing unfunded mandates.[7]

Nor was the fiscal crisis of 1991 confined to California. Connecticut was attempting to close a budgetary gap that amounted to 37 percent of its general fund expenditure. New York had a 10 percent deficit. In April 1991 thirty of the fifty states were known to be on the verge of running in the red.[8] For all state and local governments, short- and long-term debt had shot up by over $55 billion in just one year. In the four years between 1987 and 1991 debts acquired by state and local governments had increased by nearly $200 billion, or over 27 percent. Short-term debt had escalated by nearly 38 percent.[9]

These deficits may seem modest by comparison with deficits of $200 billion to $300 billion that the national government was accumulating annually in the late 1980s and early 1990s. But state and local governments lack the national government's power to print money. Any debt acquired by state and local governments must be borrowed from investors; if a state borrows too much money, financiers may simply refuse to lend more. State and local governments risk bankruptcies that the national government can avoid simply by printing additional dollars.

The California crisis thus poses a more general question: Is the modern federal system beginning to exact too high a price? Is the national government shirking its responsibilities? Is it asking states and localities to do too much? Is it not giving states and localities enough help? Are state and local governments under political pressure to assume responsibilities they cannot afford? Are they evading duties they need to perform?

Or was the crisis of 1991 simply a temporary phenomenon? After all, between 1987 and 1991 the new indebtedness of state and local governments constituted a gain of only 0.3 percent of GNP (from 15.8 to 16.1 percent). By 1994 revenue from the state sales tax in many states was reported to be increasing at double-digit rates, state coffers were reported to be "swelling with revenue," states were restoring budget cuts and worker salaries, and "nearly half the states" were said to "have enacted election-year tax cuts." Even California's fiscal picture was characterized as having improved from "disastrous" to merely "severe."[10] Are budgetary crises experienced in California and elsewhere simply political mechanisms by which a federal system self-corrects? Recessions are times when businesses eliminate waste and reallocate resources to more productive activities. Are recessions also times when governments put their houses in order?

Answers to these and other questions about the future of American federalism tumbled onto the national agenda with the election of a Republican Congress in 1994. Republican leaders have called for cutbacks in a wide range of federal grant-in-aid programs—from transportation and crime control to food stamps and welfare benefits. They have also called for elimination of many federal regulations that have traditionally accompanied aid to states and localities, and they propose to combine specific federal programs into a few broad grants over which states and localities can exercise wide discretion. Despite his earlier proposals to strengthen the role of the national government, President Bill Clinton has endorsed many of these new initiatives. He has proposed combining specific transportation programs into a single grant and suggested reducing the number of education and manpower training programs. He has signed into law a bill prohibiting Congress from imposing any new mandates on states and localities unless these are accompanied by enough aid to pay for their cost. Are these steps in the right direction? Or are they merely raising the price of federalism?

To address these questions, I shall set forth two theoretical perspectives on federalism: functional and legislative. The functional perspective is optimistic. It says that the American federal system is well designed to carry out the tasks assigned to it. Its basic orientation and the direction in which it is moving are consistent with the country's economic and political needs. It regards the California crisis as little more than the grunts and groans of an adapting political organism. Though it applauds some of the new Republican proposals as further steps in the right direction, it has doubts about others. It says that the

price Americans have been paying for their federal system has been—
up through 1994—quite acceptable.

The legislative perspective is more pessimistic. It says that the incentives shaping the decisions made by political leaders are becoming
increasingly perverse. They can claim credit for actions that weaken
federalism. They are blamed for actions that strengthen it. Political
pressures have hiked the price of federalism. In the chapters that follow
I subject the two theories to a series of empirical tests, seeking to
ascertain whether the price of federalism is climbing or falling.

The narrative I shall relate cannot be reduced to either theoretical perspective. The American federal system is too complex to be captured
within any single theoretical framework that has yet been developed. Both
the optimistic functional theory and the pessimistic legislative theory help
tell the story that unfolds in the pages that follow. But if the narrative is not
a fairy tale, its ending is not unhappy. Federalism requires a price, but the
price is one worth bearing.

The Price of Early Federalism

As a principle of government, federalism has had a dubious history.
It remains on the margins of political respectability even today. I was
recently invited to give a presentation on metropolitan government
before a United Nations conference. When I offered to discuss how the
federal principle could be used to help metropolitan areas govern themselves more effectively, my sponsors politely advised me that this topic
would be poorly received. The vast majority of UN members had a
unified form of government, I was told, and they saw little of value in
federalism. We reached a satisfactory compromise. I replaced "federal"
with "two-tier form of government."

Thomas Hobbes, the founder of modern political thought, would have
blessed the compromise, for he, too, had little room for federalism in
his understanding of the best form of government. Hobbes said that
people agreed to have a government over them only because they
realized that in a state of nature, that is, when there is no government,
life becomes a war of all against all. If no government exists to put
malefactors in jail, everyone must become a criminal simply to avoid
being a victim. Life becomes "nasty, brutish and short." To avoid the
violent state of nature, people need and want rule by a single sovereign.
Division of power among multiple sovereigns encourages bickering
among them. Conflicts become inevitable, as each sovereign tries to

expand its power (if for no other reason than to avoid becoming the prey of competing sovereigns). Government degenerates into anarchy and the world returns to the bitter state of nature from which government originally emerged.

The authors of the *Federalist* papers defended dual sovereignty by turning Hobbes's argument in favor of single sovereignty on its head. While Hobbes said that anything less than a single sovereign would lead to war of all against all, the *Federalist* argued that the best way of preserving liberty was to divide power. If power is concentrated in any one place, it can be used to crush individual liberty. Even in a democracy there can be the tyranny of the majority, the worst kind of tyranny because it is so stifling and complete. A division of power between the national and state governments reduces the possibility that any single majority will be able to control all centers of governmental power. The national government, by defending the country against foreign aggression, prevents external threats to liberty. The state governments, by denying power to any single dictator, reduce threats to liberty from within. As James Madison said in his defense of the Constitution, written on the eve of its ratification,

> The power surrendered by the people is first divided between two distinct governments, and then the portion allotted to each subdivided among distinct and separate departments. Hence a double security arises to the rights of the people. The different governments will control each other, at the same time that each will be controlled by itself.[11]

Early federalism was built on the principle of dual sovereignty. The Constitution divided sovereignty between state and nation, each in control of its own sphere. Some even interpreted the Constitution to mean that state legislatures could nullify federal laws. Early federalism also gave both levels of government their own military capacity. Congress was given the power to raise an army and wage war, but states were allowed to maintain their own militia.

The major contribution of early federalism to American liberties took place within a dozen years after the signing of the Constitution. Liberty is never established in a new nation until those in authority have peacefully ceded power to a rival political faction. Those who wrote the Constitution and secured its ratification, known as the Federalists, initially captured control of the main institutions of the national government: Congress, the presidency, and the Supreme Court. Those opposed to the new constitutional order, the antifederalists, had to content themselves with an opposition role in Congress and control over a number of state governments, most notably Virginia's.

The political issues dividing the two parties were serious. The Federalist party favored a strong central government, a powerful central bank that could facilitate economic and industrial development, and a strong, independent executive branch. Federalists had also become increasingly disturbed by the direction the French Revolution had taken. They were alarmed by the execution of thousands, the confiscation of private property, and the movement of French troops across Europe. They called for the creation of a national army and reestablished close ties with Britain.

The antifederalists, who became known as Democratic-Republicans, favored keeping most governmental power in the hands of state governments. They were opposed to a national bank, a strong presidency, and industrial government. They thought the United States would remain a free country only if it remained a land of independent farmers. They bitterly opposed the creation of a national army for fear it would be used to repress political opposition. Impressed by the French Revolution's commitment to the rights of man, they excused its excesses. The greater danger, they thought, was the reassertion of British power, and they denounced the Federalists for seeming to acquiesce in the seizure of U.S. seamen by the British navy.

The conflict between the two sides intensified after George Washington retired to his home in Mount Vernon. In 1800 Thomas Jefferson, founder of the Democratic-Republican party, waged an all-out campaign to defeat Washington's Federalist successor, John Adams. In retrospect, the central issue of the election was democracy itself. Could an opposition party drive a government out of power? Would political leaders accept their defeat?

So bitter was the feud between the two parties that Representative Matthew Lyon, a Democratic-Republican, spit in the face of a Federalist on the floor of Congress. Outside the Congress, pro-French propagandists relentlessly criticized Adams. To silence the opposition, Congress, controlled by the Federalists, passed the Alien and Sedition Acts. One of the Alien Acts gave President Adams the power to deport any foreigners "concerned in any treasonable or secret machinations against the government." The Sedition Act made it illegal to "write, print, utter, or publish . . . any false, scandalous and malicious writing . . . against . . . the Congress of the United States, or the President."[12]

The targets of the Sedition Acts soon became clear. Newspaper editors supporting the Democratic-Republicans were quickly indicted, and ten were brought to trial and convicted by juries under the influence of Federalist judges. Matthew Lyon was sentenced to a four-month jail term for claiming, presumably falsely, that President Adams had an "unbounded thirst for ridiculous pomp, foolish adulation, and selfish avarice."[13] Even George Washington lent his support to this political repression.

Federalism undoubtedly helped the fledgling American democracy survive this first constitutional test. When the Federalists passed the Alien and Sedition Acts, Democratic-Republicans in the Virginia and Kentucky state legislatures passed resolutions nullifying the laws. When it looked as if Jefferson's victory in the election of 1800 might be stripped away by a Federalist-controlled House of Representatives, both sides realized that the Virginia state militia was at least as strong as the remnants of the Continental Army. Lacking the national army they had tried to establish, the Federalists chose not to fight. They acquiesced in their political defeat in part because their opponents had military as well as political power, and because they themselves could retreat to their own regional base of power, the state and local governments of New England and the mid-Atlantic states.[14]

Jefferson claimed his victory was a revolution every bit as comprehensive as the one fought in 1776. The Alien and Sedition Acts were discarded, nullified not by a state legislature but by the results of a national election. President Adams returned to private life without suffering imprisonment or exile. Many years later, he and Jefferson reconciled their differences and developed through correspondence a close friendship.[15] They died on the same day, the fiftieth anniversary of the Declaration of Independence. To both, federalism and liberty seemed closely intertwined.

The price to be paid for early federalism became more evident with the passage of time. To achieve the blessings of liberty, early federalism divided sovereign power. When Virginia and Kentucky nullified the Alien and Sedition Acts, they preserved liberties only by threatening national unity. With the election of Jefferson, the issue was temporarily rendered moot, but the doctrine remained available for use when southerners once again felt threatened by encroaching national power.

The doctrine of nullification was revived in 1830 by John C. Calhoun, sometime senator from South Carolina, who objected to high tariffs that protected northern industry at the expense of southern cotton producers. When Congress raised the tariff, South Carolina's legislature threatened to declare the law null and void. Calhoun, then serving as Andrew Jackson's vice-president, argued that liberties could be trampled by national majorities unless states could nullify tyrannical acts. Andrew Jackson, though elected on a state's rights ticket, remained committed to national supremacy. At the annual Democratic banquet honoring the memory of Thomas Jefferson, Calhoun supporters sought to trap Jackson into endorsing the doctrine. But Jackson, aware of the scheme, raised his glass in a dramatic toast to "Our federal union: it must be preserved!" Not to be outdone, Calhoun replied in kind: "The union, next to our liberty, most dear!"[16]

A compromise was found to the overt issue, the tariff, but it was not so easy to resolve the underlying issue of slavery. In the infamous Dred Scott decision, the Supreme Court interpreted federalism to mean that boundaries could not be placed on the movements of masters and slaves. Northern territories could not free slaves that came within their boundaries; to do so deprived masters of their Fifth Amendment right not to be deprived of their property without due process of law. The decision spurred northern states to elect Abraham Lincoln president, which convinced southern whites that their liberties, most dear, were more important than federal union.

To Lincoln, as to Jackson, the union was to be preserved at all costs. Secession meant war. War meant the loss of 1 million lives, the destruction of the southern economy, the emancipation of African Americans from slavery, the demise of the doctrine of nullification, and the end to early federalism. Early federalism, with its doctrine of dual sovereignty, may have initially helped to preserve liberty, but it did so at a terrible price. As Hobbes feared, the price of dual sovereignty was war.

Since the termination of the Civil War, Americans have concluded that they can no longer trust their liberties to federalism. Sovereignty must be concentrated in the hands of the national government. Quite apart from the dangers of civil war, the powers of state and local governments have been used too often by a tyrannical majority to trample the rights of religious, racial, and political minorities. The courts now seem a more reliable institutional shelter for the nation's liberties.

But if federalism is no longer necessary or even conducive to the preservation of liberty, then what is its purpose? Is it merely a relic of an outdated past? Are the majority of the members of the United Nations correct in objecting to the very use of the word?

The Rise of Modern Federalism

The answers to these questions have been gradually articulated in the 130 years following the end of the Civil War. Although the states lost their sovereignty, they remained integral to the workings of American government. Modern federalism no longer meant dual sovereignty and shared military capacity. Modern federalism instead meant only that each level of government had its own independently elected political leaders and its own separate taxing and spending capacity. Equipped with these tools of quasi-sovereignty, each level of government could take all but the most violent of steps to defend its turf.

Although sovereignty and military capacity now rested firmly in the hands of the national government, modern federalism became more complex rather than less so. Power was no longer simply divided between the nation and its states. Cities, counties, towns, school districts, special districts, and a host of additional governmental entities, each with its own elected leaders and taxing authority, assumed new burdens and responsibilities.

Just as the blessings bestowed by early federalism were evident from its inception, so the advantages of modern federalism were clear from the onset. If states and localities were no longer the guarantors of liberty, they became the engines of economic development. By giving state and local governments the autonomy to act independently, the federal system facilitated the rapid growth of an industrial economy that eventually surpassed its European competitors. Canals and railroads were constructed, highways and sewage systems built, schools opened, parks designed, and public safety protected by cities and villages eager to make their locality a boomtown.

The price to be paid for modern federalism did not become evident until government attempted to grapple with the adverse side effects of a burgeoning capitalist economy. Out of a respect for federalism's constitutional status and political durability, social reformers first worked with and through existing components of the federal system, concentrating much of their reform effort on state and local governments.[17] Only gradually did it become clear that state and local governments, for all their ability to work with business leaders to enhance community prosperity, had difficulty meeting the needs of the poor and the needy.

It was ultimately up to the courts to find ways of keeping the price of modern federalism within bounds. Although dual sovereignty no longer meant nullification and secession, much remained to be determined about the respective areas of responsibility of the national and state governments. At first the courts retained remnants of the doctrine of dual sovereignty in order to protect processes of industrialization from governmental intrusion. But with the advent of the New Deal, the constitutional power of the national government expanded so dramatically that the doctrine of dual sovereignty virtually lost all meaning. Court interpretations of the constitutional clauses on commerce and spending have proved to be the most significant.

According to dual sovereignty theory, article 1 of the Constitution gives Congress the power to regulate commerce "among the states," but the regulation of intrastate commerce was to be left to the states. So, for example, in 1895 the Supreme Court said that Congress could not break up a sugar monopoly that had a nationwide impact on the price of sugar, because the monopoly refined its sugar within the state of Pennsylvania.[18] The mere fact that the sugar was to be sold nationwide was only "incidental" to its production. As late as 1935, the Supreme Court, in a 6 to 3 decision, said that Congress could not regulate the sale of poultry because the regulation took effect after the chickens arrived within the state of Illinois, not while they were in transit.[19]

Known as the "sick chicken" case, this decision was one of a series in which the Supreme Court declared unconstitutional legislation passed in the early days of President Franklin Roosevelt's efforts to establish his New Deal programs. Seven of the "nine old men" on the Court had been appointed by Roosevelt's conservative Republican predecessors. By declaring many New Deal programs in violation of the commerce clause, the Supreme Court seemed to be substituting its political views for those of elected officials. In a case denying the federal government the right to protect workers trying to organize a union in the coal industry, the Republican views of the Court seemed to lie just barely below the surface of a technical discussion of the commerce clause. Justice George Sutherland declared, "The relation of employer and employee is a local relation . . . over which the federal government has no legislative control."[20]

The Roosevelt Democrats were furious at decisions that seemed to deny the country's elected officials the right to govern. Not since Dred Scott had judicial review been in such disrepute. Roosevelt decided to "pack the court" by adding six new judges over and above the nine already on the Court. Although Roosevelt's court-packing scheme did not survive the political uproar on Capitol Hill, its effect on the Supreme Court was noticeable. In the midst of the court-packing debate, Justices Charles Hughes and Owen Roberts, who had agreed with Sutherland's opinion in the coal case, changed their mind and voted to uphold the Wagner Act, a new law designed to facilitate the formation of unions. In his opinion, Hughes did not explicitly overturn the coal miner decision (for which he had voted), but he did say: "When industries organize themselves on a national scale, ... how can it be maintained that their industrial labor relations constitute a forbidden field into which Congress may not enter?"[21] Relations between employers and their workers, once said to be local, suddenly became part of interstate commerce.

The change of heart by Hughes and Roberts has been called "the switch in time that saved nine." The New Deal majority that emerged on the court was soon augmented by judges appointed by Roosevelt. Since the New Deal, the definition of interstate commerce has continued to expand. In 1942 a farmer raising twenty-three acres of wheat, all of which might be fed to his own livestock, was said to be in violation of the crop quotas imposed by the Agricultural Adjustment Act of 1938. Since he was feeding his cows himself, he was not buying grain on the open market, thereby depressing the worldwide price of grain.[22] With such a definition of interstate commerce, nothing was local.

The expansion of the meaning of the commerce clause is a well-known part of American political history. The importance to federalism of court interpretations of the "spending clause" is less well known. The constitutional clause in question says that Congress has the power to collect taxes to "provide for the ... general welfare." But how about Congress's power to collect taxes for the welfare of specific individuals or groups?

The question first arose in a 1923 case, when a childless woman said she could not be asked to pay taxes in order to finance federal grants to states for programs that helped pregnant women. Since she received no benefit from the program, she sued for return of the taxes she had paid to cover its costs. In a decision that has never been reversed, the Supreme Court said that she had suffered no measurable injury and therefore had no right to sue the government. Her taxes were being used for a wide variety of purposes. The amount being spent for this program was too small to be significant.[23] The court's decision to leave spending issues to Congress was restated a decade later when the social security program was also challenged on the grounds that monies were being directed to the elderly, not for the general welfare. Said Justice Benjamin N. Cardozo for a court majority: "The conception of the spending power . . . [must find a point somewhere] between particular and general. . . . There is a middle ground . . . in which discretion is large. The discretion, however, is not confided to the Court. The discretion belongs to Congress, unless the choice is clearly wrong."[24]

The courts have ever since refused to review Congress's power to spend money. They have also conceded to Congress the right to attach any regulations to any aid Congress provides. In 1987 Congress provided a grant to state governments for the maintenance of their highways, but conditioned 5 percent of the funds on state willingness to raise the drinking age from eighteen to twenty-one. The connection between the appropriation and the regulation was based on the assumption that youths under the age of twenty-one are more likely to drive after drinking than those over twenty-one. Presumably, building more roads would only encourage more inebriated young people to drive on them. Despite the fact that the connection between the appropriation and the regulation was problematic, the Supreme Court ruled that Congress could attach any reasonable conditions to its grants to the states.[25] State sovereignty was not violated, because any state could choose not to accept the money.

In short, the courts have virtually given up the doctrine of judicial review when it comes to matters on which Congress can spend money. As a consequence, most national efforts to influence state governments come in the form of federal grants. Federal aid can also be used to influence local governments, such as counties, cities, towns, villages, and school districts. These local governments, from a constitutional point of view, are mere creatures of the state of which they are part. They have no independent sovereignty.

The Contemporary Price of Federalism

If constitutional doctrine has evolved to the point that dual sovereign theory has been put to rest, this does not mean that federalism has come to an end. Although ultimate sovereignty resides with the national government, state and local governments still have certain characteristics and capabilities that make them constituent components of a federal system. (Throughout the book, I shall follow the practice of the early federalists of referring to the "national" rather than the "federal" government. "Federal" will be saved for references to relationships among the three-tier system of government.) Two characteristics of federalism are fundamental. First, citizens elect officials of their choice for each level of government. Unless the authority of each level of government rests in the people, it will become the agent of the other. Second, each level of government raises money through taxation from the citizens residing in the area for which it is responsible. It is hard to see how a system could be regarded as federal unless each level of government can levy taxes on its residents. Unless each level of government can raise its own fiscal resources, it cannot act independently.

Although the constitutional authority of the national government has steadily expanded, state and local governments remain of great practical significance. Almost half of all government spending for domestic (as distinct from foreign and military) purposes is paid for out of taxes raised by state and local governments.[26]

The sharing of control over domestic policy among levels of government has many benefits, but federalism still exacts its price. It can lead to great regional inequalities. Also, the need for establishing cooperative relationships among governments can contribute to great inefficiency in the administration of government programs. In the pages that follow I examine the costs and benefits of modern American federalism.

In chapter 2, I set forth two theories of federalism or, it might be said, two perspectives on modern federalism. The first, functional theory, says that economic development is the main objective of state and local governments, while the national government has assumed the main responsibility for redistribution. If a federal system continues to organize itself along these lines, and functional theory says that the system is moving in the right direction, then the price of federalism can be kept to an acceptable level. Legislative theory, however, says the needs of legislators interfere with the effective functioning of a federal system.

Chapter 3 examines the power of each theory to explain the direction in which modern federalism is heading. The evidence will suggest that the United States has been evolving toward a more functional federal system. Chapter 4 shows that policies promoting economic development are produced by a somewhat different set of political and economic factors than those that produce redistributive policy. The data reveal three problems in modern federalism: the cost of welfare, fiscal inequities, and the expense of providing public services in central cities. The next three chapters explore these three issues in more detail. Chapter 5 analyzes welfare policy by looking closely at the most prominent of state redistributive policies, aid to families with dependent children. Chapter 6 analyzes federal grant programs to see whether they reduce fiscal inequities among the states. On the whole, they do not. States with more fiscal capacity actually receive more federal aid than states with less. The chapter considers some of the reasons. Chapter 7 seeks to determine whether big-city governments are more costly than other local governments. I find that big cities of the Rust Belt pay more for their public services. I also find that big cities are treated more or less fairly both by Congress and by state legislatures, except that Sun Belt cities are discriminated against by their state legislatures. Assessing and reducing the price of federalism are the topics of the concluding chapter.

2

Functional and Legislative Theories of Federalism

One can hardly imagine how much [the] division of sovereignty contributes to the well-being of each of the states that compose the Union. In these small communities ... all public authority [is] turned toward internal improvements. ... The ambition of power yields to the less refined and less dangerous desire for well-being. ...

Alexis de Tocqueville, *Democracy in America*

Among the popular and representative systems of government, I do not approve of the federal system: it is too perfect; and it requires virtues and political talents much superior to our own.

Simon Bolivar

I have constructed two contrasting theories of federalism from earlier research. The first, functional theory, identifies distinctive areas of competence for each level of government. It predicts that each level will expand in its arena of competence but will remain limited or will diminish in its less competent arena. The second, legislative theory, says that the modern federal system is shaped by the political needs of legislators responsible for its design. Legislators at all levels of government will seek to distribute governmental benefits for which they can claim credit and, if at all possible, will shift governmental burdens to other levels of the federal system.

The two theories might better be called perspectives because they are embryonic rather than full-grown. Their names are original to this study. Neither has been integrated into a mathematical model. In many instances they generate different, even competing hypotheses, yet they are not altogether inconsistent with one another.

Many scholars have contributed to their development. My syntheses do not do justice to the diversity of their views. The syntheses are not intended to be a summary of the ideas of any particular scholar, but they constitute reasonably consistent frameworks codified from a variety of sources. Throughout most of this book, I shall call them theories to highlight their ambition to be all-encompassing. But in the concluding chapter I shall treat them as perspectives in order to examine the ways they complement and illuminate one another, with the hope that future scholars will find ways of bringing them together into a single, integrated theory of modern federalism.

Functional Theory

Functional theory identifies the two main economic purposes of domestic government as developmental and redistributive.[1] Developmental programs provide the physical and social infrastructure necessary to facilitate a country's economic growth. The physical infrastructure includes roads, mass transit systems, sanitation systems, public parks, and a vast array of other basic utilities. The social infrastructure includes institutions that protect persons and property from unlawful activity, guard against conflagrations, protect the public health, and educate the next generation. Unless these and other basic social services are provided, modern industrial societies are unlikely to develop.[2]

Redistributive programs reallocate societal resources from the "haves" to the "have-nots." They transfer economic resources from those who have gained the most from economic development to those who have gained the least: the elderly, the disabled, the unemployed, the sick, the poor, families headed by single parents, and others lacking in material resources. Some analysts believe that these redistributive programs indirectly contribute to economic development in the long run; others think they retard economic development by reducing incentives to work and save. Most people regard at least a minimal level of redistribution as justifiable regardless of the developmental consequences. Most people also think that the higher the level of economic development, the more a society should redistribute some resources to the poor and the needy.[3]

Locus of the Developmental Function

For federal governments to function effectively, the division of responsibilities among levels of government must respect the comparative advantage of each level of government.

Specifically, the national government should assume the primary responsibility for redistribution, while state and local governments assume primary responsibility for development. As Lord James Bryce wrote nearly a century ago,

> It is the business of a local authority to mend the roads, to clean out the village well or provide a new pump, to see that there is a place where straying beasts may be kept till the owner reclaims them, to fix the number of cattle each villager may turn out on the common pasture, to give each his share of timber cut in the common woodland.[4]

Local governments are best equipped to design and administer development programs because their decisions are disciplined by market forces as well as by political pressures. Local governments must be sensitive to market considerations when designing and administering roadways, sanitation systems, public safety services, and educational programs. Unless local public services are provided in ways that meet the needs of local business and residents, residents will consider moving to another locality better attuned to their needs. Since 17 percent of the population changes its residence each year,[5] the effects of locational choices on property values can be quickly felt.

Business and residential choices are, of course, influenced by factors other than the quality of local public services. Businesses want to be close to both their sources of supply and the markets for their products. Residential choices are affected by family ties, job opportunities, and the quality of the natural environment. But even though these and other factors affect the decisions of many firms and many residents, the quality of publicly provided infrastructure affects locational choices on the margins. For some businesses and for some residents, all other factors balance one another out and the quality of the social and physical infrastructure becomes decisive when choosing a location. According to standard economic theory, it is the marginal business and the marginal resident that determine the market value of property in the locality.

Since small changes in supply or demand can have a significant effect on price, residents of a community, eager to maintain their property values, can be expected to pressure government officials to meet local expectations and employ public resources efficiently to facilitate economic development. Most of the time, the continuing need to attract newcomers to a town shapes policies so that adjustments are made long before any seriously adverse economic developments take place. Inefficient and inappropriate policies can have fairly rapid effects on a town's property values and government revenue flows. As a result, most local governments can be expected to be relatively competent at designing and executing developmental policies. Admittedly, there is a certain "narrowness of mind and the spirit of parsimony," among local officials, as Lord Bryce was the first to admit, but if it were otherwise, "there would be less of that shrewdness which the practice of local government forms."[6]

A system of local government also gives citizens some choice in the level and type of basic governmental services they are to have. Some people favor sex education programs and condom distribution in school; others do not. Some people think refuse collection should be publicly provided; others prefer to recycle their own garbage. Some people think police protection should be intensive; others think intrusive police invade the civil liberties of citizens. Some people favor instruction of children in a multicultural curriculum; others think the emphasis should be placed on the traditional Western classics. Inasmuch as a system of local government gives citizens some choice among these alternatives, it helps to reduce conflict and enhance citizen satisfaction.

Providing basic services through local governments also facilitates the gathering of information about the best way of organizing public services. Each city or town is a laboratory where experiments are tried. If successful, the experiment is copied by other town governments. If it fails, the experiment is soon abandoned.[7] Also, localities pay close attention to the wages and salaries paid employees in adjacent communities. If town salaries are comparatively high or low, pressures to bring the town into line with its neighbors can be expected to develop.

Local governments eschew progressive income taxes when raising revenue to pay for local services. No more than 3.1 percent of local revenues have ever come from this source (see table 2-1). When an income tax is imposed, it is typically a flat-rate tax applied equally across income levels. If local governments did otherwise, many people

TABLE 2-1. *Sources of Revenue for National, State, and Local Governments, Selected Years, 1957–90*

Percent

| | Sources of revenue | | | | | |
| | Income tax | | | User and miscellaneous taxes | | |
Year	National	State	Local	National	State	Local
1957	40.9	7.5	0.9	10.0	21.3	32.8
1962	42.8	9.1	1.0	8.9	22.5	32.9
1967	38.1	10.5	2.1	9.4	19.3	32.2
1972	42.4	15.4	3.0	8.1	20.2	31.5
1977	41.0	16.4	3.1	9.6	17.1	34.5
1982	43.5	17.4	2.6	11.1	17.3	40.2
1987	41.3	18.3	2.4	12.3	17.5	41.5
1990	40.5	19.0	2.4	12.4	17.3	38.7

SOURCES: See appendix.

would move from the town. Local governments rely instead on the property tax for much of the revenue they need. Property is fixed to the land and cannot be moved, making it easier to place a local tax on it. But the property tax, too, is a flat tax. The big home in the fancy part of town is usually taxed at the same rate as the small home on the other side of the tracks. Were it otherwise, the rich would be tempted to leave.

Local governments also depend heavily on user fees and miscellaneous taxes levied in return for specific services received from local government. These taxes have the advantage of being closely calibrated to citizens' demand for public goods. If they want the service, they have to pay for it. If they do not need it, they do not need to pay. In 1957 nearly a third of local revenue was raised from these fees and taxes. By 1990 the percentage had reached nearly 40 percent (table 2-1).

Diseconomies of Scale

Not all local governments are equally efficient. There seem to be noticeable diseconomies of scale within the public sector. The larger the governmental unit, the more costly service provision seems to be per person. In the Pittsburgh metropolitan area, for example, the large central city of Pittsburgh imposes a higher tax per household than do any of the surrounding suburban communities. Also, the per pupil local tax revenue collected for schools is greater than that collected by any suburban community, yet the educational services are of poorer quality than in most suburban communities.[8] Similarly, a study of the Chicago metropolitan area discovered that police services in poor black suburbs are as effective at preventing crime as police services in poor black neighborhoods in Chicago—even though the costs of operating the suburban police departments are less than one-fourteenth of those in Chicago.[9]

Some of the diseconomies of scale are related to the way the public-sector work force is organized. When governmental organization has a large geographical reach, workers become well organized and unions are able to gain considerable influence over public policy. Wages tend to be higher, and unions place greater constraints on labor-saving, cost-reducing technological innovations. Thus a study of Pittsburgh reports that "the city's large number of public employees, combined with their relatively high salaries and fringe benefits, makes delivery of basic public services relatively more expensive" than it is in the surrounding suburbs.[10]

Pittsburgh is not an isolated example. In general, the larger and the more centralized the governmental institutions, the more powerful are public-sector unions. Public-sector strike threats are more threatening to public safety and welfare when they have a broader geographical reach. Finding replacement workers or designing alternative strategies for service delivery are more difficult if the number of strikers is large. As a result, employee wages and working conditions impose a much higher burden on the fiscal resources of larger governmental jurisdictions.

Big-city governments are also less likely than town governments to have market-based information on the cost of public services. When negotiating contracts with outside providers, purchasing materials, or designing service delivery systems, they are more likely to find themselves in a unique situation. Unlike town governments, they typically do not have within their state and region many other governments with similar physical settings and social problems. They can communicate with big cities in other parts of the country, but differences in state law, regional economies, and historical practices make it more difficult to draw clear conclusions. For these reasons, recent research has shown that in the United States economic growth occurs more rapidly when service delivery is provided by a decentralized system of local governments than when it is provided by any single metropolitanwide system.[11]

Fiscal Disparities

Although developmental services can be efficiently provided by local governments, a price is to be paid for this efficiency: significant disparity in the provision of government services is likely if developmental policies are determined exclusively by local governments. For example, richer communities are more likely to provide more and better educational services than poor communities. In the Pittsburgh area, for example, the town of Cornell raised $4,104 in revenues per student in 1985 with a tax rate no higher than one that raised only $2,087 in the town of Clairton City. One town could enjoy twice as expensive a school system as its neighbor without imposing a higher tax rate.[12]

Some functional theorists regard these inequities as an acceptable price to be paid in return for the benefits of a federal system. Disparities in the quality of public services are simply to be expected in a market economy. Just as some individuals and families have the income to obtain better homes and cars, so they will be able to purchase homes in communities that provide a higher level of public services, whether these be schools, parks, or police services. If society wants to engage in redistribution, it should give monies directly to needy individuals regardless of where they live.[13]

These functional theorists accept such inequities in part because they expect them to diminish with increasing integration of the national economy. Economic investment gravitates from places where wages and land values are high to places where the factors of production command a lower price. As the less expensive parts of the country attract business investments, they acquire the fiscal capacity to provide better social and physical infrastructure. Convergence among states and localities is hastened by improvements in communication and transportation systems. As both labor and capital become increasingly mobile, less economically developed regions find it easier to close the gap.

Other functional theorists are more concerned about fiscal disparities among states and localities. They are less sanguine about the imminent disappearance of regional differences in wages, property values, and fiscal capacity. They think major differences in expenditure for schools, public safety, and other public services should be avoided so as to provide children with equal opportunity and communities with equally adequate safety services. For this reason, functional theorists typically recommend that national and state grants to local governments be designed to offset inequalities in local tax resources.[14]

Grants

National grants may be either closely regulated categorical grants or block grants that give state and local governments considerable discretion. Categorical grants, which are generally used for redistributive purposes, are discussed below. Block grants are characteristically designed to help state and local governments perform their developmental objectives.[15] Although the House of Representatives has approved a block grant for welfare programs, state and local governments generally use block grants for developmental purposes.[16]

Block grants may be used to induce local governments to adequately fund programs whose benefits spill over into other jurisdictions.[17] For example, roads integrated into a state and national transportation system benefit users who neither live nor pay taxes within a local community charged with the responsibility for maintaining them. A grant from a higher level of government is sometimes thought necessary to induce adequate local support of transportation.

According to functional theory, the amount of the national grant should exactly match the amount of the benefit enjoyed by nonlocal residents (beyond the benefit enjoyed by residents themselves). If half the benefits of good schools are enjoyed not by local residents themselves but by the many other places to which well-educated students may move upon graduation, then half the cost of the good schools should be paid for by higher levels of government. National grants should thus be matching grants, though it is often extremely difficult to estimate the appropriate matching ratio.

The block grant, if matched to some level of local expenditure, can not only stimulate local expenditure along appropriate lines but can also help offset disparity in local fiscal capacity. Indeed, block grants (sometimes referred to as revenue sharing or power equalizing) are sometimes thought to be almost a panacea for all that is wrong with the federal system. Equity can be achieved by raising monies at the national level and directing it to the most needy places. It can be used to offset spillover effects. Yet the specific use of block grants can be determined by state and local governments for purposes these governments deem most appropriate. The advantages of national equity can be combined with those of state and local efficiency.[18]

Equity block grants pose two difficulties, however. The first is political. The national government may not have the political capacity to reallocate monies from well-off parts of the country to less fortunate areas. Functional theorists overlook this political fact of life.[19] Legislative theorists, as I shall show, are more realistic.

In addition to the political obstacles, block grants, if relied upon too heavily, reduce incentives for local governments to manage their resources efficiently. If monies are received from national grants rather than local tax dollars, local officials are no longer subject to the discipline of the marketplace. Each city or town needs to see direct fiscal benefits from operating efficiently and effectively if local officials are to have appropriate incentives. If a town becomes too dependent on block grants, it loses this incentive. If block grants become too generous, the national government will need to impose accompanying regulations that deny local governments requisite political autonomy.[20]

In the Netherlands, for example, block grants from the central government to local governments account for two-thirds of local government resources. The results are not altogether beneficial. According to one study, "With the amount of general grant far exceeding that of local taxes and charges, municipal authorities need make little effort to secure their sources of income and those in the cities who benefit from general municipal spending do not need to worry about its source."[21] As a result, local governments in the Netherlands have few direct incentives to facilitate the economic development of their communities, and the central departments impose tight restrictions on local operations. Similarly, cities in northern England have been so helped by block grants, so burdened by regulations, and so lacking in fiscal incentives that they have been unable to develop effective development strategies.[22]

Block grants thus need to find an appropriate balance between two competing considerations. On the one hand, they need to offset extreme inequities such as those in the Pittsburgh metropolitan area. On the other hand, they should not be so large that they eliminate the incentive to operate services prudently.

The State Role in Development Policy

Quite apart from considerations of fiscal disparity, development policy cannot be an exclusively local prerogative. Many development policies are best coordinated across a substantial geographical area. Major systems of transportation, sanitation, air and water pollution control, higher education, and other critical components of the social and physical infrastructure can be designed efficiently only if governments with broad territorial reach are involved in their planning and financing. Both state governments and special authorities having metropolitanwide authority are often called upon to provide the necessary coordinating function. State governments can thus be expected to be significant participants in the provision of the social and physical infrastructure necessary for economic development.

Environmental pollution cannot be controlled without a plan that extends across metropolitan areas, states, or even regions. Any program of pollution control will necessarily impose costs on particular neighborhoods and communities. If such decisions are left to local government, each will insist that the problem must be addressed but the solution should be located somewhere else. This happens so frequently it is known as the NIMBY (not in my backyard) problem. Each community tries to shift the cost of pollution control to its neighbors. In order to keep the NIMBY problem from thwarting provision of necessary components of the social and physical infrastructure, responsibility for certain kinds of development must be assigned to state governments.[23]

The National Role in Development Policy

Although some developmental tasks must be undertaken by higher levels of government, the national government, on the whole, is the least efficient provider of development policies. Unlike local and state governments, it operates under few marketlike constraints. If it designs the physical infrastructure poorly or situates it in a less efficient location, the long-term economic development of the country suffers. But economic signals to the national government indicating the relative efficiency of its policies are not as clear or as rapidly conveyed as the signals available to local governments. Because of constraints on the flow of labor and capital across national boundaries, the revenue flows of the national government do not quickly feel the effect of policy mistakes. As a result, the national government receives less information from the marketplace about the effectiveness of its policy choices.

Developmental infrastructure provided by a national government also tends toward uniformity. It is typically designed by professionals responsive to the dominant political coalition. A national government is not likely to tailor its policies to suit the particular developmental needs of specific places and regions. As Lord Bryce once observed, "A highly trained [national] civil service . . . tends to lay undue stress upon uniformity, becomes attached to its settled habits, dislikes novelties, [and] contracts bureaucratic methods. . . . The more the central bureaucracy controls local affairs, the wider will be the action of these tendencies."[24]

Despite the success local governments have had at facilitating economic growth, many have advocated national direction of economic development.[25] Alexander Hamilton favored promotion of domestic manufacturing, Daniel Webster and Henry Clay sought to use tariff revenues to pay for internal improvements, Herbert Hoover signed into law the Economic Recovery Act, and Richard Nixon froze prices and wages. Hamilton, Webster, and Clay failed to win much congressional support for their schemes; Hoover and Nixon discovered that manipulation of the national economy through controls on prices and wages had disastrous economic consequences.

The latest round of suggestions for a national economic policy travels under the label of industrial policy. These suggestions have been inspired by declining employment in the manufacturing sector and by a continuing trade deficit, especially with Japan. According to industrial policy advocates, the United States needs to copy the Japanese and use the power of the national government to manage trade relations, retrain workers, and facilitate expansion of industries in which future growth is likely to occur.

Critics of industrial policy give both economic and political reasons for rejecting most industrial policy proposals. Guessing the economic future is a risky enterprise, they point out. Heads of departments in the national government are unlikely to be able to make more sophisticated guesses with the taxpayers' money than are a multiplicity of businesses and financiers, whose own fiscal resources are at stake. And even if government experts ascertain the correct options, they are unlikely to be able to act on their impulses. Instead of placing bets on future winners, they will be expected to bail out current losers, who characteristically blame their losses on unfair competition rather than their own misjudgments. Government is more likely to bet on a sagging automobile industry, supported by senators from Michigan and Ohio, than on the vagaries of virtual reality, which is more appealing to visionaries than to currently powerful economic and political interests.[26]

Although the issue has been placed repeatedly on the national agenda, neither proponents or opponents have given sufficient consideration to the fact that industrial policy is a regular part of governmental action at the state and local level. Junior colleges retrain workers; counties build roads; sanitation districts dig tunnels for sewage lines; states yield tax concessions to attract manufacturing plants; and governors promote state products overseas.[27] Although some states and localities may fail to seize attractive opportunities and others may concede too much, they have one great advantage over the national government: they constitute a multiplicity of decisionmakers, each constrained by a competitive market consisting of other state and local governments. It is not a matter of whether or not to have an industrial policy; it is a matter of which level of government should have the responsibility for economic development.

Although many development policies can be carried out at state and local levels, some must nonetheless be carried out on a national scale and therefore can be performed effectively only by the national government. Health regulations for the food and drug industry are nationally determined because the gains from a common framework very likely outweigh any losses that come from the fact that it is a less efficient governmental entity making the decisions. A set of national standards has created an integrated interstate highway system of great benefit to the country's economic development, though the interests expressed through state and local governments were also taken into account. Functional theorists therefore do not expect the national government to be entirely removed from the processes of formulating development policy.

Locus of the Redistributive Function

The appropriate locus of the redistributive function of government is the inverse of the appropriate locus for most developmental activities. If the national government is the least efficient formulator of developmental policy, it is the most competent agent of redistribution. Local governments are the least capable. State governments are substantially less competent agents of redistribution than the federal government, but they are to be preferred over local governments.

Constraints on Local Government

Local governments are unable to redistribute wealth effectively because labor and capital are mobile in an economically and political integrated nation-state. If a locality attempts in any serious way to tax the rich and give to the poor, more poor people will enter the locality, even as the rich will depart. One liberal Massachusetts town became a convenient locale for a range of social services, including apartments for poor families, group homes for recovering drug and alcohol abusers, halfway homes, counseling centers, and other programs for the poor. Despite the fact (or because?) the programs were well administered, the growing number of agency clients eventually provoked complaints from town leaders that the community was becoming "a magnet for everyone else's problems." Complaining that taxpayers were being asked to foot the bill for the education, security, and fire protection of low-income nontaxpayers, one candidate appealed effectively to local voters by insisting, "We can't afford this anymore."[28] Even if local officials ignore such opposition and persist in efforts to assist the poor and the needy, their effort, if carried too far, will almost necessarily fail. If no other force is able to stop large-scale redistribution, bankruptcy will.

The smaller the territorial reach of a local government, the more open its economy and the less its capacity for redistribution. Most small suburbs in metropolitan areas have almost no capacity to meet the special needs of low-income citizens, because such actions would immediately affect the suburb's tax rate, property values, and attractiveness to business. Big cities are somewhat better able to undertake redistributive activities because their geographical reach is greater. Businesses and residents will have to absorb higher relocation costs if they wish to escape the cost of paying for redistribution.

Some towns and cities can engage in redistribution because they enjoy control over a natural monopoly. Most big cities have certain geographical features that give them an advantage. New York, Boston, Baltimore, Charleston, and Seattle all have wonderful natural harbors. Chicago is located at the point where the Great Lakes system reaches furthest into the interior of the continent. St. Louis is located at the confluence of the Missouri and the Mississippi Rivers, Pittsburgh at the point where three rivers combine to form the Ohio River, and Minneapolis and St. Paul at the point where the Mississippi no longer becomes navigable by steamer.

These natural advantages are typically reinforced by additions to a fixed transportation grid. Canals are dug, railroads constructed, highways built, and airports erected. Industry and commerce become so dependent upon access to this transportation grid that the big city can collect a higher tax than would be possible if it did not have something like a natural monopoly.

Nowhere are the consequences of a natural monopoly for local politics and policy more evident than in the city of San Francisco. Located at the tip of the peninsula that helps to form the marvelous San Francisco Bay, the city's climate, location, and historic settlement patterns have blessed it with unparalleled advantages. So free is San Francisco from the competitive considerations that typically constrain local politics that Richard DeLeon has dubbed it a " 'semisovereign city'—a city that imposes as many limits on capital as capital imposes on it." In his fascinating study of this "left coast city," the author finds that "San Francisco has asserted its local autonomy, expanded the public sphere, . . . spurned the dictates of investor prerogative, severely restricted business use of its urban space, and inured itself to threats of private-sector disinvestment." Well, almost. In the epilogue to his effusive account of progressive success, DeLeon admits that California's 1991 recession undermined the power of the city's dominant left-wing coalition. A local columnist gloated that the progressively more "Wicked Witch of the West" was now dead. But the city's new mayor assessed the situation more accurately: "San Francisco will always be a progressive city."[29] Its marvelous monopoly makes it so.

Some smaller communities may also be able to redistribute income without suffering undue economic hardship because of the advantages their location gives them. Aspen sits in a beautiful valley; San Mateo and Pacific Palisades are nestled in hills overlooking the Pacific Ocean; Berkeley's hills overlook San Francisco Bay; and Cambridge holds hostage both the Massachusetts Institute of Technology and Harvard University. If these towns wish to control rents or impose burdensome taxes, they can do so without incurring a significant economic penalty. Citizens will accept these costs as part of the price of obtaining access to the special advantages the community provides.

Although natural monopolies will always exist, there is reason to think they are less prevalent than they once were. Technological advances have reduced the advantages of natural harbors and fixed transportation grids. As communication substitutes for transportation and as products become lighter, permitting shipment by truck and plane instead of by rail, big cities no longer dominate their hinterlands in the same way they did in the nineteenth century. As the playing field on which cities and towns compete becomes increasingly level, local governments become even less capable of engaging in redistributive activities.

States and Redistribution

Just as big cities are better able to redistribute than small suburbs, so states are better able to redistribute than are most local governments. Often encompassing more than one metropolitan area, states have substantially greater territorial reach. The cost of moving across state lines is more substantial than changing residence within a metropolitan area. Whereas 17 percent of the population changes residence every year, only 3 percent moves across a state line.[30] Functional theory thus expects to find state governments to be more engaged in redistributive activities than local governments are.

But even though states are better able to redistribute than local governments, their capacity for redistribution still is limited by the mobility of labor and capital. The Supreme Court has ruled that newcomers to a state must be given equal access to government services, including welfare assistance.[31] To avoid becoming a magnet for the poor, the sick, and the needy, states must be cautious that they do not design a system of welfare considerably more lavish than that of other states.

It was once thought that states need not worry about becoming a welfare magnet because poor people were said to be geographically immobile. Dependent on friends and family for assistance and lacking the economic resources to transport themselves to a new location, the poor were thought to be quite impervious to any differences in welfare policies among the states.[32] But poor people have been shown to be just as likely to move across state lines as the nonpoor, and people receiving welfare benefits have been shown to be just as likely to uproot themselves and head for another part of the country as those not dependent upon governmental aid.[33] It was also thought that poor people move to seek new economic opportunities or renew family ties, not to obtain welfare benefits. But as I will show in chapter 5, the decision to move or not to move is also affected by interstate differences in welfare benefits.

The National Government and Redistribution

The national government has the greatest capacity to engage in redistributive programs, because it can prevent the in-migration of labor from foreign countries and can impose some constraints on capital flow. The largest redistributive programs in the United States—social security and medicare—are designed and administered by the federal government. If any state or local government had attempted to mount a comparable program by itself, it would have gone bankrupt long before becoming a haven for the aged. National policymakers have established a national system of publicly funded medical services for those over sixty-five and have debated creating a comparable program for all age groups. Only Hawaii has been willing to undertake a similar set of services. Had any of the forty-eight contiguous states promised its citizens universal health insurance, it would have become an attractive new home for thousands of the profoundly ill.

The national government also levies heavier taxes on the well-to-do than on low-income people, most notably in the form of an income tax. The income tax is waived for people below the poverty line but can reach as high as 39 percent for those in the highest income bracket. This tax generates 40 percent of the revenue of the national government. By comparison, states rely on the income tax for less than 20 percent of their revenue, and local governments get only 2 to 3 percent of their income from this source (table 2-1). What is more, the income tax levied by most state governments lacks the progressive feature of the national tax. The state of Massachusetts, for example, considered changing its flat 6 percent income tax to a progressive tax in which the top rate would approach 10 percent. The governor said even this modestly progressive income tax would discourage businesses and higher-income people from staying in Massachusetts. In November 1994 state voters responded favorably to this argument and rejected the progressive tax, even though a majority of voters would have received a tax break. The argument is less compelling at the national level.

The increasing integration of the international economy has begun to erode some of the redistributive capacities of even the national government. The cost of communication and transportation is falling rapidly. Products can be shipped from one part of the globe to another at greatly reduced costs. Large corporations can have bills prepared by low-wage workers in Ireland instead of high-paid workers in Illinois, because the cost of transmitting the information across the Atlantic is less than the wage differentials. The ease with which foreigners can illegally enter the United States places further pressures on the welfare state. This caused the House of Representatives to include in its 1995 welfare bill provisions that would deny welfare benefits to both legal and illegal immigrants.

Although the increasing flow of labor among nations is posing an increasing challenge to the American welfare state, the effects of the free flow of capital among nations are even greater. In the period immediately following World War II the United States could impose a tax on business activity without fear of a significant diversion of economic activity to another country. Compared with the rest of the world, U.S.

FIGURE 2-1. *Revenue Received by National Government from Payroll and Corporate Taxes, 1957–90*

Percent

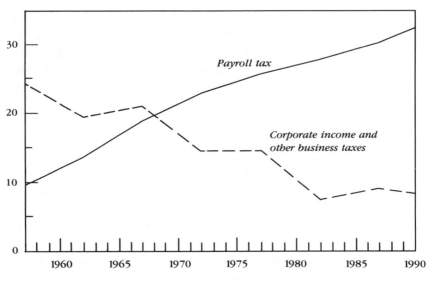

SOURCES: See appendix.

politics were so predictable and its economy so robust that businesses were willing to accept lower returns on U.S. investments than foreign ones. But as the economies of Europe and Asia have continued to expand and as their political systems have proven increasingly durable, businesses are now more willing to accept the risk associated with shifting economic activity out of the United States.

The major response of the national government to the internationalization of the world economy has been to cut the direct tax on business activity. As late as 1957, the corporate income tax and other direct taxes on business accounted for nearly one-fourth of the revenue received by the federal government. By 1990 they amounted to less than one-twelfth (see figure 2-1). Significantly, the federal government chose not to replace the revenue lost from a declining corporate income tax with an increase in personal income taxes. Instead, it increased a broad-based, nonprogressive payroll tax levied to finance the growing cost of social security and medicare.

But if changes in the international economy are beginning to limit the national government's capability for redistribution, it still remains the level of government that has the greatest redistributive capacity. Taxes on business have never been more than a trivial portion of the revenue stream of state and local governments, and the state and local taxes of choice, the sales and property taxes, are much less progressive than the national income tax. And despite increasing international competition, there is no reason to believe that the country's redistributive policies are excessive. The overall level of taxation in the United States is well below that of its major industrial competitors in Europe (though not in Asia).[34]

Categorical Grants

The national government may ask state and local governments to assist in the performance of its redistributive activities. By paying part or all of the costs, it may ask lower tiers to perform certain redistributive activities, such as providing rent subsidies for low-income people. There is much to be said for categorical grants. If all lower-tier governments are asked by the national government to make similar contributions to redistributive activities, each can participate in the redistributive function without placing itself at risk of becoming a haven for the poor and the needy. For example, the national government has required all school districts to provide for the education of disabled children, and federal monies have been given to local school districts to help pay for some of the additional cost of special education. Before the national government imposed this requirement, special education programs were hopelessly inadequate and many local school districts refused to let disabled children attend school. Some have attributed such hard-heartedness to overrepresentation on local school boards of the spiritual descendants of Simon Legree. But functional theory offers a less personalized explanation: any district that provided a substantial set of special education services ran the risk of becoming a haven for families with disabled children. Once a national requirement was imposed on all school districts, each was able to establish an appropriate set of educational services without placing itself at undue economic risk.

Redistributive federal grants, such as educational aid for the handicapped, are called categorical grants, because, unlike block grants, they are accompanied by detailed regulations to make sure the funds are not diverted to developmental activity. These regulations help ensure that monies are used for the purposes for which they were intended. By controlling the use of federal grants, federal regulations prevent local governments from using the grants to gain an advantage on their competitors.

Functional theory expects national regulation of state and local redistributive activities to create conflicts within the federal system. The conflict is greatest in the early stages of a program, when state and local governments are most likely to divert monies to developmental objectives. To forestall cheating, the national government begins to impose tighter regulations, which impede needed flexibility in the administration of the program. After a period of experimentation and the recruitment of professionals trained to carry out the functions of the program, regulations are relaxed and a modus vivendi is worked out within the federal system. In short, the price to be paid for the administration of intergovernmental categorical grants gradually falls.

The experience of the compensatory education program, an educational program directed toward improving the education of the disadvantaged, illustrates this pattern. When the program was initially established, the national government had few guidelines and there was widespread local diversion of compensatory funds to other educational purposes. Tight federal regulations were then imposed on local districts. The regulations were so restrictive that they were interpreted as requiring the removal of disadvantaged children from the regular classroom and giving them instruction in separate quarters, a practice that many felt stigmatized those the program was supposed to help. Eventually, national regulations were loosened, programming became routinized, and the gap between the performance of white and minority students declined substantially.[35]

Localities also resisted national objectives during the first years of the federal housing program. The Housing Act of 1949 was expected to enhance the housing stock for low-income Americans. Amendments to the legislation in 1954 gave local governments the discretion to use the money for construction for a broader range of income groups and for commercial as well as residential purposes. When given the opportunity to exercise discretion in the use of housing funds, cities concentrated an ever increasing percentage of the funds in upper-income housing and commercial construction. In response to complaints that urban renewal was tantamount to black removal from areas adjacent to the central business district, housing policy was revised during the Johnson and Nixon administrations so as to concentrate funds on low- and moderate-income housing.[36]

An Empirical Theory

Although functional theory has been mainly used for normative evaluation of public policies,[37] it has at times been employed as an empirical theory to account for the greater degree of redistribution carried out by the national government than by state and local governments.[38] Yet, as an empirical theory, functional theory has been criticized for failing to specify the political processes by which policy is formulated.[39]

Functional theorists have responded to this criticism by asserting that voters take into account the economic prosperity of their state or community when evaluating public issues and candidates for public office. State and local officials who enhance the property values and economic prosperity of their constituency are more likely to be rewarded with reelection. Because the market will respond fairly quickly to policy choices adversely affecting state and local prosperity, public officials have political as well as policy incentives to pursue efficient, effective development policies. In most states and localities, however, there are few incentives to enact large-scale redistributive policies, for which the economic and political costs are likely to be very high.

According to functional theory, officials elected to national office are also rewarded for concentrating on policies within their sphere of competence. Unlike state and local officials, they cannot ignore redistribution in the hope that some other level of government will address politically compelling needs. Instead, they must ascertain the politically appropriate degree of redistribution that the voting majority prefers. National officials find it easier to shift the responsibility for development policy to state and local officials, who have strong incentives to provide appropriate social and physical infrastructure from their own resources. If the national government becomes involved, it runs the risk of being accused of encouraging fraud, waste, and abuse. Its relative inability to ascertain appropriate strategies for economic development discourages national officials from running the political risks of pursuing these policies. As a result, federal policymakers tend to shun economic development policies.[40]

The debate over redistribution becomes most intense in presidential election contests. The president is the very personification of American government for many people. The doings of presidents command media attention, fascinate ordinary citizens, and affect the strategies and calculations of organized groups, members of Congress, and presidential hopefuls. Voter turnout in presidential elections runs approximately 50 percent higher than turnout in state elections held in nonpresidential years. (The size of the electorate in local elections is typically less than half the size of the electorate in presidential elections.)[41] Since the percentage of the vote cast by low-income and minority citizens is larger in high-turnout elections, the pressure for redistribution is most intense when presidential candidates are on the ballot. The specter of cuts in social security haunts every presidential election. Taxes, welfare, medical care, environmental protection, consumer rights, protection for the disabled: these are staples of presidential politics trumped only by the public demand that jobs be plentiful and wars be short.

The victor in presidential campaigns, needless to say, is not necessarily the candidate who promises to do the most to help the poor by taking from the rich. Conservative presidential candidates have won the presidency more often than have liberal ones. But functional theorists point out that major changes in the degree of redistribution have occurred only at presidential instigation. The welfare state was legitimated by Roosevelt's New Deal, Harry Truman placed civil rights on the national agenda, Lyndon Johnson founded the Great Society, and Richard Nixon called for welfare reform and signed into law food stamps, aid to the disabled, and the indexation of the social security program. The political fate of redistribution depends heavily on the outcome of the struggle for the presidency.

Interest group activity reinforces the propensity of governments to act within their sphere of competence. Groups favoring redistribution concentrate their attention at the national level, because the lower economic cost of national redistribution makes it easier to secure political support for their policy preferences. The American Association of Retired Persons, the Children's Defense Fund, the Center on Budget and Policy Priorities, and a host of consumer and environmental advocacy organizations concentrate their energies on the national government. Anticipating that they will encounter greater resistance at state and local levels, potentially comparable groups often decide it is not worth the effort to organize there. As a recent study of interest group politics at the state level concluded, "Senior citizen, environmentalist, and women's and minority groups have enjoyed limited success."[42]

Interest groups interested in economic development, on the other hand, typically focus their attention on local and state officials. The costs of government failure to promote the economic development of a state or community are more immediate and apparent than a failure to act by the federal government. It is thus easier for developmentally oriented groups to make a persuasive argument for their policies in conversations with state and local officials than with those in Washington. Perhaps this is one reason that over two-thirds of the country's trade associations do *not* locate their headquarters in Washington, D.C.[43] According to one major study, the kinds of groups participating in state politics represent business, labor, farmers, education, and local government.[44] Business groups will also try to influence national policy, but the main focus of their efforts is often to limit government action.[45]

Congressional Decisionmaking

Functional theorists assume that Congress is organized so as to formulate policies that make best use of the competencies of the national government. For example, functional theorists assume the main function of congressional committees is to gather the information necessary to design effective national policy. Congress is divided into committees so that each committee can acquire the knowledge necessary to make policy recommendations that will win majorities on the chamber floor. Committees are thought not to exercise inordinate power over national policy, because they must craft proposed legislation that can obtain passage on the floor of Congress.[46]

Functional theorists also say that Congress tends to distribute benefits widely, a tendency known as the universalism rule. This rule says that legislation is designed so as to win nearly universal support from among the members of a legislative body so that policy is not dependent upon fluctuating, temporary majorities. The rule is enforced by the fact that all legislation must navigate a tortuous passage that requires votes in committees, passage on the floors of both Houses, renegotiation in a conference committee that includes representatives from both chambers, repassage on the chamber floors, and, finally, a presidential signature or, in the case of a presidential veto, a two-thirds vote by each legislative chamber.

Proponents of legislative initiatives have long known that any proposal that is to survive this labyrinth must be constructed in such a way as to weld together a broad, diverse set of interests. Legislative proponents would be taking a great risk if they left any major region or type of community seriously shorthanded. Not every program must benefit every district equally, but, taken together, the sum total of federal aid to localities needs to be reasonably well balanced.[47] Politically, it is preferable to find ways of building stable coalitions through logrolling that will distribute federal aid more or less evenly to almost all parts of the country.[48]

Not only do functional theorists expect Congress to follow the rule of universalism, but they also expect federal grants will be used to soften the territorial inequity in fiscal resources among states. Informed of differences in state and local capacities to facilitate economic development, and unable to perform this task efficiently, the national government will provide resources to needy parts of the country.

Predicting the Direction of Change

Functional theorists predict that over time policymakers at local and, to a lesser extent, state levels will increasingly concentrate their attention on economic development policies. The national government, on the other hand, will increasingly concentrate its attention on redistributive policies. The theory further predicts that over time the national government will provide increasing assistance to state and local governments in order to help them perform their redistributive tasks. However, the national government will be increasingly disinclined to help state and local governments perform their developmental responsibilities.

Some functional theorists also would expect increases in federal developmental grants to local governments. The national government would simply be providing local governments with additional resources to help carry out the tasks that they are best able to perform.

Others have quite the opposite expectation. If the national government supplies the resources, state and local political leaders are less constrained to justify expenditures. Lower-priority projects are undertaken even when benefits do not exceed costs. Developmental grants to local authorities do not enhance state and local development; instead, they introduce distortions and inefficiencies.

Redistributive grants to state and local authorities are more easily justified by functional federalism. If the federal government wishes to pursue a set of redistributive policies that require the coordinated efforts of all levels of government, it must provide financial support. Otherwise, state and local governments can be expected to refuse to participate in the redistributive undertaking. Coordination of redistributive programs is seldom simple, especially in the early years when a program is being established. The program may well become bogged down in delays and bureaucratic red tape. But since only the national government has the capacity to carry out an effective redistributive program, it is likely to come under interest group pressure to continue the coordination. In a society where demands for redistribution steadily increase, national redistributive grants to state and local governments can be expected to expand steadily.

In sum, functional theory is optimistic about the future of American federalism. Each level of government has an appropriate set of responsibilities, and the political forces at work encourage each level of government to concentrate on those responsibilities at which it is most competent. The system is capable of self-correction. Inconsistencies and problems are temporary, not enduring. The California fiscal crisis was not the agonized gasp of a patient suffering a terminal illness but merely the groan of a convalescent on the mend.

Legislative Theory

A second theory of federalism, best characterized as legislative theory, is much less optimistic. It thinks that the political incentives that shape the decisions of policymakers induce them to make the wrong choices. The national government takes on responsibilities it should best avoid. It imposes unaffordable tasks on lower levels of the system.

The theory bears the legislative label because it assumes that policies are shaped by the political needs of those who write the country's laws. It also gives a less important policy role for presidents than does functional theory. It assumes that, in general, the preferences of presidents (and governors) have much less effect on domestic public policy than do preferences of the members of Congress (and state legislatures).

The Role of Presidents

The theory's second assumption accords well with much that is known about American constitutional theory and practice. Harry Truman expressed the frustration of many presidents when he predicted what would happen to his successor, Dwight Eisenhower: "He'll sit here and he'll say, 'Do this! Do that!' *And nothing will happen.* Poor Ike— it won't be a bit like the Army. He'll find it very frustrating."[49] Or, in the words of George Bush, "I don't want to sound sanctimonious about this, but I was elected to govern."[50]

Bush may have thought the voters elected him to govern, but this was not what the makers of the U.S. Constitution intended. They remembered clearly the struggle for independence against the armies of King George III, and they were not about to give presidents anything remotely resembling royal power. The Constitution gives the president the duty to faithfully execute the laws of the United States, but Congress is given the authority to make these laws. The president may veto laws passed by Congress, but Congress can still pass the law over the president's veto by a two-thirds vote. The president cannot expend any monies without congressional approval. The president may negotiate and sign treaties with other nations, but two-thirds of the Senate must consent before the treaty can take effect. The president may appoint others to assist in executing the laws, but these officials can take office only if a majority of the Senate approves. The subordination of presidents to Congress is ultimately established by the congressional power of impeachment, by which Congress can remove a president from office.

The American party system further limits the power of the president. During his first two years in office, Bill Clinton had Democratic majorities in both the Senate and the House. But the mere fact that the president and Congress were controlled by the same party did not guarantee cooperation on legislative matters. Clinton had to make important compromises to win congressional approval of his tax legislation, voter registration bill, trade agreement with Mexico, and crime bill. He was unable to win passage of his proposal for universal health insurance. Clinton's experiences are not unusual. A recent study indicates that presidents are able to win congressional approval for proposed legislation without significant compromise in less than 20 percent of the major legislative items they propose.[51]

Congressional influence is especially great when it comes to the distribution of federal programs among states and congressional districts. Members care a lot about the impact of national programs in their home territory. Presidents care more about their overall consequences for the nation and less about the distributional consequences of these policies.[52] In any bargaining between the president and Congress over distributional issues, legislative theory assumes congressional preferences will prevail.

Legislative Incentives

Legislative theory assumes that elected representatives' primary goal is their own reelection. In pursuit of that goal, representatives seek to secure benefits for—and screen costs from—their constituencies.[53] Legislators also seek credit for all good things that happen to constituents and avoid blame for anything bad that might occur. As Oklahoma

Representative Mike Synar put it, "It's ambition that gets you [to Congress]. It's paranoia that keeps you here."[54]

Legislative theory further assumes that constituents easily recognize spatially concentrated costs and benefits, but that spatially dispersed costs and benefits are less perceptible. Legislators therefore support projects that have geographically concentrated benefits but diffuse costs, and they oppose policies that have diffuse benefits but spatially concentrated costs.

Legislators and Development

Developmental policies expected to generate economic activity within a district are generally perceived to be a concentrated benefit worthy of legislative support. Members of Congress favor expenditure on dams, courthouses, sports stadiums, museums, atomic colliders, and other visible signs of government stimulation of the local economy. In Barry Goldwater's words, "I don't care what the piece of equipment is—or how bad it is—if it's done in his state, the senator has to stand up and scream for it."[55] Legislators support developmental projects for their districts even though the total cost of these projects, dispersed throughout the country, might outweigh any benefits the projects might have. Programs not worth their cost are usually dubbed "pork" or "pork barrel" projects. But it is often difficult to tell whether a particular developmental project is really worth the investment. As Speaker of the House Thomas Foley once said, "One person's pork barrel project is another person's wise investment in the local infrastructure." Or as Representative James Howard put it, "Pork barrel spelled backwards is infrastructure."[56] In sum, legislators often find it easy to justify their support for additional monies to improve state and local infrastructure and carry out other developmental projects of interest to their constituents.

The way in which Joe McDade of Scranton, Pennsylvania, used his position as ranking Republican on the House Appropriations Committee is regarded by legislative theorists as a quintessential example of legislative decisionmaking. Although under indictment on charges of "racketeering, conspiracy and accepting about $100,000 in illegal gratuities," McDade won reelection to Congress in 1994 in part because of his success in winning federal grants for his district. He secured federal monies to help build a center for the performing arts and fund a microbiology institute for cancer research at the University of Scranton (even though it has no medical school or research scientists), restore an antique aqueduct, construct McDade Park (including a tourist-friendly museum on the history of coal mining), turn the home of second-rate author Zane Grey into a national monument, finance a flood control project, and convert a railroad station into a fancy hotel and restaurant.[57]

The propensity of members of Congress to get more pork for their constituents has been used to explain the pressure on the national government to spend more than it receives in tax revenues. Legislative theorists suggest that representatives and senators can nearly ensure their reelection if they hand out observable benefits to the geographic area from which they come—regardless of the fiscal cost to U.S. taxpayers. The political benefits that accrue from expenditures for bridges, dams, tunnels, and colliders outweigh the political costs of paying for them, which are spread diffusely among taxpayers across time and space. Legislative theory says the result is spiraling public expenditure.

Legislative theory also suggests that the propensity for pork is less heavily concentrated in the Senate than the House of Representatives. Senatorial elections are more visible, more issue oriented, and more likely to be decided by national partisan trends. For all these reasons, pork is less likely to determine senatorial electoral outcomes.[58]

Legislative theory is less sanguine than functional theory about the likelihood that fiscal inequities at state and local levels can be offset by federal grants. According to legislative theory, members vote for programs that provide a net fiscal benefit for their constituents. Constituents expect to receive back in benefits as much as they pay in taxes. When a study indicated that the share of national expenditures spent in Massachusetts had dropped from 2.8 percent in 1988 to 2.7 percent in 1993, so that the state was receiving only 97 cents back for every dollar paid in taxes (instead of the $1.01 it had received in 1988), the finding fetched the following headline in a local newspaper: "State's Share of Federal Dollars Drops: Kennedy's Record in Last Decade, a Campaign Issue." Senator Edward Kennedy had six years earlier run on the campaign slogan, "He can do more for Massachusetts." His Republican opponent now accused him of not having "done the hard work to do very much [for Massachusetts] at all."[59] The critique of Kennedy's alleged laziness was hardly unusual. Voters in most states think benefits received should keep pace with taxes paid. This means that senators from states with high fiscal capacity, whose constituents contribute a disproportionate share to the federal treasury, demand that federal programs give back to their state a level of benefits equivalent to what has been paid in taxes. Senators elected from these states can hardly be expected to vote for legislation that targets aid to states with few fiscal resources.

One way Congress can design programs so as to distribute benefits to states in proportion to the taxes their residents pay is to make federal grants conditional on the contribution of a matching amount by state or local government. The higher the state or local share, the more likely that states with greater fiscal capacity will get more federal dollars, simply because these states have more resources to pay for their share.[60] In the case of medicaid, for example, every federal dollar must, in most states, be matched by a state dollar.

Functional and legislative theory differ with regard to the importance of committees for congressional decisionmaking. As I have discussed, functional theory assumes that the role of committees is to provide information to all members of Congress and that no particular influence over policy accrues to members simply by virtue of their membership on a particular committee. Legislative theory assumes that legislators gravitate toward committees that control policies of special concern to their constituents and that committee membership confers on representatives a capacity to exercise disproportionate influence over policy.[61] Since most legislation is written within committees, members can use their influence within the committee to secure additional pork for the constituents back home.

Legislators and Redistribution

Legislators' opinions about redistribution are, according to legislative theory, strongly influenced by constituency pressures. A legislator who represents a low-income, needy population or a liberal constituency is likely to favor the expansion of redistributive programs. Those who represent middle-income constituents less likely to need government aid are more likely to resist redistribution. Political support for redistribution is expected to be greater in cities and states with higher poverty rates.[62]

Geographical politics are likely to affect redistributive decisions less than developmental ones. Both the costs and benefits are geographically diffuse. In addition, legislators apparently do not gain votes from securing more redistributive dollars for their district.[63] Legislators need to balance the demands of those anticipating geographically diffuse benefits against those anticipating the equally diffuse tax burdens neces-

TABLE 2-2. *Public Support for Developmental and Redistributive Programs, 1988–93*

Type of program	Percentage of respondents who said too little is spent on this type of program
Developmental	
Environmental protection	66
Education	69
Drug control	62
Crime	63
Highways	38
Parks and recreation	30
Mass transportation	32
Average for all developmental programs	**51**
Redistributive	
Welfare	44
Big cities	36
Conditions of blacks	31
Social security	50
Average for all redistributive programs	**40**

SOURCE: James Allan Davis and Tom W. Smith, *General Social Surveys, 1972–1993* (Chicago: National Opinion Research Center, 1993).

sary to finance them. Legislators find themselves caught between intense demands for redistribution and equally intense opposition to tax increases. Whether they choose to raise taxes or to cut benefits, they are likely to be criticized.

Surveys of public opinion indicate that spending for most types of redistributive spending is less popular than most kinds of developmental spending (see table 2-2). When people are asked whether they think too little is spent on welfare, the problems of cities, or improving conditions for black Americans, only a little more than one-third say yes. But when people are asked whether too little is spent on education, efforts to halt crime and drug use, or environmental protection, two-thirds agree. Not all developmental spending is popular: only about one-third think more should be spent on highways, parks, or mass transportation. And not all redistributive spending is unpopular: half the public still favors spending more money on social security. Nonetheless, the politics of redistribution can be expected to generate considerable legislative conflict.

The conflict can generally be expected to fall along partisan lines, although one can cite numerous exceptions to this pattern. In general, it is the Republicans who worry more about economic development and the Democrats who worry more about securing a more equitable division of the economic pie.

Because redistributive policies are more likely to generate partisan conflict, they often become highly visible. It is thus especially important in the redistributive arena that legislators try to avoid blame for the harms they must impose. Blame avoidance is even more important to political leaders than credit claiming. When politicians take credit for something that happens, many will remain skeptical. But voters are unlikely to forget a politician whom they blame for a harm they have suffered.[64]

To avoid blame, legislators try to construct devices that help disguise the connections between their actions and the harms that occur. The blame-avoidance mechanisms members of Congress have devised are legion: voice votes instead of roll call votes; delegation of difficult decisions to presidents, bureaucrats, commissions, or state and local governments; legislation so complex and internally contradictory few can figure out its impact; and incorporation of a vast amount of legislation into a single bill that contains such obvious benefits they seem to outweigh the harms imposed.

One way of avoiding blame when responding to demands for redistribution is to require lower levels of government to pay for the redistributive benefits. The legislator gets the credit for benefiting needy constituents, but the cost is paid by a lower governmental tier. The connection between the legislator's actions and the cost to the taxpayer is at least partially disguised.

In 1990 Congress passed and President Bush signed a bill requiring that state and local governments ensure equal opportunity and equal access to public facilities by disabled persons. But very little money was given to state and local governments to help pay for the cost of providing the improved opportunity and access. Members of Congress and the president received credit for the civil rights legislation; the costs have been borne by state and local governments. The welfare reform enacted in 1988 required many states to garnish the wages of absent fathers and provide 50 percent of the cost of assisting two-parent as well as single-parent families.[65] Congress has added many new regulations to medicaid programs, contributing to their rising cost and diverting monies from other state programs.[66] The Clean Air Act Amendments Act of 1990 also placed many new environmental obligations on state and local governments. Congress and the president got the credit for addressing environmental problems, while state and local governments were asked to bear the burden of imposing additional costs on energy users.[67] Federal transportation regulations require state and local governments to test city truck drivers for alcohol and drug use. Environmental regulations require local governments to move city fuel tanks above ground.[68] Congress requires all school districts to provide for the special educational needs of handicapped children, but it pays for little more than a tenth of the cost. Congress has not taken the steps necessary to limit the influx of illegal immigrants into the United States, perhaps because illegal immigrants seem to have had an overall positive affect on the nation's economy. But the social cost borne by governments in the seven most heavily affected states is nearly $2 billion a year more than tax revenues received.[69] Congress is unwilling to make up the difference.

The shifting of national responsibilities to state and local governments prompted many state and local officials to organize a "National Unfunded Mandates Day" in October 1993. Officials asked Washington to stop imposing further rules and regulations on local officials unless the necessary compliance monies were made available. Citing a report by the U.S. Conference of Mayors that claimed cities would need to spend $54 billion dollars on ten major mandates over the next five years, one mayor claimed that cities were suffering "spending without representation."[70]

A ban on any further unfunded mandates was promised by Republican candidates for Congress during the 1994 election campaign as part of their "Contract with America." To fulfill their campaign commitments, the Republican-controlled Congress approved a bill banning the passage of any new laws regulating the actions of states and localities without compensating them for costs incurred as a result of the mandate. Any proposed legislation that imposes an unfunded mandate will be subject to a point of order, which can be raised by any member of Congress. Although the legislation won widespread support and was enthusiastically signed into law by President Clinton, it may mean less in reality than appears on the surface. The legislation is entirely prospective. No existing federal regulation is in any way affected by the law. But a law that has only a prospective effect can be nullified by any future law, which automatically supersedes any law already enacted. If Congress chooses at any time in the future to impose an unfunded mandate on a state or locality, it can vote down a point of order by majority vote and enact a mandate, despite apparently sweeping language to the contrary.

Despite the passage of the unfunded mandate law, legislative theory expects the mandate issue to continue. As members of Congress come under increasing electoral pressure, they will try to shift redistributive responsibilities to state and local governments. In that way they can provide more services without being blamed for the tax increases necessary to pay for them.

A Theory of Change

In the immediate postwar period, pork barrel propensities were thought to be held in check by strong parties, the presence of conservatives on key appropriation committees, and an informal club that kept power in the hands of hard-working insiders.[71] But beginning in the late 1960s and continuing into the 1970s, several trends changed the nature of legislative politics. First, the American voter paid less attention to partisan affiliation when voting for a member of Congress. Improved systems of transportation and communication allowed citizens to obtain direct impressions of their representatives and have given members of Congress the ability to tell their story directly to constituents. The mediating role of political parties became less important.

Second, members introduced changes in Congress that enabled them to capitalize on the opportunities the new technologies provide. Members of Congress hired more staff, extended their use of the franking privilege, voted themselves more free trips to their home district, opened up more offices in their district, and set up sophisticated TV and radio communication facilities on Capitol Hill. They also reorganized Congress by increasing the number and autonomy of subcommittees. More issues were brought to the chamber floor, and more of the issues were decided by a recorded vote. As the cost of campaigning exploded, fund-raising became a full-time preoccupation. All of these trends made members more independent, autonomous, and sensitive to the needs and concerns of their constituents.[72] As members became more sophisticated, they came to regard themselves as professional politicians who expected to make their job the basis for a career. In the process, reelection became ever more important.

As members became more professionalized and were more bent on reelection, they devised more and more pork barrel schemes, accelerating government expenditure and pushing deficits ever higher.[73] Government expenditure continues to grow in response to the legislators' need to respond to the geographically defined needs of their constituents.

An Empirical Theory

Legislative theorists seldom, if ever, offer their theory as a normative guide. Only the most polite applause is reserved for legislators' responsiveness to the geographic area that elected them. Most legislative theorists think that the price the nation pays for such responsiveness is exorbitant. Government expenditures rise; the public debt climbs; state and local mandates remain unfunded; the common interests of the country as a whole are given scant attention. Some legislative theorists have gone so far as to call for wholesale changes in systems of representation: term limitations; tight restrictions on resources available to incumbents; elimination of first-past-the-post, single-election districts; and even moves toward a parliamentary form of government.[74]

Predicting the Direction of Change

Calls for reform are persuasive to many legislative theorists, because the theory seems to predict perverse policymaking in a legislatively directed federal system. Government is likely to continue to grow indiscriminately. Even worse, each level of government is likely to grow in the very domain where it is least competent.

The federal government is likely to expand its development policies, because these policies generate the pork in greatest demand by local constituencies. State governments are forced to expand their redistributive activities in response to the new mandates placed upon them by federal officials. Local governments, subject to both national and state mandates, will be under still additional pressure to increase their redistributive efforts.

Conclusions

Functional theory and legislative theory offer contrasting assessments of the health of the modern federal system. According to functional theorists, the federal system is capable of adapting to the increasing integration of the American economy. Each level of government focuses on those responsibilities for which it is best adapted.

Legislative theory is much less optimistic. The electoral incentives facing legislators induce them to act in ways that contribute to increasing federal disequilibrium. Congress does little to offset the fiscal inequalities existing at state and local levels. Instead, members of Congress, to gain reelection, add to the burdens of state and local governments and inefficiently allocate resources among them. In the chapter that follows I shall examine information on fiscal trends in American federalism to see whether the direction in which the federal system has been moving better supports functional or legislative theory.

3

The Changing
Federal System

*I have never been more struck by the good sense and the
practical judgment of the Americans than in the manner in
which they elude the numberless difficulties resulting from
their Federal Constitution.*
Alexis de Tocqueville, *Democracy in America*

Functional and legislative theories of federalism disagree about the
direction in which the federal system is moving. Functional theory says
the price of federalism is diminishing. Each level of government is
focusing more on the function it can best perform. As the nation's
economy becomes increasingly integrated, the federal government
gradually assumes responsibility for redistributive programs, while
state and local governments concentrate their attention on economic
development.

Legislative theory anticipates that the price of federalism will climb.
It foresees legislators at higher levels of government taking credit for
financing popular developmental programs. These legislators also try
to avoid blame by assigning redistributive tasks to lower levels of government. As a result, the federal system becomes increasingly inefficient, ineffectual, and prone to fiscal crisis.

In this chapter I will show that legislative theories can account for
some of the dynamics of the federal system, especially during the 1960s
and 1970s. But for the most part I find the direction of change to be
consistent with functional theory. Each level of government is increasingly focused on the policy arena in which it has the greatest
competence.[1]

50

The Adolescence of Modern Federalism

Federalism is thought to be an ancient, even hoary component of the country's constitutional structure. But the transformation in American federalism that has produced the modern system is of recent vintage. It was born during the New Deal. The growth spurt that characterizes its adolescence dates only from the Great Society.

The narrow conception of an appropriate federal role dominant throughout the nineteenth century was initially challenged by Franklin Roosevelt's New Deal. To stimulate economic recovery, Congress provided fiscal aid to cities under the Federal Emergency Relief Act of 1933; homeownership was made more accessible to middle- and working-class families in 1934 when their bank mortgages were reinsured by the Federal Housing Authority; states and localities received funds for roads and highways under the Interstate Highway Act of 1934; the poor and the elderly received public assistance as part of the Social Security Act of 1935; and the Public Works Administration (PWA), established by the National Industrial Recovery Act of 1933, built roads, dams, and public housing. Taken all together, federal aid to local governments increased from $68.3 million in 1934 to $2.6 billion in 1940.[2] (Unless otherwise specified, all dollar figures have been converted into 1990 dollars.) The Supreme Court, after initially questioning the constitutional basis for New Deal policy, eventually handed down a series of decisions that legitimated an expanded federal role.

If modern federalism was born during the Great Depression and the New Deal, it was not until after World War II that intergovernmental programs became something more than a stepchild of American government. Much of the initial impetus for a more sustained federal role came from growing problems of large central cities. Beginning in the 1950s, it became increasingly apparent that their difficulties were not just by-products of the depression but a consequence of broader social and economic forces.

The congressional response to these demands went through three major stages in the postwar era. Congress first tried to revive the economic vitality of central cities by redeveloping areas surrounding central business districts. It then turned to the amelioration of urban social and fiscal problems. Finally, Congress backed away from urban America, cutting back much of the assistance it had been providing.

Direct federal grants to all local governments in 1957 totaled less than $1.6 billion (see table 3-6 below). Although many of these grant programs were of marginal significance, one of them, the 1954 urban renewal program, constituted the first major attempt by the federal government to shape the urban future. Significantly, this attempt was never explicitly conceptualized by Congress as an urban policy. Instead, it was tucked away in a series of seemingly minor amendments to the Housing Act of 1949.

Public housing had long been controversial. When the PWA set aside 30 percent of its public housing units for African Americans, southerners complained that the program was encouraging racial integration. When it began buying land and constructing houses, lower federal courts said PWA had exceeded its constitutional authority. Congress responded to this constitutional attack in 1937 by taking the authority to build public housing away from PWA and giving it to the U.S. Housing Authority, which, instead of erecting its own housing, gave housing construction loans to local governments. Although this delegation of direct responsibility to local governments placed the program on stronger constitutional footing, it did not end the criticism that government was unfairly competing with private developers, and, as a result, not much public housing was constructed until the passage of the 1949 housing act.

As originally signed by Harry Truman, this act stated as its national goal the provision of a decent home and suitable living environment for every American family. To facilitate this objective, it offered low-interest grants and loans for the redevelopment of blighted areas within cities. Nearly all expenditure was limited to residential construction for low- to moderate-income people.

To expand political support for housing legislation, congressional supporters loosened the low-income residence restriction in 1954, 1959, and 1961 with amendments that allowed states and localities to use an ever-increasing share of the monies appropriated under the act for commercial revitalization and the construction of higher-income housing. Many central-city leaders recognized that these revisions in the legislation provided them with an opportunity to revive their central business districts. From their perspective, big cities needed to provide better access and more ample parking for trucks and automobiles as well as relaxing, mall-like atmospheres for retail shopping. Residential construction was needed for college-educated employees hired to work in the new high-rise offices. Poor minorities could be asked to move to areas more distant from the central business district.

Although these plans seemed in theory to give big cities a chance to renew their economic vitality, they were, in practice, a mixed blessing. Some cities combined federal dollars with private development monies to facilitate their transformation from a manufacturing to an office-oriented economy. Chicago may be the outstanding case in point. Faced with the loss of millions of manufacturing jobs, Chicago managed to redesign its central-city core so that its position as the heartland's dominant commercial, financial, and administrative center was strengthened and reinforced. Building on Chicago's past architectural triumphs, city fathers constructed a skyline of unsurpassed variety and monumentality. Capitalizing on the city's magnificent lake front, they attracted a young, prosperous population to newly constructed and refurbished condominiums. Anticipating the college boom, they used urban renewal monies to stabilize the racially changing neighborhood near the University of Chicago and to help construct an entirely new Chicago campus for the University of Illinois within a stone's throw of the city center.

In other cities, outcomes were not as favorable. In New Haven, the urban renewal program was expected to revitalize the downtown business district and attract middle-class residents back to areas adjacent to the city center. Despite the infusion of federal funds and private development money, New Haven, unlike Chicago, could not make a successful transition from the industrial city it once had been to the commercial city it needed to become. Too close to New York City to become an independent financial and administrative center, yet too far away to become a satellite office center, New Haven was unable to benefit from the office boom of the 1980s. And without the presence of central-city office workers, retailer efforts to compete effectively with suburban shopping centers failed dismally.

The benefits from urban renewal varied from city to city, but the costs were evident almost everywhere. Residents of blighted neighborhoods were usually the minority poor. When they lost access to housing in areas adjacent to central business districts, they migrated to aging neighborhoods farther from the city center. This migration, reinforced by an influx of African Americans from the South, accentuated the racial tensions that culminated in civil rights demonstrations, racial violence, and, eventually, a white backlash. Urban renewal was criticized for contributing to—rather than reversing—the processes of urban decline. With the election of President Lyndon Johnson, federal urban

TABLE 3-1. *Developmental and Redistributive Expenditure of National Government and State-Local Governments, Selected Years, 1962–90*

Type of expenditure and level of government	Percentage of GNP						Amount (billions of 1990 dollars)					
	1962	1967	1972	1977	1982	1990	1962	1967	1972	1977	1982	1990
Developmental												
National	4.2	3.9	4.4	5.0	4.5	5.2	101	118	157	194	190	286
State and local	9.3	8.7	9.9	9.2	9.1	10.8	201	267	346	358	380	590
Total[a]	**13.6**	**12.6**	**14.3**	**14.2**	**13.6**	**16.0**	**301**	**385**	**497**	**552**	**570**	**875**
Redistributive												
National	4.8	5.5	7.4	9.4	10.8	10.3	114	167	257	368	451	561
State and local	2.2	2.0	2.6	3.2	3.4	3.5	52	61	91	125	141	188
Total[a]	**7.0**	**7.4**	**11.0**	**12.6**	**14.1**	**13.7**	**167**	**228**	**347**	**493**	**591**	**749**
Total national expenditure[a]	**9.0**	**9.3**	**11.7**	**14.4**	**15.3**	**15.5**	**215**	**285**	**408**	**562**	**641**	**846**
Total state and local expenditure[a]	**11.6**	**10.8**	**12.6**	**12.4**	**12.4**	**14.3**	**253**	**329**	**436**	**484**	**520**	**778**
Total domestic expenditure[a]	**20.6**	**20.0**	**25.3**	**26.8**	**27.8**	**28.8**	**467**	**614**	**844**	**1,045**	**1,161**	**1,624**

SOURCES: See appendix.
a. Totals may not add because of rounding.

policy, as will be discussed below, would take a new, more redistributive direction.

If urban renewal represents one of the early and more uncertain steps taken toward the creation of a modern federal system, the involvement of the national government in domestic policy formation still had not reached puberty. As late as 1962 national domestic expenditures amounted to only 9 percent of GNP. Over the next twenty-eight years these expenditures would increase from $215 billion to $846 billion (see table 3-1). Much of this fiscal growth was a by-product of population and economic growth. But governmental expenditure did more than keep pace with overall economic expansion; it also grew relative to GNP. The proportion of GNP spent by the national government increased from 9 percent in 1962 to 15.5 percent in 1990. Expenditures by state and local governments from their own fiscal resources also increased during this period, though at a somewhat lesser rate. In 1962 state and local expenditure amounted to $253 billion and accounted for 11.6 percent of GNP; in 1990 it had increased to $778 billion, or 14.3 percent.

Not only was each level of government expanding, but the relationships among levels of government were becoming more complex. This increased complexity was justified by the doctrine of cooperative or "marble-cake" federalism. As initially propounded by political scientist Morton Grodzins, cooperative federalism criticized the old dual sovereignty theory of federalism as outmoded. Dual sovereignty theory claimed that governments in the United States constituted a layer cake, each level separate from and independent of the other. Grodzins pointed out that, in practice, agencies from different levels of government typically worked together to solve problems, combining and intertwining their functions to such an extent that the intergovernmental system resembled a marble cake.[3]

According to Grodzins, all levels of government can work effectively together for three reasons. First, the involvement of all levels ensures that many different interests in society are involved in making policy. Federal, state, and local officials all have their own constituencies, and they each bring a distinctive perspective to bear. Cooperative federalism is thus democratic in nature. Second, the fact that state and local interests are represented in Congress means that federal officials take into account the needs and concerns of those to whom they make grants. Local officials are hardly ever compelled to take action; relations tend to be cooperative. Finally, the professional administrators of intergovernmental programs tend to share common values. They attend similar college and graduate programs, they read the same journals, and they frequent the same meetings of professional associations.

Grodzins's ideas about cooperative federalism were quickly absorbed into Lyndon Johnson's vision of a Great Society. All levels of government could work together, the president claimed, though the combination of governments appropriate to any given program would differ. Some federal grants went to states to assist in state-run programs. Other federal funds were allocated directly to local governments. Still other federal grants were to be distributed by each state to its local governments.[4]

This new marble-cake federalism was well leavened. In 1962 dollars granted in aid from the national to state and local governments amounted to no more than 1.4 percent of GNP. By 1977 this had increased to 3.1 percent of GNP (see table 3-5 below). Federal monies were directed toward ending poverty, financing welfare reform, educating disadvantaged children, subsidizing low-income housing, encouraging mass transit, and providing general fiscal support for cities. At the same time the national government issued an ever-growing number of regulations to accompany its grants-in-aid (figure 3-1). A brief review of the largest and politically most salient of these programs will reveal how widely the concept of cooperative federalism was being applied.

War on Poverty

If any one initiative symbolizes the era of cooperative federalism, it was the modestly funded but politically explosive war on poverty. Announced in the aftermath of the Kennedy assassination and on the eve of Johnson's triumphant 1964 presidential campaign, the Economic Opportunity Act of 1964 (the statutory basis for the war on poverty) directed the bulk of its fiscal resources to cities.

Several accomplishments remain evident two decades later. The popular Head Start program for preschoolers anticipated and paved the way for the child care and nursery school programs that subsequently diffused throughout the country. The job corps, a residential education and training program, though expensive, paid off in better wages and employment prospects. The legal services program changed the standing of poor people in the courts by challenging the constitutionality of a wide variety of local police and administrative practices. And by providing political, administrative, and employment opportunities to emerging African American, Latin American, and other minority activ-

FIGURE 3-1. *Growth in Federal Regulations, 1949–93*

1949 = 100

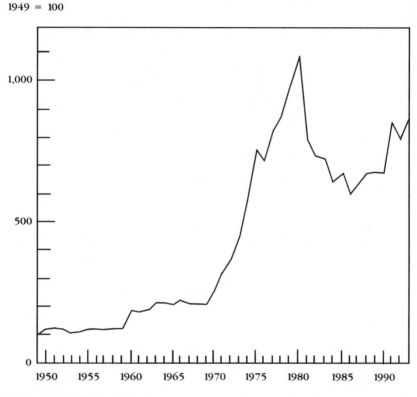

SOURCES: *Federal Register*, various pages.

ists, the poverty program facilitated the incorporation of minority leaders into the fabric of urban political life. From the poverty warriors of the 1960s and 1970s emerged many minority mayors, state legislators, and members of Congress elected in the 1980s and 1990s.

Despite these achievements, the war on poverty is better known for its warring factions than its substantive results. Its modest size—an average of $4.9 billion was expended annually over the nine-year life of its existence—belied its pretension to be a warlike enterprise. Its efforts to coordinate local social services failed dismally. Most of its job search, worker readiness, summer job, and other short-term manpower training programs had few long-term economic benefits.[5]

The main objection to the war on poverty was its emphasis on political action. In many cities, it antagonized local agencies and elected officials by encouraging protests, demonstrations, legal action, and minority electoral mobilization.[6] To some Washington policy analysts, an emphasis on political action made sense. Involving the impoverished in the system could forestall political alienation and perhaps even reverse the social apathy that seemed endemic to inner-city life. From a narrow partisan standpoint, energized African American and Latin American communities, newly enfranchised by civil rights legislation, could give Democrats a massive, energized bloc of supporters. These policy and partisan objectives may have made sense to some in Washington, but local officials wondered why federal monies should fund their political opposition. Not surprisingly, the program was blamed for the wave of civil violence that swept through American cities in the two years immediately after its adoption. Some argued that it broke up the biracial Democratic coalition that had made a war on poverty possible. Except where minority leaders had come to power, few local tears were shed in 1974 when Richard Nixon, who had campaigned against the poverty war, persuaded Congress to transfer its popular components to other agencies and shut down the remainder.

Education

Before cooperative federalism, Congress had authorized only three small education programs: impact aid, vocational education, and a combination of mathematics, science, and library programs. A larger federal role had been inhibited by conservative opposition to federal control of education, southern opposition to desegregation, and public school opposition to sharing federal funds with nonpublic, sectarian schools.

To overcome these sources of opposition, Johnson proposed that federal aid to education be designed to help fight the war against poverty. Proposed in these terms, Johnson was able to obtain compromises on which public and nonpublic school officials could agree, and the large Democratic majority in Congress quickly passed the legislation. The resulting compensatory education programs had a strong urban emphasis: 37 percent of the pupils participating in compensatory education programs in 1985 lived in central cities (compared with 26 percent of all pupils).[7] Congress also appropriated in subsequent years monies for special education for the handicapped, bilingual education, and aid to assist in school desegregation. In 1978 Congress acknowledged the increased federal role in education by transforming the Office of Education into a cabinet-level department.

The compensatory education program, though controversial, continued into the 1990s. Its propensity to pull out students from regular classrooms and teach them in special remedial settings has been criticized for stigmatizing educationally disadvantaged children. But it has been praised for symbolizing the country's commitment to equal educational opportunity and given some of the credit for the gains in educational achievement made by minority groups.[8]

Housing and Urban Development

Despite the fact that housing and urban development was given cabinet-level status in 1965, two of its major programs, public housing and urban renewal, suffered from disrepute. Public housing was symbolized by ugly, dirty, crime-infested, segregated high-rise apartment buildings, while urban renewal became synonymous with black removal. To correct these failings, housing policy under the new cooperative federalism undertook two new initiatives.

The first, the 1966 Demonstration Cities and Metropolitan Development Act, called for a comprehensive, coordinated, carefully planned attack on a wide variety of physical and social problems within designated inner-city neighborhoods. Known as the model cities program, it came as close to a specifically urban policy as Congress had ever passed. But the program became bogged down in bureaucratic and intergovernmental infighting and, in the end, mainly demonstrated that the intergovernmental system could not easily plan comprehensive solutions to urban problems.

The second strategy relied more on the private market to provide low-income housing units. It encouraged developers to build low- and moderate-income housing by subsidizing the interest rates on construction. Between 1968 and 1972 more than 1.6 million units were constructed, more than the total number of federally subsidized public housing previously erected. Then in 1970, 42,000 additional low-income families were assisted under a new rent subsidy program that paid for the portion of the cost of renting an approved housing unit above 25 percent of the family's income.[9] Congress then expanded the rent subsidy program in section 8 of the Housing and Community Development Act of 1974 so that it was reaching an estimated 300,000 new families a year by the late 1970s.[10]

Transportation

In 1956 Congress enacted the interstate highway act, which created a highway trust fund made up of revenues from a sales tax on gasoline. From this fund the federal government paid for 90 percent of the cost of the construction and maintenance of the comprehensive system of limited-access highways that revolutionized American transportation. But even while the program was contributing to economic growth, it was helping to intensify traffic congestion within central cities. As commuters used the new interstate highways to get to work, usage of buses, trains, and trolleys declined. By 1960 only 26 percent of central-city workers were using public transportation systems.[11]

When central-city officials asked for help in shoring up mass transit systems, Congress responded in 1961 by funding demonstration projects and offering to help cities better plan their mass transportation systems. In subsequent years, the scope of federal involvement increased. Congress authorized aid for mass transit construction in 1964; two years later, it established a Department of Transportation; in 1973, it antagonized the highway lobby by diverting funds that had accumulated in the highway trust account to mass transit; and in 1974, for the first time, it appropriated funds for transit operations. Despite these efforts to support mass transit, Americans became increasingly dependent upon the automobile; by 1980 the percentage of central-city workers commuting by public transport had declined to 14.3 percent.[12]

Block Grants and Fiscal Relief

The shape of cooperative federalism was modified somewhat with the election of two Republican administrations after 1968. Local officials had been complaining that federal bureaucrats were burdening local governments with unnecessary regulations. In his campaign for the presidency, Richard Nixon made these demands his own. Instead of a system of categorical grants, which regulated the way state and local governments used federal dollars, he proposed block grants that distributed federal monies for locally defined purposes.

Block grants were popular with state and local officials for the obvious reason that they gave them money they could spend without having to ask for more from state and local taxpayers. Indeed, they were a local politician's dream—"free" money to be spent on whatever legal purpose one wanted without having to tax the local voters.

Nixon's block grant proposals were also consistent with Republican philosophy that local control was to be preferred to federal regulation. But in order to win support for his proposals in a Congress controlled by the Democratic party, Nixon was forced to agree to continue many of the categorical programs that Democrats favored. As a result, block grants did not so much replace categorical grants as supplement them.

The total size of the intergovernmental grant program continued to grow throughout the administrations of Richard Nixon and Gerald Ford, and by 1977 these grants constituted a surprisingly large 3.1 percent of the country's gross national product (table 3-5 below).

Three major block grant programs were enacted into law. The first, the General Revenue Sharing Act of 1972, corresponded most closely to the Nixon administration's conception of an ideal federal system. Monies were distributed according to a strict formula that gave virtually no discretion to Washington bureaucrats. Local governments needed to submit no more than the most minimal application in order to receive the funds for which they were eligible. And monies were distributed with only minimal restrictions on their use. The program was expected to marry the federal government's ability to raise large amounts of funds equitably with the ability of local government officials to expend monies sensibly and efficiently.

The second block grant, the Community Development Block Grant Act of 1974 (CDBG), established the section 8 rent subsidy program and consolidated model cities, urban renewal, and five other categorical programs into a single grant that was to be used to provide decent housing, suitable environments, and economic opportunities for community residents, particularly those of low and moderate income. The legislation represented a compromise between the Nixon administration and the Democratic Congress. On the one side, the Republican administration succeeded in achieving a substantial amount of deregulation: the number of pages contained in the relevant regulations was reduced from 2,600 to 120, and the average application was 50 instead of 1,400 pages in length. On the other side, the Democratic Congress was able to establish the section 8 rent subsidy program for low-income families.[13]

Since CDBG distributed its funds widely to communities of all sizes and fiscal capacities, Congress, at the prompting of the Carter administration, created an additional community development program known as the urban development action grants (UDAGs). A throwback to the days of urban renewal, this short-lived program, passed in 1977, assisted the economic and commercial development of cities with especially disadvantaged populations.

The third block grant, the Comprehensive Employment Training Act of 1974 (CETA), replaced seventeen manpower training programs established by the war on poverty and related programs with a block grant that gave local governments considerable flexibility in designing training for jobless community residents. Congressional Democrats supported the legislation because it authorized funds for public-sector employment in any community where the unemployment rate exceeded 6 percent. When Carter became president, the public-sector employment component of CETA expanded rapidly, so that by 1978 it "provided jobs for more than a million unemployed persons and job training and work experience for thousands more."[14]

Retrenchment

Block grants, including general revenue sharing, were so popular locally that few realized in 1977 that the dramatic expansion in federal grants to state and local governments would soon be reversed by an almost equally rapid contraction. Yet the marble cake was beginning to crumble under the impact of both intellectual and political change. The intellectual charge against cooperative federalism came from a group of scholars who focused on the implementation of federal programs.[15] Implementation studies showed that the many different groups that influence intergovernmental policymaking often check and block one another, making it impossible to get much done. When Lyndon Johnson tried to build "new towns" for the poor on vacant federal land in big cities, he encountered the opposition of local officials, who responded to neighborhood complaints about the effects of these new towns on their property values.[16] Virtually no new towns were built. Implementation studies also found that when many different governmental agencies must agree before action can be taken, delays and confusion are almost inevitable. If success ever occurs, it becomes evident only years, maybe decades, later, long after political support has begun to wane.[17] Finally, these studies pointed out that when small-scale, experimental, minimally funded programs are justified with grandiose rhetorical flourishes, program outcomes necessarily disappoint constituents.

The intellectual case against marble-cake federalism was reinforced by the conservative surge to power in 1980. Two pieces of legislation urged on Congress by the newly elected Reagan administration provided the framework for the retrenchment in the intergovernmental grant system: the Economic Recovery Tax Act and the Omnibus Budget Reconciliation Act, both passed in 1981.[18] By cutting taxes more sharply than at any time in the nation's history, the first ushered in a decade or more of deficit politics that tightly constrained domestic spending programs. The second deregulated and cut expenditures for most intergovernmental programs. Between 1980 and 1990 mass transit was cut from $5.0 billion to $3.7 billion. Compensatory education was reduced from $5.3 billion to $4.4 billion. Desegregation assistance was eliminated altogether. By 1990 public-sector employment was abolished, urban development action grants were eliminated, and only 52,000 new families were receiving rent subsidies.[19]

Congress was even less enthusiastic about block grants during the Reagan years. General revenue sharing was eliminated in 1985, and CDBG was cut from $6.1 billion in 1980 to $2.8 billion in 1990.[20] Democrats on Capitol Hill acquiesced in the Reagan administration's proposed cuts in revenue sharing and many block grants because they wanted to save monies for entitlement programs. Also, it was easier to cut block grants when local government coffers were swelling with additional revenues generated by the economic growth of the mid-1980s. Then, too, block grants were difficult to defend in times of budgetary constraint. The very reason the block grants were popular with local politicians became the reason the program was difficult to justify as national policy. Why, it was asked, should the federal taxpayer give unrestricted money to local governments? Would not local officials be more accountable to their own citizens and taxpayers if they were not so dependent on federal assistance?

As a result of cuts in both categorical and block grant programs, the remarkable feast provided by federal grants over a fifteen-year period was then followed by a fifteen-year famine. The size of federal grants contracted substantially, falling back to 2.5 percent of GNP in 1990 (table 3-5 below). The great spurt in national regulatory activity begun in the late 1960s also ended with the election of Reagan in 1980. During the 1980s the number of regulations issued by the national government fell markedly, but it began to resume an upward direction in the 1990s (see figure 3-1).

In short, in the past thirty years modern federalism has changed dramatically in size and shape. In this era the New Deal baby became of age. Federalism had both an adolescent growth spurt and the ups and downs that seem to be an inevitable part of that stage in the life cycle.

The question posed by this adolescent period is whether the system is now becoming mature enough to be granted a driver's license. What changes have been occurring in the purposes—developmental or redistributive—for which federal, state, and local governments expend monies? What changes have occurred in the purposes for which money is transferred from higher to lower levels of government? Has the system been heading recklessly toward a cliff? Or is it increasingly able to steer itself in the correct direction?

Classifying Government Expenditure

To provide some answers to these questions, I have collected data on the overall fiscal trends within the federal system at various points between 1962 and 1990. The appendix provides details on sources of information and procedures used to collect and classify the data.

I have classified expenditures by each level of government in a manner that differs from methods used in many other fiscal studies of the federal system. I have counted only expenditures paid for out of a government's own fiscal resources. Any expenditure for which a government is compensated by a transfer from another level of government is regarded as an expenditure by the government making the transfer, not by the government that actually carries out the substantive activity. For example, highway expenditures paid for by the national government are counted as national expenditures, even though state and local governments may receive these funds and hire the contractors to pave the roads. I classify the data in this manner because I want to distinguish between instances when governments are spending their own money and instances when they are spending someone else's. Just as I am spending the money when I hire someone to paint my house, so it makes sense to say the national government is spending the money when it pays local governments to build a road. This procedure also has the advantage of eliminating any double counting that might otherwise occur.[21]

I have also classified the expenditures from the fiscal resources of each level of government into two broad categories of expenditure: developmental and redistributive. Redistributive expenditures include monies spent on pensions (including social security), medicare, welfare assistance, housing, medicaid, food stamps, supplemental social insurance, special educational programs for the disabled, and other programs directed at dependent groups in the population.[22] All other domestic programs are classified as developmental, because their main function is to assist in the creation of the physical and social infrastructure necessary for economic development.

My classification scheme does not pretend to establish whether development monies spent actually facilitated economic growth or whether the redistributive monies actually aided low-income citizens.

I consider only the implied intention or purpose of the policy—whether it is primarily justified as conducive to economic growth or as a help for the aged, the poor, the sick, the disabled, or some other dependent group.

Advocates for particular programs often justify public expenditure as having both developmental and redistributive purposes. Monies given for highway construction and to assist technological innovation are often said to benefit not only economic development but also to help the unemployed, who will benefit from newly created jobs. Although the claim may be correct, I still classify such a program as developmental, because the redistributive consequences, if they occur, are a secondary by-product of the program's developmental objective. After all, jobs could be created simply by building thousands of replicas of Stonehenge; mere job creation is not a good enough reason to justify developmental programs. Similarly, monies given to help the disabled are often said to contribute to economic development because the program enhances the productivity of the labor force. Although the claim may be correct, the developmental consequence is secondary to the program's primary purpose of assisting a disadvantaged group of individuals.

Some people may think that my system of classification incorrectly identifies education as a developmental rather than a redistributive function of government. But classifying education as primarily redistributive ignores the fact that investments in education have been routinely shown to be among the best predictors of national economic growth and economic productivity. Any country, state, or locality that did not provide schooling for its residents would suffer an immediate, dramatic economic reversal. Families with school-age children would leave the community; businesses in need of skilled workers would follow almost immediately.

Critics of my classification scheme may wish to concede that education performs a developmental function but insist that it is also redistributive in nature. Public schools are open to all residents regardless of income, race, national origin, or even legal residence in the country. The common school, it may be said, constitutes the country's primary symbol of its commitment to equal opportunity, the melting pot that homogenized an immigrant nation, the ladder that allowed many a Horatio Alger to climb from poverty to riches. Many educational programs are focused on the educationally disadvantaged, those whose first language is not English, and those in need of special services.

TABLE 3-2. *Developmental and Redistributive Expenditure of National Government, by Category, Selected Years, 1962–90*

Function and category	Percentage of GNP						Amount (billions of 1990 dollars)					
	1962	1967	1972	1977	1982	1990	1962	1967	1972	1977	1982	1990
Developmental												
Transportation	0.64	0.61	0.66	0.61	0.62	0.38	15.2	18.8	23.1	23.6	26.4	20.8
Natural resources	1.98	1.05	1.02	1.04	1.45	1.30	47.2	32.1	35.3	40.7	60.6	70.8
Safety	0.47	0.48	0.50	0.82	0.58	0.50	11.3	14.6	17.2	31.9	24.4	27.1
Education	0.33	0.76	1.08	1.10	0.80	0.74	7.8	23.3	37.6	42.8	33.2	40.2
Utilities	0.72	0.76	0.77	0.73	0.68	0.72	17.1	23.3	26.8	28.6	28.6	39.1
Miscellaneous	0.08	0.19	0.32	0.68	0.40	1.60	2.0	5.8	11.0	26.4	16.9	87.6
Total	4.22	3.85	4.35	4.98	4.53	5.24	100.6	117.9	151.0	194.0	190.1	285.6
Redistribution												
Pensions/medical insurance	3.04	3.60	4.61	6.13	7.34	7.29	72.7	110.9	160.1	238.1	306.8	398.4
Welfare	1.25	1.26	1.95	2.56	2.30	1.98	29.9	38.6	67.9	99.0	96.1	108.3
Health and hospitals	0.34	0.39	0.45	0.52	0.50	0.45	8.1	12.0	15.7	19.3	20.7	24.6
Housing	0.15	0.20	0.38	0.29	0.65	0.54	3.7	6.2	13.2	11.1	27.0	29.3
Total	4.78	5.45	7.39	9.37	10.79	10.26	114.3	166.9	256.8	367.5	450.6	560.7
Total domestic expenditure[a]	9.00	9.30	11.74	14.35	15.32	15.50	214.6	284.9	407.9	561.5	640.7	846.1

SOURCES: See appendix.
a. Totals may not add because of rounding.

I do not dispute the fact that investments in education may have some redistributive consequences. The distinction between developmental and redistributive is not dichotomous but forms a continuum along which governmental programs fall. But research has shown that the main functional consequences of educational expenditure have been developmental, not redistributive. The characteristics of a student's family—education, income, occupation, and commitment to educa- tion—predict much more accurately the amount a pupil learns in school than school characteristics do. Once family background char- acteristics have been taken into account, the separate and independent effect of schools on student achievement turns out to be very small. This does not mean that pupils do not learn in school. It only means that they learn pretty much in proportion to the resources they bring to the school setting. Although recent efforts to focus on the needs of the disadvantaged have may have had some limited success, both the size of these programs and their effects are too small to justify classi- fying the bulk of educational expenditure as redistributive (though I have classified as redistributive specific federal educational programs directed toward needy groups).[23]

The Redistributive Focus of the National Government

Once the data are classified in these ways, it can be seen that the greatest growth in the expenditure of the national government oc- curred within the redistributive sector, more than doubling from 4.8 percent of GNP to 10.3 percent over the twenty-eight-year period be- tween 1962 and 1990 (table 3-1). The greatest increase occurred in medical and social security programs for senior citizens. In constant dollars, they increased from $73 billion to $398 billion (see table 3-2). Welfare and poverty programs also grew substantially—from $30 bil- lion in 1962 to $108 billion in 1990.

It should not be surprising to see that these redistributive programs expanded rapidly during the Great Society years of Lyndon Johnson.[24] In addition to the war on poverty, compensatory education programs for the educationally disadvantaged, and several new low-income hous- ing programs, the most important new programs were medicare for the elderly and medicaid for citizens whose incomes were below the pov- erty line. The continued steep growth in the size of the welfare state during the Nixon and Ford administrations is less well known—proba- bly because both political parties have a vested interest in keeping the fact a secret. Democrats are reluctant to admit that the welfare state expanded as rapidly under two Republican administrations as at any time in American history. Republicans have been hardly more eager to take credit for the fact that it was under Richard Nixon and Gerald Ford that the poor were given food stamps, impoverished disabled Americans were given supplemental social insurance that was indexed to inflation, educational programs for disabled children were mandated and partially funded, rent subsidies were given to many below the poverty line, job training programs were expanded, and social security benefits were indexed to inflation.[25]

Equally noteworthy is the modest effect on redistributive spending of what has come to be known as the Reagan retrenchment. It is true that national redistributive expenditure as a share of GNP declined from 10.8 percent to 10.3 percent between 1982 and 1990 (table 3-1). It is also true that the amount expended for welfare programs for the very poor declined from 2.3 to 2.0 percent of GNP (table 3-2). But these reductions and limitations barely justify being characterized as "retrenchment." After all, the actual expenditures on redistributive programs (in constant dollars) rose by over $110 billion. The Reagan and Bush administrations may have slowed the growth of the redistributive welfare state. They did not dismantle it.

In contrast to the doubling of the size of redistributive expenditure, the increase in developmental outlays by the national government was quite modest—from 4.2 percent of GNP in 1962 to 5.2 percent in 1990 (table 3-1). National expenditures for transportation, for example, increased from $15 billion to just $21 billion (table 3-2). As a percentage of GNP this constitutes an actual decline—from 0.64 percent to 0.38 percent. National expenditures for police, fire, and other safety programs increased from $11 billion to $27 billion, but this growth, while noticeable, did not significantly change the percentage of GNP the national government devoted to these basic governmental services. Once again, it is worth looking specifically at the effects of the policies of the Reagan administration. Its greatest success in cutting domestic expenditure occurred during its first year in office. Through a series of brilliant maneuvers designed by David Stockman, the Reagan administration persuaded Congress to cut both taxes and expenditures. These efforts did not keep redistributive expenditures from climbing between 1977 and 1982. But the story is strikingly different when it comes to developmental policy. In this arena, national expenditure fell between 1977 and 1982 from 5.0 to 4.5 percent of GNP—almost back to the level existing in 1962. Developmental expenditure climbed back upward in subsequent years, however, reaching 5.2 percent of GNP in 1990 (table 3-1).

The impact of the Reagan years on the expenditure policies of the national government is worth underlining. The president and his party were committed to cutting waste in government. Redistributive programs were high on the party's budget-cutting agenda, though the president was sensitive to opposition charges that he was trying to balance the budget on the backs of the poor. Many Democrats in Congress wanted to retain as many existing programs as possible. In the struggles between the two branches, many compromises had to be reached. Despite the fact that the greatest growth in national expenditure had occurred in the redistributive arena, the conservative president found it difficult to make more than modest cuts in these programs. Through all the twists and turns of partisan conflict, the end result over nearly three decades was a greater focus of national government expenditure on redistributive purposes. In 1962 only one dollar in two went toward redistribution. In 1990 two dollars out of three were so allocated (figure 3-2). Theorists of functional federalism could only applaud the change.

The Developmental Focus of State and Local Governments

The change in the state and local system was almost the mirror opposite of changes in federal expenditure policy. Even in 1962 developmental expenditure at the state and local level was more than twice as high as at the national level—9.3 percent of GNP, compared with 4.2 percent (table 3-1). Despite increases in developmental expenditure by all levels of government, the national government never closed the gap. Over the twenty-eight-year period, states poured new money into education, increasing outlays from $41 billion to $167 billion. States also sharply increased their support for police, fire, and other safety services from $15 billion to $55 billion (table 3-3). At the local level, the biggest growth was in basic safety and utility expenditures (table 3-4).

Although states and localities were playing a dominant role in the developmental arena, they were falling behind in the redistributive arena. While the national government was more than doubling its commitment to redistribution, state and local redistributive spending edged up only slightly—from a very low 2.2 percent of GNP in 1962 to only

TABLE 3-3. *Developmental and Redistributive Expenditure of State Governments, by Category, Selected Years, 1962–90*

Function and category	Percentage of GNP						Amount (billions of 1990 dollars)					
	1962	1967	1972	1977	1982	1990	1962	1967	1972	1977	1982	1990
Developmental												
Transportation	0.91	0.88	0.87	0.54	0.87	0.59	21.7	27.0	30.1	21.0	24.0	32.5
Natural resources	0.15	0.19	0.16	0.11	0.14	0.14	3.5	5.9	5.7	4.3	6.0	7.7
Safety	0.63	0.71	0.50	0.71	0.58	1.00	15.1	21.8	17.3	27.3	24.3	54.8
Education	1.71	2.18	2.67	2.76	2.88	3.05	40.9	66.7	92.9	107.5	120.6	166.8
Utilities	*	*	*	0.13	0.18	0.18	*	*	*	4.9	7.4	9.6
Miscellaneous	0.15	0.14	0.50	0.11	0.10	0.12	3.7	4.4	17.6	4.3	4.1	6.3
Total[a]	**3.55**	**4.10**	**4.71**	**4.36**	**4.45**	**5.08**	**84.9**	**125.8**	**163.6**	**169.3**	**186.4**	**277.7**
Redistributive												
Pensions/medical insurance	0.73	0.52	0.77	1.17	1.10	1.01	17.5	15.9	26.9	45.4	46.1	55.0
Welfare	0.32	0.35	0.49	0.68	0.74	0.79	7.6	10.8	16.9	26.5	31.1	42.9
Health and hospitals	0.38	0.40	0.49	0.57	0.63	0.69	9.0	12.2	16.9	22.1	26.4	37.6
Housing	0.01	0.01	-.03	-.03	0.01	0.03	0.3	0.3	-0.9	-1.2	0.6	1.4
Total[a]	**1.44**	**1.28**	**1.72**	**2.39**	**2.48**	**2.52**	**34.4**	**39.2**	**59.8**	**92.8**	**104.2**	**136.9**
Total domestic expenditure[a]	**4.99**	**5.38**	**6.43**	**6.75**	**6.93**	**7.60**	**119.0**	**165.1**	**223.4**	**262.1**	**290.6**	**414.7**

SOURCES: See appendix.
*Less than 0.01 percent of GNP or less than $0.1 billion.
a. Totals may not add because of rounding.

TABLE 3-4. *Developmental and Redistributive Expenditure of Local Governments, by Category, Selected Years, 1962–90*

Function and category	Percentage of GNP						Amount (billions of 1990 dollars)					
	1962	1967	1972	1977	1982	1990	1962	1967	1972	1977	1982	1990
Developmental												
Transportation	0.47	0.37	0.38	0.31	0.32	0.37	11.3	11.3	13.3	12.0	13.4	20.1
Natural resources	0.06	0.06	0.04	0.04	0.03	0.04	1.5	1.9	1.5	1.5	1.4	2.3
Safety	1.56	1.48	1.71	1.71	1.54	2.03	37.4	45.2	59.4	66.7	64.1	110.8
Education	1.95	1.97	2.13	1.73	1.48	1.81	46.6	60.2	74.1	67.6	61.7	98.8
Utilities	0.77	0.73	0.80	0.98	1.26	1.20	18.4	22.4	27.8	38.3	52.5	65.3
Miscellaneous	0.02	0.02	0.17	0.07	0.01	0.27	0.6	0.5	5.9	2.9	0.3	14.5
Total[a]	**5.83**	**4.63**	**5.23**	**4.84**	**4.64**	**5.72**	**115.8**	**141.5**	**182.0**	**189.0**	**193.3**	**311.8**
Redistributive												
Pensions/medical insurance	0.11	0.12	0.13	0.13	0.14	0.16	2.6	3.8	4.4	5.1	6.0	8.9
Welfare	0.15	0.14	0.18	0.14	0.09	0.10	3.5	4.3	5.9	5.7	3.8	5.5
Health and hospitals	0.36	0.38	0.50	0.50	0.57	0.60	8.5	11.4	17.4	19.5	23.8	32.5
Housing	0.14	0.08	0.09	0.06	0.07	0.08	3.3	2.6	3.1	2.1	2.9	4.4
Total[a]	**0.76**	**0.72**	**0.90**	**0.83**	**0.87**	**0.94**	**18.0**	**22.1**	**30.8**	**32.4**	**36.5**	**51.3**
Total domestic expenditure[a]	**6.59**	**5.35**	**6.13**	**5.67**	**5.51**	**6.66**	**133.7**	**163.6**	**212.8**	**221.4**	**229.8**	**363.2**

SOURCES: See appendix.
a. Totals may not add because of rounding.

FIGURE 3-2. *Government Expenditures Devoted to Redistributive Purposes, by Level, 1962–90*

Percent

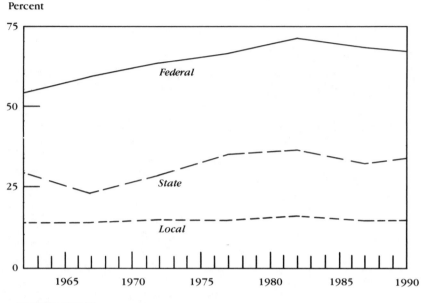

SOURCES: See appendix.

a slightly higher 3.5 percent in 1990 (table 3-1). During this period the civil rights movement rose to power, the Great Society was built, and entitlements became an entrenched part of American social policy. Yet the share of state expenditures devoted to redistribution increased only from 28.9 percent to 33.0 percent; at the local level the increase was barely detectable—from 13.5 percent to 14.1 percent (figure 3-2).

State and local reluctance to participate in the redistributive movement can hardly be attributed to the political climate. Over most of this period Democrats controlled at least part of state government in a majority of states and held unified control over both houses of the state legislature as well as the gubernatorial chair in several. Unified Republican control of state government was the exception.[26] At the local level, blacks and Latinos were exercising newfound voting power, electing minority leaders at record rates.[27] But neither the strength of the Democratic party nor minority success at local levels brought major changes in the pattern of public expenditure.

All in all, the findings are strikingly consistent with a functional theory of federalism. National government expenditures became increasingly concentrated in the redistributive arena, for which the national government was uniquely suited. State and local expenditure continued to focus on developmental undertakings.[28]

My discussion thus far has lumped states and localities together, a justifiable procedure up to a point. According to legal doctrine, local governments are creatures of the state. States can countermand any action taken by a local government, even to the point of eliminating a local government altogether. Secondly, functional theory does not draw the same sharp distinction between the role of states and localities that it does between the role of the national government and the state and local system.

Functional theory nonetheless identifies some differences between state and local governments. Local governments are more efficient than state governments because they are more immediately disciplined by the marketplace. Although this gives local governments greater ability to promote economic development, it leaves them with less capacity for redistribution. Legislative theory also distinguishes between state and local governments. Since state governments can mandate actions by local governments, local governments are potentially threatened by redistributive mandates that state governments might impose. Given these theoretical considerations, it is worth examining differences between state and local fiscal policies.

Once again, the data are consistent with functional theory. State redistributive expenditure has risen more rapidly than local redistributive expenditure. In 1962 states spent nearly twice as much as localities on redistributive programs—1.4 percent of GNP compared with 0.8 percent. Over the following twenty-eight-year period state expenditure increased to 2.5 percent of GNP while local redistributive expenditure remained almost flat (tables 3-3 and 3-4).

The story with respect to developmental expenditure is less consistent with functional theory. In 1962 localities spent 5.8 percent of GNP on development, whereas states spent only 3.6 percent. Local developmental expenditure declined in subsequent years but edged back up to 5.7 percent by 1990; in the meantime, state expenditure on development grew substantially to 5.1 percent (tables 3-3 and 3-4). The increasing developmental role of state governments may be explained by functional theorists as a response to the need to coordinate infrastructure over a broader geographical area in a period of increasing economic integration. But legislative theory more persuasively explains the relatively large increase at the state level in terms of the credit-

TABLE 3-5. *Developmental and Redistributive Federal Grants to State-Local Governments, by Category, Selected Years, 1957–90*

Function and category	Percentage of GNP							Amount (billions of 1990 dollars)						
	1957	1962	1967	1972	1977	1982	1990	1957	1962	1967	1972	1977	1982	1990
Developmental														
Transportation	0.2	0.5	0.5	0.4	0.3	0.3	0.3	4.3	11.6	15.4	14.7	12.7	11.6	15.5
Natural resources	0.0	0.0	0.0	0.1	0.0	0.0	0.0	0.6	0.6	0.9	1.8	1.9	1.3	2.2
Safety	0.0	0.0	0.0	0.0	0.2	0.2	0.1	0.2	0.3	0.6	1.7	1.0	1.7	2.8
Education	0.1	0.3	0.5	0.6	0.6	0.5	0.4	2.7	4.9	14.6	20.7	22.1	19.6	23.2
Utilities	0.0	0.0	0.0	0.0	0.0	0.0	0.0	0.0	0.0	0.0	0.0	0.0	0.0	0.0
Miscellaneous	0.1	0.1	0.2	0.1	0.7	0.5	0.3	1.6	3.0	6.0	4.7	36.8	25.2	16.4
Total[a]	**0.4**	**0.9**	**1.2**	**1.2**	**1.8**	**1.5**	**1.1**	**9.4**	**20.4**	**37.5**	**43.6**	**74.5**	**59.4**	**60.1**
Redistributive														
Pensions/medical insurance	0.0	0.1	0.0	0.1	0.1	0.1	0.1	0.0	1.9	0.0	2.2	3.0	2.8	2.8
Welfare	0.4	0.4	0.5	1.1	0.9	1.0	1.1	7.0	10.2	15.8	37.9	37.0	41.8	60.0
Health and hospitals	0.0	0.0	0.0	0.1	0.1	0.1	0.1	0.5	0.7	1.5	3.8	3.5	3.8	5.9
Housing	0.0	0.1	0.1	0.1	0.2	0.2	0.2	0.5	1.5	2.5	4.4	7.1	9.8	10.8
Total[a]	**0.4**	**0.6**	**0.7**	**1.3**	**1.3**	**1.3**	**1.4**	**8.0**	**14.3**	**19.8**	**48.3**	**50.6**	**58.2**	**79.5**
Total domestic expenditure[a]	**0.8**	**1.4**	**1.9**	**2.7**	**3.1**	**2.8**	**2.5**	**17.4**	**34.7**	**57.3**	**91.9**	**125.1**	**117.6**	**139.6**

SOURCES: See appendix.

a. Totals may not add because of rounding.

claiming needs of state legislators. As Morris Fiorina has shown, state legislatures have in recent years become increasingly professionalized.[29] With more resources to establish themselves as independent entrepreneurs within their districts, state legislators may be using developmental dollars to secure their reelection.

Even though the shift of developmental responsibilities from the local to the state level suggests an increase in the price of federalism, all other trends point in the opposite direction. Local governments resist allocating monies for redistribution. The national government has more than doubled its redistributive commitment. Meanwhile, the national government has only modestly increased its expenditure for developmental purposes, whereas substantial increments have occurred at the state level.

Intergovernmental Grants

The system of intergovernmental grants has the potential for alleviating some of the disadvantages of American federalism. Federal grants can help equalize expenditures among state and local governments, and they can assist in meeting the needs of those dependent on government services. But these benefits come at a price. The larger the grant from the higher tier of government, the less disciplined by market forces is the lower tier. The more regulations imposed by the higher level of government, the more bureaucratized, inefficient, and ineffective the federal system becomes.

The price of federalism can be reduced if intergovernmental grants are used sparingly. Developmental grants should be made only to the extent necessary to achieve territorial equity in the provision of public services (such as equalizing educational expenditure among localities) or to facilitate closer intergovernmental coordination of large-scale improvements in the infrastructure (such as the establishment of an interstate highway system). Redistributive grants are more easily justified, because in their absence state and local governments are unlikely to meet the needs of dependent populations.

Changes in Federal Grant Policy

Developmental grants to state and local governments increased rapidly between 1957 and 1977, climbing from $9 billion to $75 billion (table 3-5). Legislative theory provides a persuasive explanation for this increase in developmental pork. Developmental expenditures were growing at the very time that congressional reelection rates were climbing, congressional resources were expanding, and congressional subcommittees were becoming more influential.

Growth in developmental pork was also facilitated by a tax system that operated so as to generate virtually blame-free growth in the revenue of the national government. To finance World War II, Congress had enacted a tax that contained numerous income brackets, each of which was taxed at a higher rate. Beginning in the 1960s and continuing throughout the 1970s, inflation regularly shifted taxpayers into higher tax brackets. This inflation-induced "bracket creep" was a continuous, relentless source of additional government revenue for which political leaders could not easily be blamed. Congress and the president watched governmental revenues increase without lifting a finger. Although the president and Congress were sometimes accused of doing nothing to prevent these tax increases, it was difficult for political opponents to pinpoint blame for something that did not happen.[30]

Inflation was such an effective blame-avoidance mechanism that Congress hardly ever raised income taxes overtly during the first decades of the cold war. Eisenhower asked for a modest tax on gasoline to pay for the creation of the interstate highway system. And Lyndon Johnson asked for and obtained a temporary 10 percent surtax to pay for the rising costs of the Vietnam War, an unpopular tax that was soon discontinued. But for the most part tax legislation enacted during the postwar period cut taxes as a way of offsetting the new revenues generated by inflation-induced bracket creep. The popular Kennedy tax cut in 1963 was the largest and best known.[31]

But if legislative theory can convincingly account for changes in the intergovernmental system between 1957 and 1977, it provides little help in accounting for more recent changes. Instead of a continued distribution of additional morsels from the larder, developmental grants to state and local governments fell from $75 billion in 1977 to $60 billion in 1990 (table 3-5). As a percentage of GNP, the drop was from 1.8 percent to 1.1 percent, a decrease of 42 percent.

As developmental grants fell through the floor, redistributive federal grants continued to grow. Between 1957 and 1977 redistributive grants increased from $8 billion to $51 billion; they continued to climb to $80 billion in 1990 (table 3-5). The growth was from 0.4 to 1.3 percent of GNP during the first twenty years, with a continued upward creep to 1.4 percent of GNP during the more recent period.

The percentage of federal grants allocated to redistributive purposes fell during the years of inflation-driven bracket creep, dropping from 46 percent in 1957 to 41 percent in 1977. But after 1977 the system began moving in a more functional direction: the percentage of federal grants focusing on redistribution had increased to 57 percent by 1990.[32] Instead of spinning out of control, as legislative theory had feared, the intergovernmental grant system was adapting to the realistic requirements of a functional federal system. Each level of government was finding its appropriate role.

Changes in budgetary politics that brought the era of inflation-induced bracket creep to an end help to account for the greater explanatory power of the functional theory of federalism during the 1980s. In earlier decades, the political costs of federal expenditure were relatively modest. Ever-higher revenue flows could be realized without overtly imposing tax increases on citizens. But in 1981 marginal income tax rates were indexed. Increased revenue could be realized only by explicitly raising taxes. Legislators could no longer escape blame for the rising cost of government operation.

The consequences of tax indexation for budget deficits were reinforced by simultaneous sharp cuts in marginal tax rates. The Reagan administration had not originally intended to combine tax cuts with tax indexation. The president's advisers had in fact explicitly decided not to include indexation in the president's proposals. One of the political advantages to excluding indexation from the Reagan tax cuts was that such exclusion would have helped enable Reagan to realize sufficient government revenues and still fulfill his campaign promise to reduce taxes by 30 percent over the next three years. The advisers expected a relatively high rate of inflation-induced bracket creep to take away roughly half of the tax cut as fast as it was being implemented. But Senator Robert Dole, Republican majority leader in the Senate, saw the 1981 tax bill as an opportunity to enact tax indexation proposals he had long advocated. Dole recognized that the consequences of indexation for revenue flows could well be disastrous, so he agreed to a delay of indexation for two years in order that inflation could induce a fair bit of bracket creep in the meantime.[33]

Little did Dole, Reagan, or anyone else realize that Paul Volcker at the Federal Reserve was simultaneously restricting the money supply so sharply that both inflation and the economy would soon plummet. In the two years after the passage of the law but before indexation came into effect, very little inflation-induced bracket creep occurred. As a result, taxes were indexed at the lowest rate they had reached in the entire cold war period. Any modifications of tax policy would now have to take place through explicit, blame-inducing government action.

Budget deficits ballooned. With the automatic process of bracket creep no longer in place, tax policymaking became a costly political task. At first the political costs were dodged. Congress hurriedly rescinded—and Reagan signed—several of the tax cuts included in the 1981 legislation. But since these cuts had not yet become effective, the blame that had to be accepted was moderate, not severe. Congress also agreed in 1982 to modest spending cuts and tax increases within the social security program. But since most cuts mainly affected future recipients, the blame to be suffered was once again only moderate, not severe. Yet even in this case Congress and the president felt they needed to construct an elaborate, bipartisan, independent commission to help take the heat.[34]

Other schemes to deal with the deficit were less successful. The Gramm-Rudman-Hollings Deficit Reduction Act of 1985 was expected to reduce the deficit automatically (much as indexation automatically increased entitlements and cut taxes), but automatic deficit reduction (scheduled to become severe in years four and five of the legislation) failed to work in practice. When the Gramm-Rudman-Hollings act threatened to disrupt government operations, its effect was postponed until it was finally replaced by the Budget Enforcement Act of 1990, signed into law by President Bush. Despite the claim made at the time of its passage that the deficit would be cut by $500 billion over the next five years (mainly in years four and five), the 1990 budget compromise, though making some progress, failed to forestall a continued increase in the debt-GNP ratio. In 1993 the Clinton administration once again proposed to reduce the deficit by $500 billion over the next five years. Finally, budget deficits began to recede.

The deficit-reducing efforts of the Bush and Clinton administrations were politically costly. Bush was harshly criticized by his own party for rescinding his promise not to increase taxes that had been so deeply etched in the public mind by his pledge, "Read my lips, no new taxes." Clinton secured passage by only one vote in the Senate and two votes in the House of a tax increase that was concentrated on only a small percentage of the population with the highest incomes. Presidents and members of Congress now found it very difficult to impose new taxes on the American public. There was no going back to the days of Eisenhower, Kennedy, Johnson, Nixon, Ford, and Carter, all of whom were able to enjoy increased revenues from a rise in tax rates that was occurring quietly every week as a function of bracket creep.

Since blame avoidance was less feasible after 1981, legislative theory became less applicable. In the 1960s and early 1970s, House members gained votes if federal spending in their state increased. In the late 1970s and 1980s, these electoral benefits from increased spending disappeared.[35] Members of Congress now had to apply a tougher cost-benefit test to the grants they were making.

In this more austere fiscal climate, Congress introduced institutional changes that facilitated its ability to contain developmental expenditure. During the 1980s power shifted upward from the subcommittees to the congressional party leadership, who established budget priorities in large "omnibus" pieces of legislation passed under strict time pressures at the close of the fiscal year. Both subcommittees and rank-and-file members lost many of the prerogatives they had enjoyed a decade earlier.[36] Members no longer sought membership on pork barrel committees with the eagerness they had once displayed.[37]

The news media has been slow to recognize the decline of pork in American national politics. Raking the muck in search of pork is at the heart of the journalist's trade. In search of newsworthy copy, reporters search diligently for any vestige of pork remaining. It is thus remarkable that a reporter for the *Boston Globe* admitted in 1994 that "in an era of closer public scrutiny, massive federal debt and tighter spending rules, the days of influential lawmakers coasting back to their districts with easy federal money ... are growing ever shorter." The reporter quotes a representative as saying that "the pork barrel process is coming to an end."[38] And the *Wall Street Journal* reported that "a surprising number of candidates across the nation are wooing voters by promising to cut federal pork-barrel spending right at home." In New Jersey, for example, two candidates for Congress were said to be competing for votes by out-campaigning one another against a $1.4 billion federal flood tunnel for the district. Said one: "We need people in Congress who will say, 'This is wasteful spending in our own district, and I don't want it.' "[39] Pork has become so unpopular that in 1995 each house of Congress passed a bill giving the president the line-item veto, said to be an effective tool for thwarting special interest legislation.

Hopes for the line-item veto may be exaggerated, and pork may not be coming to an end. But with power in Congress more centralized, deficits rising, and bracket creep eliminated, legislators have begun to leave developmental policy to state and local governments.

TABLE 3-6. *Developmental and Redistributive Federal Grants to Local Governments, by Category, Selected Years, 1957–90*

Function and category	Percentage of GNP							Amount (billions of 1990 dollars)						
	1957	1962	1967	1972	1977	1982	1990	1957	1962	1967	1972	1977	1982	1990
Developmental														
Transportation	*	0.01	*	*	0.01	0.01	0.01	*	0.1	0.1	0.1	0.3	0.2	0.4
Natural resources	*	*	*	*	*	*	*	*	*	*	*	*	*	*
Safety	0.01	0.01	0.02	0.05	0.24	0.18	0.05	0.2	0.3	0.6	1.7	1.0	1.7	2.8
Education	0.04	0.05	0.09	0.09	0.09	0.05	0.04	0.7	1.2	2.6	2.9	3.5	2.3	1.9
Utilities	*	*	*	*	*	*	*	*	*	*	*	*	*	*
Miscellaneous	0.01	0.01	0.04	0.10	0.34	0.18	0.06	0.1	0.1	1.1	3.5	21.6	13.5	3.0
Total[a]	**0.06**	**0.08**	**0.15**	**0.24**	**0.68**	**0.42**	**0.16**	**1.0**	**1.7**	**4.4**	**8.2**	**26.4**	**17.7**	**8.1**
Redistributive														
Pensions/medical insurance	*	*	*	*	*	*	*	*	*	*	*	*	*	*
Welfare	*	*	*	0.01	0.01	0.01	0.01	*	*	0.1	0.2	0.4	0.4	0.6
Health and hospitals	*	*	*	0.01	0.01	0.01	0.01	*	*	0.1	0.4	0.5	0.5	0.4
Housing	0.03	0.06	0.06	0.12	0.13	0.22	0.17	0.5	1.5	1.9	4.2	5.1	9.3	9.3
Total[a]	**0.03**	**0.06**	**0.07**	**0.14**	**0.16**	**0.24**	**0.19**	**0.5**	**1.5**	**2.1**	**4.8**	**6.0**	**10.2**	**10.3**
Total federal grants[a]	**0.09**	**0.14**	**0.22**	**0.38**	**0.84**	**0.66**	**0.35**	**1.6**	**3.2**	**6.5**	**13.0**	**32.3**	**27.9**	**18.4**

SOURCES: See appendix.
*Less than 0.01 percent of GNP or less than $0.1 billion.
a. Totals may not add because of rounding.

Until 1994 these developments had less impact on redistributive spending in large part because redistributive questions have always been decided in a bargaining process that includes the president and the major congressional leaders of both parties. Shifts in social security, medicare, and medicaid occur only with broad shifts in public sentiment and partisan political power. It is not merely a matter of altering the locus of decisionmaking or the visibility of the issue. As a result, federal grants were increasingly for redistributive purposes, the national government's area of relative competence. It remains to be seen whether the protected status redistributive spending has enjoyed will continue into the late 1990s.

Differences between State and Local Governments

A comparison of federal grants to state governments with those of local governments provides further evidence that the pork barrel has lost its luster. Legislative theory anticipates that developmental aid will be given primarily to local governments, because money given directly to localities can be more precisely directed to the constituents of the members of the House of Representatives (who derive greater benefits from pork than their Senate colleagues).

Again, legislative theory does well in predicting the trends occurring between 1957 and 1977. Developmental grants to local governments expanded the most rapidly during the heyday of legislative federalism, threatening to make local governments so dependent on the federal government that they would no longer be disciplined by economic markets. Just as legislative theory would expect, federal grants grew from $1.0 billion to $26.4 billion (table 3-6). Grants for basic safety services grew from $0.2 billion to $1.0 billion, highway grants jumped from $9 million to $260 million, and education grants soared from $0.7 billion to $3.5 billion. But the direction of change dramatically reversed itself during the 1980s; developmental grants fell to just $8.1 billion in 1990. General revenue sharing, block grants, and other miscellaneous grants fell from $21.6 billion to $3.0 billion between 1977 and 1990. Education grants fell from $3.5 billion to $1.9 billion. Highway grants increased in real dollar terms, but the increase was at a slower rate than that of the overall economy.

As developmental grants were contracting, redistributive aid to localities (mainly for low-income housing) moved upward. Starting at $517 million in 1957, housing grants rose to $5.1 billion in 1977 and $9.3 billion in 1990.

TABLE 3-7. *Developmental and Redistributive Federal Grants to State Governments, by Category, Selected Years, 1957–90*

Function and category	Percentage of GNP							Amount (billions of 1990 dollars)						
	1957	1962	1967	1972	1977	1982	1990	1957	1962	1967	1972	1977	1982	1990
Developmental														
Transportation	0.2	0.5	0.5	0.4	0.3	0.3	0.3	4.3	11.5	15.3	14.6	12.4	11.4	15.1
Natural resources	0.0	0.0	0.0	0.1	0.0	0.0	0.0	0.6	0.6	0.9	1.8	1.9	1.3	2.2
Safety	*	*	*	*	*	*	*	*	*	*	*	*	*	*
Education	0.1	0.2	0.4	0.5	0.5	0.4	0.4	2.0	3.7	12.0	17.8	18.6	17.3	21.3
Utilities	0.0	0.0	0.0	0.0	0.0	0.0	0.0	0.0	0.0	0.0	0.0	0.0	0.0	0.0
Miscellaneous	0.1	0.1	0.2	0.0	0.4	0.3	0.2	1.5	2.9	4.9	1.2	15.2	11.7	13.4
Total[a]	**0.4**	**0.8**	**1.1**	**1.0**	**1.2**	**1.0**	**0.9**	**8.4**	**18.7**	**33.1**	**35.4**	**48.1**	**41.7**	**52.0**
Redistributive														
Pensions/medical insurance	0.0	0.1	0.0	0.1	0.1	0.1	0.1	0.0	1.9	0.0	2.2	3.0	2.8	2.8
Welfare	0.4	0.4	0.5	1.1	0.9	1.0	1.1	7.0	10.2	15.7	37.7	36.6	41.4	59.4
Health and hospitals	0.0	0.0	0.0	0.1	0.1	0.1	0.1	0.5	0.7	1.4	3.4	3.0	3.3	5.5
Housing	0.0	0.0	0.0	0.0	0.1	0.0	0.0	0.0	0.0	0.6	0.2	2.0	0.5	1.5
Total[a]	**0.4**	**0.5**	**0.6**	**1.2**	**1.1**	**1.1**	**1.2**	**7.5**	**12.8**	**17.7**	**43.5**	**44.6**	**48.0**	**69.2**
Total federal grants[a]	**0.8**	**1.3**	**1.7**	**2.3**	**2.3**	**2.1**	**2.2**	**15.9**	**31.5**	**50.8**	**78.9**	**92.7**	**89.7**	**121.2**

SOURCES: See appendix.
*Less than 0.01 percent of GNP or less than $0.1 billion.
a. Totals may not add because of rounding.

The ups and downs of federal grants to localities are neatly captured by a calculation that identifies the percentage of federal grants to localities devoted to redistributive purposes. In 1957, 31 percent of national grants were for redistributive purposes. In the twenty years of legislative federalism that followed, the redistributive share fell to 18 percent. The federal system seemed to be moving out of equilibrium, as more and more pork was being poured through the legislative process. But after 1977 trends reversed themselves so that by 1990 56 percent of federal grant dollars directed toward localities had a redistributive objective.[40]

Change at the state level was less pronounced, as befits the interstitial role that states play in the federal system. As a percentage of GNP, developmental grants expanded significantly in the 1960s and 1970s and contracted moderately in more recent decades (table 3-7). In the meantime, redistributive grants continued to grow throughout much of the period between 1957 and 1990. The biggest increases in redistributive grants to state governments were those for welfare. The real value of welfare grants rose from $7 billion in 1957 to $37 billion in 1977 and to $59 billion in 1990. As a result, by 1990 federal redistributive grants to states were exceeding developmental ones.

Conclusions

Legislative theory helps to account for the extraordinary growth of federal development grants over the twenty years between 1957 and 1977. During this period the political benefits of pork barrel legislation seem to have exceeded the political costs of increased taxation. This imbalance seems to have been due to the increasing decentralization of Congress and to the fact that the cost of government expansion was hidden by a tax system that generated additional revenues without requiring explicit legislative enactments.

In recent years, however, tax indexation, congressional centralization, fiscal deficits, and budgetary crises have imposed greater political costs on legislative spending proposals. As a result, a broader, more diffuse set of interests must be taken into account when designing federal programs. In this new political environment, the claims of geographically specific interests have less political clout.

As a result, functional federalism provides an increasingly powerful framework for explaining trends in the federal system. Quite apart from political developments in Washington, economic forces in society are forcing each level of the federal system to concentrate on issues within its area of competence. As improvements in transportation and communication systems produce an increasingly integrated economy, capital, entrepreneurial activity, and skilled labor become ever more mobile. State and local governments are placed in an increasingly competitive relationship with one another, forcing each to attend ever more strictly to developmental objectives. As Thomas J. Anton has observed,

> The national government has increasingly concentrated its funds on social insurance and assistance benefits [while] state (and local) governments have focused their energies on education, health, transportation, and housekeeping programs, [and] ... promot[ion of] state economic development. These differences in policy interests do not preclude one level of government from entering another's sphere of interest, but they do help to restrain such entry.[41]

Recent trends in American politics provide one clue to the reasons legislative and functional theories are both needed to understand the American federal system. Functional theory is too Panglossian to be entirely satisfying. The federal system is "good enough" but it is still "government work." It still has the warts of a democracy, warts that Churchill thought were ugly enough to make it the "worst possible system except for all alternatives." A democratic system must be run by politicians who respond to electoral pressures. The decisions they take will often be shaped by considerations other than the best long-term interests of the country. But although legislative theory identifies powerful incentives that can distort the appropriate role of the national government, it tends to overstate its case. If allocating developmental benefits to constituents were a foolproof, cost-free method of gaining reelection, the distribution of such benefits would never cease to escalate. Eventually the system would break down. But long before reaching the point of collapse, the system is likely to correct itself in ways that functional theory can better explain. Excessive pork will generate a taxpayer revolt upon which members of Congress and, especially, presidential candidates will seek to capitalize. It is not an accident that every president since Jimmy Carter has not only endorsed the line-item veto but has been fairly successful in curtailing developmental spending. Legislative theory is not so much inaccurate as incomplete.

4

Why States Choose Different Policies

Is variety within a country more a gain or a loss?
Lord James Bryce, *The American Commonwealth*

Both functional and legislative theory expect government expenditures in a federal system to vary from place to place. Functional theorists expect expenditures to vary depending on a state's taxable resources, the needs and wants of local residents, and the competitive position of a state vis-à-vis other parts of the country. According to functional theory, the determinants of developmental expenditure are different from the factors affecting redistribution.[1] For example, the amount of taxable resources available to a state can be expected to have a larger effect on developmental than redistributive expenditure; those in wealthier states will be inclined to spend more of their marginal dollars on overall social and physical infrastructure than on the needy. Functional theory also expects differentials among states to dissipate as the nation's economy becomes increasingly integrated.

Legislative theorists also expect state policy to vary. Each state has had a distinctive political and institutional history, and its legacy can be expected to have fiscal consequences. Politics has become more professionalized in some states, while other states have continued to rely on political amateurs. The more professionalized states can be expected to increase spending more rapidly. Also, states vary in their partisan orientation. Some states are controlled by Democrats, others by Republicans, and still others enjoy (or suffer) divided government. These partisan differences will shape fiscal policy. Republicans will be willing to spend more on the economic development of the state, while Democrats prefer to spend more on redistribution.

Both theories are needed to explain the findings on state fiscal policies reported in this chapter. I shall show that the variation in state fiscal policies remains as large today as it was thirty years ago. States spend more on developmental policy if they are wealthier, have more residents living in a large central city, are controlled by professional legislators, and have more Republican legislators. Factors affecting redistributive spending differ in a number of respects. Redistributive spending is unaffected by a state's poverty rate but goes up if a state has more taxable resources. Redistributive spending also is greater if a state is densely populated, has more residents living in central cities, is managed by professional legislators, and is Democratic in its partisanship. If the minority population is larger, it spends less.

The Variation in State Expenditure

Many of the most extreme disparities existing within the United States when the federal system was established have disappeared. There is no longer a distinction between slave and free states. Formal, state-enforced racial segregation has been abolished everywhere. Social security and medicare are available to citizens of all states. So is the guarantee that all children be given an appropriate education regardless of their physical or mental disability.

As the political and legal framework has become increasingly similar throughout the United States, and as the cost of transportation and communication continues to fall, the United States might be expected to become an increasingly homogeneous society. Under these circumstances, classical economic theory expects economic activity to drift to those parts of the country where the factors of production cost less. Economic growth is expected to be concentrated disproportionately where land is cheap and wages are low. Over time, the cost of all the factors of production is expected to become more or less uniform. As wages, incomes, and prices become increasingly uniform, the demand for and cost of government services should become more or less the same throughout all states and regions.[2]

Certain transformations in American society are quite consistent with classical economy theory. As the South's political and legal framework became more similar to that of the North, economic activity moved southward to take advantage of the relatively inexpensive land

and low wages found in that part of the country. More recently, similar forces have caused economic activity to shift from California to the mountain states. But despite trends toward uniformity in many dimensions of economic life, differences among states continue to persist. They differ in their social problems, their fiscal resources, their partisan makeup, and their per capita governmental expenditure. Many of the differences observable when John F. Kennedy was president in 1962 are equally evident more than thirty years later.

The coefficient of variation (CV) provides one of the best measures of the extent to which the fifty states differ from one another on any particular characteristic. This coefficient is simply the standard deviation of a variable divided by its mean. The coefficient varies between zero and infinity. If a characteristic is normally distributed among the states and if its value is as high as 1.0, the states are so different from one another that one-third of the states deviate from the average state by an amount greater than the value the characteristic takes in that average state.[3] For example, in 1991 Michigan had a density of only sixty-two persons per square kilometer, close to the national average, but many states—Rhode Island, Connecticut, and Maryland, for example—had a much higher density and other states—Montana, Alaska, and North Dakota, to mention just three—had a much lower density. As a result, the standard deviation was over eighty persons per square kilometer and the CV took an extremely high value of 1.37. For most state characteristics the standard deviation is less than the mean, producing a CV of less than 1.0. Even a coefficient of 0.33 indicates substantial variation among the states, however. It suggests that a third of the states differ from the average state by an amount that is as much as one-third the value in the average state. For example, in 1982 the poverty rate in the average state (Arizona) was 13.2 percent. But in one-third of the states the poverty rate was either 4.5 percentage points higher or lower than this average rate, producing a CV of 0.35.

The CV is a useful statistic because it permits direct observation of changes in the distribution of a variable over time. Yet it does not change when all states are changing at the same rate. For example, the median per capita income of the residents of all states increased from $3,456 to $17,772 between 1962 and 1991. But because interstate differences in income changed hardly at all, the CV remained close to 0.16 throughout the period.

In short, the CV is a shorthand way of detecting the extent to which variations among the states are increasing or decreasing. If its value is falling, differences among states are disappearing. If its value is increasing, states are becoming more unlike one another. One caveat should be mentioned. The statistic captures overall trends among most states: it does not identify each and every detail.

To ascertain whether state developmental and redistributive per capita expenditures were becoming more divergent or more uniform, I classified the expenditures of all fifty states according to the categories used in chapter 3. The amount that states spent for which they were reimbursed by federal grants-in-aid was excluded from the calculation.[4]

I combined expenditures by each state's government and its local governments paid for out of their own fiscal resources into a single overall expenditure level for each state. I did so because decisions taken at each level of government within a state are so dependent on decisions at the other level. If states give more money to local school districts, then the local school districts need to raise less money from their own resources. Conversely, if local districts levy a higher property tax and raise more of their own funds, states need to grant them less from the state treasury. The interconnections between decisions at various levels of government within a state are so complicated that it makes more sense to treat each state, and all the local governments within the state, as a single decisionmaking unit. The courts recognize this interdependency among governments within a state. From a legal standpoint, all local governments are creatures of the state. Any action a local government takes is state action that can be countermanded or overturned by a decision of the state legislature.[5]

The amount that state governments and the localities within them spent per capita on developmental programs varied markedly among the states. Alaska spent the most for developmental purposes. (Alaska was different enough from other states that a special control for it was incorporated into the regression analysis that concludes this chapter.) New York, California, Nevada, and Hawaii were also big development spenders. Georgia, Missouri, and Arkansas spent the least for development. The variation in developmental expenditure changed considerably over the period between 1967 and 1991. The CV climbed from 0.31 in 1967 to a high of 0.57 in 1982, when a national recession forced particularly deep cuts in state expenditures in the industrial heartland (see table 4-1). The coefficient subsequently fell to 0.34 in 1991. This means that in 1991 one-third of the states spent at least 34 percent more or 34 percent less per person on development than did the average state.

TABLE 4-1. *Variations among State Characteristics, Selected Years, 1967–91*

State characteristic	Coefficient of variation					
	1967	*1972*	*1977*	*1982*	*1987*	*1991*
Developmental expenditure	0.31	0.36	0.33	0.57	0.50	0.34
Redistributive expenditure	0.32	0.65	0.36	0.35	0.37	0.28
Taxable resources	0.19	0.17	0.17	0.36	0.20	0.20
Median per capita income	0.16	0.14	0.15	0.15	0.16	0.16
Poverty rate	0.43	0.39	0.32	0.28	0.35	0.32
Percent minority	1.02	0.95	0.87	0.79	0.75	0.73
Percent living in central cities	0.83	0.80	0.79	0.79	0.84	0.83
Population density	1.48	1.48	1.44	1.39	1.38	1.37
Percent Democrats in state legislature	0.41	0.37	0.28	0.35	0.28	0.24
Legislative salary	0.99	0.89	0.83	0.79	0.79	0.79

SOURCES: See appendix.

But if the variability in developmental expenditure fluctuated significantly, the variability in redistributive expenditure, with one exception, remained more or less constant throughout the period. The CV in 1967 was 0.32; by 1991 it had declined slightly to 0.28. Those most generous with their redistributive monies included New York, California, Massachusetts, and Hawaii. The least generous included South Dakota, North Dakota, Nebraska, Utah, and New Mexico. In 1972 the variability among the states shot dramatically upward to 0.65. This short-term phenomenon was due to the uneven implementation among the states of the federal medicaid and food stamp programs. Once these programs were institutionalized in all of the states, interstate variability in redistributive expenditure returned to its pre–Great Society level.[6]

Determinants of State Developmental and Redistributive Policy

Many of the factors affecting state spending—taxable resources, population density, percentage living in a central city—appear to be economic or demographic rather than political variables. Some analysts have therefore concluded that government expenditure is determined mainly by social and economic forces, not by political ones. Even analysts who have identified a significant role for political parties, group pressures, and the organization of state legislatures often assume that demographic variables, such as poverty and minority rates, measure economic, not political, life.[7] But one should not ignore the political meaning hidden in demographic and economic variables. For example, the taxable resources of a state are not simply an economic factor that has no political significance. The variable also measures the public's demand for public services. As people become more affluent, they expect government to provide more and better public services, and, if political leaders do not respond, they will eventually be replaced by ones who will.[8] Other variables that at first glance seem to be measuring only economic and social phenomena, such as poverty rates and the size of the minority population, also measure both public preferences and governmental constraints on expenditure decisions. As is implied by the rediscovery of the concept of political economy, many demographic variables are indicators of political relationships as much as of social and economic conditions. I treat them as such in the analysis that follows.

Taxable Resources

Functional theorists expect governments in states with high taxable resources to spend more per person than more fiscally constrained governments. The demand for most publicly provided services increases with income. Just as consumers with more money purchase bigger and more luxurious homes, so citizens with more money expect their government to provide them with better roads, sanitation systems, schools, and parks. Legislative theorists also expect higher expenditures in wealthier states because electoral incentives encourage expenditure whenever feasible.

In order to test these hypotheses, it is necessary to construct a measure of the taxable resources of a state. Since there are many ways a state can extract revenues from its citizens, a variety of indicators of taxable resources may be used, including the amount of income earned by residents of a state, from which revenue can be obtained by levying a tax on income; the total value of state property, which can be assessed a property tax; the total value of all retail sales of all goods and services produced in a state, which can be made subject to a sales tax; and the value of all products mined in a state, which can be subjected to a tax on ore.

Any one of these factors is by itself misleading, because it captures only one dimension of a state's fiscal capacity. States draw on all four and still other dimensions, each to a varying degree. Some states tax property more heavily. Other states levy higher rates on retail sales.

Still other states levy a higher tax on personal income. In order to better measure a state's overall taxable resources—that is, the amount that a state can raise in revenue at any given tax rate—the Advisory Commission on Intergovernmental Relations (ACIR) has constructed an index that combines into a single measure all the factors states utilize in their taxing arrangements. Each factor in the indicator is given a weight proportionate to its importance in the taxing scheme of the average (or, as ACIR calls it, the representative) state. Since income, sales, and property taxes account for most state tax revenues, the most important factors in the index are the total value of a state's personal income, retail sales, and residential and business property.

Just as states vary in their expenditure policies, so they differ in their potential fiscal resources. In 1991 Alaska had the greatest tax capacity. Other states with very high taxable resources included Wyoming, Illinois, Nevada, and Delaware. States with very low fiscal capacities included Maine, Alabama, South Carolina, and Mississippi. Interstate variation in fiscal capacity, with one exception, has remained fairly constant since 1967 (see table 4-1). In 1967 the CV stood at 0.19; by 1991 it had nudged upward to 0.20. The coefficient did jump temporarily to 0.36 during the recession of 1982, which had a dramatically different impact on the industrial heartland than it did on the coastal states.

Since both legislative and functional theory expect developmental and redistributive expenditures to rise with an increase in taxable resources, the findings shown in figure 4-1 should come as no surprise. The ten wealthiest states spent almost $3,000 per person for developmental purposes; the ten poorest states spent only a little more than $1,500. A similar pattern is evident in expenditures for redistributive purposes. The wealthiest states spent $830 per person for social purposes; the poorest states spent $411. Although these figures are suggestive, they are not conclusive evidence that the fiscal capacity of a state has a major effect on governmental expenditure. It may be that some other variable correlated with fiscal capacity accounts for these differences among the states. Only after controlling for the other factors affecting expenditure will it be possible to identify the unique influence of a state's taxable resources on expenditure policy.

Poverty Rates

Functional theory expects poverty rates to cause lower per capita redistributive expenditures but to bring about higher developmental

FIGURE 4-1. *State Taxable Resources and per Capita Developmental and Redistributive Expenditures, 1991*

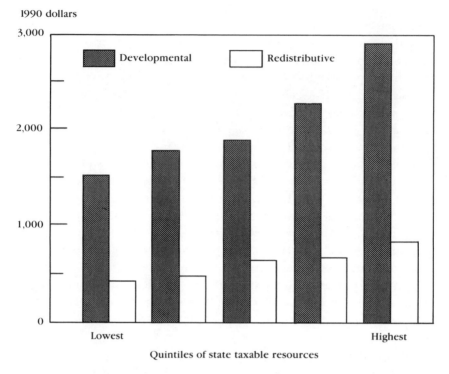

1990 dollars

Quintiles of state taxable resources

SOURCES: See appendix.

expenditures. In states with relatively high poverty rates, the cost of maintaining the state's social and physical infrastructure is higher. Concentrations of poor people impose social and fiscal costs on the general community in the form of higher spending for police, prisons, fire protection, and schools. However, redistributive expenditures will be lower in states with higher poverty levels because state officials will attempt to keep their state from becoming a welfare magnet. States with relatively low poverty rates are less concerned about becoming a haven for the poor.

Predictions from legislative theory usually go in the opposite direction. Legislative theorists expect that in states with higher percentages of poor people, the political pressures from those representing poor people will be greater and redistributive expenditures will be higher.[9] Legislative theorists also expect mandates from the national government to force states with higher poverty levels to spend more on redistributive programs.[10]

The percentage of a state's population living in poverty can be estimated by using the federal government's measure of poverty. This measure takes into account differences in family size. It has been criticized for ignoring differences in cost of living among the states and for inaccurately estimating the level of poverty in the United States, but most people agree it is the best available indicator of interstate differences in income deprivation.

States vary considerably in the percentages of their population living below the poverty line. Mississippi, Louisiana, and Arkansas are among the states with the highest poverty rates; Minnesota, Connecticut, and Wisconsin are among those with the lowest. The variation in poverty among the states declined significantly between 1967 and 1982, from a CV of 0.43 to 0.28, but then increased slightly during the 1980s to 0.32 (table 4-1).

Per capita redistributive expenditures by state and local governments are lowest where poverty rates are highest (figure 4-2). The ten states with the lowest poverty rates spent an average of about $750 on redistributive programs in 1991; the ten states with the highest poverty rates spent only $450. States with lower poverty rates also spent more on developmental programs. The ten states with the lowest poverty rates spent $2,805 per person on development, while the ten states with the highest poverty rates spent only $1,529.

These findings suggest that states try to avoid becoming welfare magnets. If their poor population is relatively large, they keep redistributive expenditure low in order to discourage any further in-migration of poor people. But these findings offer no support for the claim that the costs of maintaining the social and physical infrastructure of a state are higher if a state has a higher poverty rate. But these findings are only preliminary; a more adequate test of the welfare magnet theory is reported at the end of this chapter.

Percentage of Population Living in Central Cities

Functional theorists agree that developmental expenditure should be higher in central cities, but they do not always agree on the explanation. Some functional theorists say that the financial needs of central cities are greater because their populations are relatively poor, are of minority background, and live in close proximity to one another. But if these

FIGURE 4-2. *State Poverty Rates and per Capita Developmental and Redistributive Expenditures, 1991*

1990 dollars

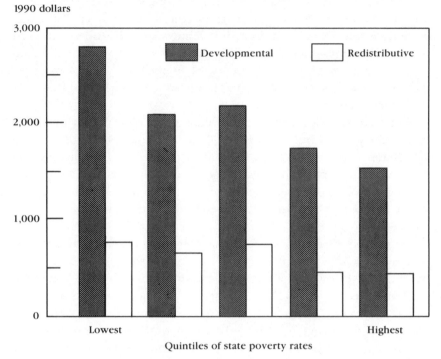

Quintiles of state poverty rates

SOURCES: See appendix.

factors are introduced separately in a model of public expenditure, then any effect of the percentage of the population living in central cities on expenditure levels must be measuring something besides public needs caused by poverty, diversity, or density. Other functional theorists expect central cities to suffer from diseconomies of scale because they are usually substantially larger than the suburban and rural communities located elsewhere in the state. Large cities are more likely to have well-organized groups of public employees who are in a strong position to demand higher salaries and better working conditions. Legislative theory also expects both redistributive and developmental expenditure to be higher in central cities. Cities enjoy a natural monopoly over the most valuable land in the region. When legislators have access to a valued resource, electoral incentives are likely to encourage them to tax the resource and spend the revenues for governmental purposes. These pressures are particularly great in central cities, where

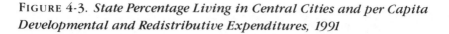

FIGURE 4-3. *State Percentage Living in Central Cities and per Capita Developmental and Redistributive Expenditures, 1991*

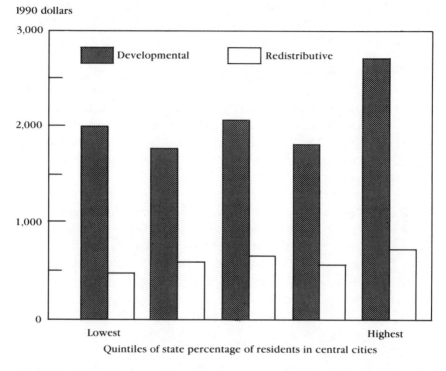

1990 dollars

Quintiles of state percentage of residents in central cities

SOURCES: See appendix.

those who own the most valuable property—in the downtown business district—cast few votes.

To test these hypotheses, I calculated for each state the percentage of the population living within central cities of 100,000 or more. The variation among the states in the percentage of a state's population living in central cities has long been and still remains very large, with a CV of 0.83 in 1991 (table 4-1). Ten states, including Maine, Montana, the Dakotas, and Wyoming, had no residents living within a central city. States with the highest percentage of residents living in central cities included Hawaii, Arizona, New York, Alaska, and Texas.

The findings reported in figure 4-3 are generally consistent with the expectations of both functional and legislative theories. The ten states with the highest percentage living in central cities spent, on average, more for both developmental and redistributive purposes than any other group of states. The ten states with the fewest central-city residents spent, on average, the least on redistribution. However, the developmental expenditures of this quintile were nearly as high as those of the middle group of states. A more exact testing of the central-city hypothesis drawn from functional and legislative theories is reported in the regression analysis below.

Minority Percentage

Functional theorists do not expect the minority percentage of a state's population to affect public expenditure of either kind. But because of racial divisions and the peculiarities of the system of representation in the United States, legislative theory readily accommodates the hypothesis that a larger minority population results in lower expenditure on redistribution.

The reasoning behind this hypothesis has to do with the distinction that white Americans seem to make between what they regard as the "deserving" poor and the "undeserving" poor. The deserving poor are deemed to have found themselves in poverty through no fault of their own. Even though they have worked hard and lived according to the conventional moral code of the society, the deserving poor have suffered ill fortune. Economic recession or foreign competition may have temporarily cost them their jobs; death may have claimed a wage-earning spouse; an accident or disease may have left them blind or otherwise disabled; or they may simply have inadequate savings to carry them through their retirement years. The undeserving poor are considered to be the long-term unemployed who have never acquired—or somehow have lost—the habits and capacities necessary to hold a full-time job. The undeserving poor also include those who have defied the conventional moral code by bearing a child out of wedlock. Some analysts feel that the distinction between the deserving and the undeserving poor has been reinforced in American political culture by racial prejudices and antagonisms. Whatever the cause of their poverty, minorities, especially African Americans, are said to be regarded as less deserving.[11]

Social welfare programs are designed in ways that reinforce the distinction between those poor perceived to be deserving and those not so perceived. Several programs are directed toward the deserving poor. The well-funded social security retirement program and medicare have greatly reduced poverty among those over the age of sixty-five. The blind, disabled, and aged not eligible for social security benefits receive aid under the supplemental social insurance (SSI) program, which has a federally funded minimum national standard indexed to changes in the cost of living. The temporarily unemployed receive unemployment benefits under an unemployment insurance program funded by a federal tax on employers. Recipients of benefits under these programs have continued to receive into the 1990s most of the benefits established in the 1960s and 1970s.[12]

Government provides cash benefits to the undeserving poor mainly by means of aid to families with dependent children (AFDC) and state-funded general assistance programs. The undeserving poor also receive food stamps, medicaid, and assistance with their home energy costs. Perhaps cuts in these programs are due to the fact that AFDC has become increasingly identified with the undeserving poor, who may also be perceived to be even less deserving than they once were.

Many white voters believe that minorities are a disproportionate percentage of the undeserving poor. White voters are also overrepresented in state legislatures. Unlike proportional systems of election, which provide proportionate representation for minority opinion, American legislative elections are typically winner-take-all or "first-past-the-post" contests. In addition, races tend to vote in blocs, and minorities usually have lower turnout rates.[13] The net result is an overrepresentation in state legislatures of white majority interests, compared with those of minorities. The overrepresentation of white interests is more likely to affect the redistributive expenditure of a state when the minority percentage in the population is larger. This perverse effect occurs because white Americans are likely to perceive minorities to be disproportionately represented among the undeserving poor. If minorities are a larger percentage of the population, they will also be a larger portion of the state's needy population. Majority white opposition to redistribution is likely to be greater.

Approximately 80 percent of the U.S. population was white in 1990. Twelve percent identified themselves as black; the remainder identified themselves as Asian, American Indian, or members of some other race. About 6.4 percent of the population is regarded as of Hispanic origin, but some of these identify themselves as white.

The variation in the minority percentage of a state's population decreased steadily from 1.02 in 1967 to 0.73 in 1991 (table 4-1). States with the highest percentages of minorities in 1991 included Mississippi, Hawaii, Louisiana, California, and South Carolina. The racially most homogeneous states included New Hampshire, Vermont, Maine, Iowa, and West Virginia.

FIGURE 4-4. *State Minority Rates and per Capita Developmental and Redistributive Expenditures, 1991*

1990 dollars

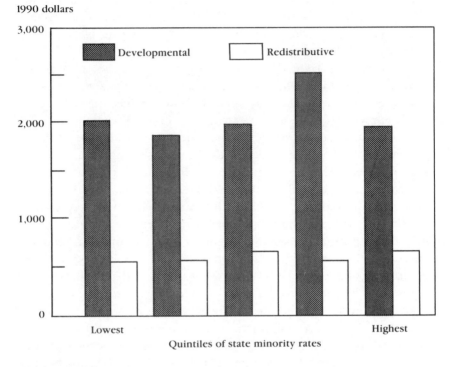

SOURCES: See appendix.

When states are grouped into quintiles according to the minority percentage of their population, no significant differences in redistributive expenditure among the states are apparent. A simple look at the relationship between minority representation and redistributive spending provides little empirical support for the hypothesis that a larger minority population will lead to lower redistributive expenditures (see figure 4-4). But the results from the more sophisticated regression analysis reported below will suggest a different conclusion.

Density

Legislative theorists expect citizens to vary in their demand for developmental services according to the density of their populations. As states become more densely populated, the actions of individuals impinge more directly upon one another and their need for governmental services increases. But the cost of supplying these services may be inversely related to density. Services to sparsely settled areas also may be more expensive, because these areas do not benefit from any economies of agglomeration. Highways and sewage systems must be extended over more distant terrain in order to serve state residents. Children must be bused to school over longer distances. The net effect of differences in demand and cost of supplying developmental services is uncertain. Some studies indicate that density is positively related to public expenditure; other studies identify a negative relationship.

The net effect of density on redistributive expenditure is less problematic. According to functional theory, demand for higher levels of redistribution is greater where density creates greater interdependency. Overall, higher density is likely to result in greater redistributive spending.

Although the U.S. population increased by 50 million between 1969 and 1991, states remained extremely diverse in the density of their population, with the CV falling only slightly from 1.48 in 1967 to 1.37 in 1991 (see table 4-1). Classifying states into quintiles according to the density of their population suggests that more densely populated states spend more on redistribution. The most sparsely inhabited quintile of states spent just over $530 per person on redistribution, while the most densely settled states spent $800 per person (see figure 4-5). The classification also reveals a curvilinear relationship between density and development expenditure. Both the most sparsely settled states and the most densely populated states spent more on development. The ten states at the middle of the density distribution spent the least. Sparsely settled states may incur high development costs in order to serve a widely dispersed population. The social interdependence occurring in densely settled states may induce a high demand for development services. States that are neither sparsely nor densely populated seem to enjoy lower costs and suffer fewer demands. This topic will be revisited in the regression analysis below.

Partisanship

Legislative theory hypothesizes that partisan divisions will influence state fiscal policy. But prior studies of state expenditure have been unable to detect interpretable partisan effects on overall levels of state expenditure, leading some analysts to conclude that the two parties were Tweedledum and Tweedledee.[14] One way of rescuing the hypothesis from these puzzling results is to distinguish between redistributive and developmental expenditure. Democrats can be expected to sup-

FIGURE 4-5. *State Population Density and per Capita Developmental and Redistributive Expenditures, 1991*

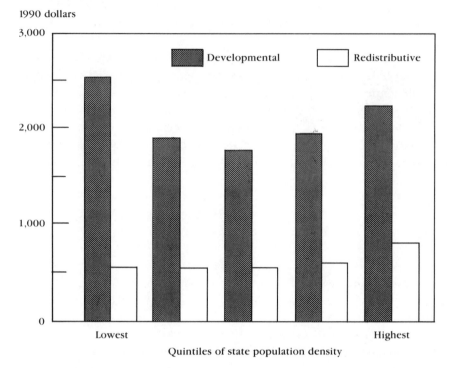

1990 dollars

SOURCES: See appendix.

port higher levels of spending on redistribution because of the party's ties to lower-income and minority groups. Republicans can be expected to support higher levels of spending on development because their upper-income constituents place a higher premium on economic growth strategies. Legislative theory further expects partisanship to have a larger effect on developmental than redistributive expenditure because the latter type is constrained by national mandates.

The partisanship of state legislatures in this study is indicated by the percentage of the state legislators who were members of the Democratic party in 1991. The measure is an imperfect measure of the balance of power between the two parties. It does not take into account the partisan affiliation of the governor of the state or whether both houses of the legislature were controlled by the same party. The measure assumes that expenditure levels are determined by the legislature currently in office, ignoring the fact that much public expenditure is historically determined. The measure also ignores the fact that state expenditure is determined in part by local governments and only in part by state legislatures. It does not distinguish between states in which the Democratic party is relatively liberal in its orientation and states (usually in the South) in which Democrats are more conserva-tive. Despite these defects, the measure may still capture the general propensity of a state to favor one political party rather than the other.

Partisan differences among the states have historically been quite large. The South was once thought to be solidly Democratic; northern states were predominantly Republican. But with the demise of the one-party system in southern states and the strengthening of the Demo-cratic party in New England, these regional differences have waned. The CV shifted downward from 0.41 in 1967 to 0.24 in 1991 (table 4-1). Perhaps it is this increasing political similarity among the states that accounts for a general impression that regional differences in the United States are dissipating.

When states are grouped into quintiles according to their partisan-ship in 1991, relationships between partisanship and expenditure are relatively small and inconsistent (figure 4-6). However, there is some suggestion that states with more Republican legislators spend more on development while states with more Democratic legislators may spend more on redistribution. The effects of partisanship may be obscured by the countervailing effects of other factors. More exact evidence testing these hypotheses will be presented in the analysis that concludes this chapter.

Professionalization of State Politics

Legislative theory expects developmental and redistributive expen-diture to be higher in states where politics has been professionalized. Professional legislators seek to make politics their career. Service in the legislature is more than a sideline to their main vocation; it is the very focus of their public life. Professional politicians, unlike amateurs, have a particularly strong interest in winning reelection or building a base of support for running for higher office.[15] For this reason professional politicians have a vested interest in the expansion of government. The more services government provides, the more constituents need legis-lative representatives to help them get desired benefits and protect them from potential harms.[16] By helping constituents, professional pol-iticians can facilitate their reelection.

FIGURE 4-6. *Democratic Percentage in State Legislatures and per Capita Developmental and Redistributive Expenditures, 1991*

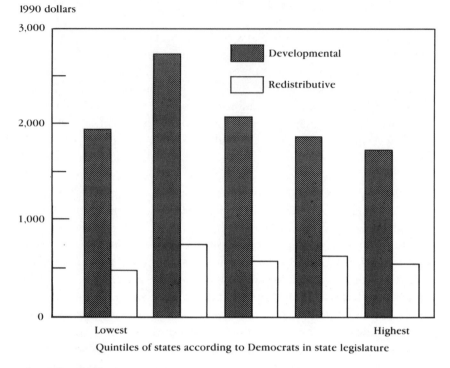

1990 dollars

Quintiles of states according to Democrats in state legislature

SOURCES: See appendix.

Professional and amateur politicians can be found in every state and locality. But some states encourage professionalization by expecting their legislative servants to take on more tasks, giving them more staff assistance, and paying them a higher salary. Probably the best single measure of the professionalization of state politics is the salary a state pays its legislators. The salary level indicates how much time the state expects legislators to devote to their job, and it determines the monetary incentive that comes with making politics a career. All other things being equal, jobs that pay better are more earnestly pursued.

State legislative salaries are not a perfect measure of the professionalization of state politics, however. State expenditures are determined not only by state legislatures but also by decisions made by local governments. Statewide politics may have become highly professionalized while local politics may have remained in the hands of amateurs. While this is possible, my analysis makes the assumption that state legislative

FIGURE 4-7. *Professionalization of State Legislatures and per Capita Developmental and Redistributive Expenditures, 1991*

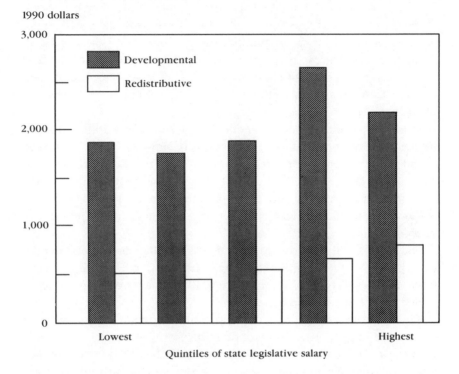

1990 dollars

Quintiles of state legislative salary

SOURCES: See appendix.

salaries indicate the degree to which politics is professionalized not only in the state capital but throughout the state more generally.

Interstate variation in professionalization, as indicated by legislative salaries, declined moderately between 1967 and 1991, with the CV falling from 0.99 to 0.79 (table 4-1). However, substantial variation remains. A third of the states still pay their legislators at least 80 percent more or 80 percent less than the average state. These differences in compensation are strongly correlated with state expenditures. The twenty states in which legislators are paid the most also have both the highest developmental and the highest redistributive expenditure (see figure 4-7). Some might think this relationship is simply due to the fact that both higher salaries and higher expenditures are a function of a state's taxable resources. But in the regression analysis that follows it will be clear that the professionalization of state politics has its own effect on state expenditures.

A Comprehensive Explanation of State Expenditure

State developmental and redistributive expenditure may be associated with the taxable resources of a state, its density, its poverty rate, the size of its minority population, the percentage of its population living in central cities, the partisan composition of the legislature, and the professionalization of state politics. The precise influence of each of these factors can be identified only by controlling for the influence of all the others.

To isolate the independent effects of each factor, per capita redistributive and developmental expenditures were simultaneously regressed on all these factors. I included data from all fifty states for six years: 1967, 1972, 1977, 1982, 1987, and 1991. Since the relationships among the variables remained relatively consistent over this period of time, it was possible to include data for all six years within a pooled time-series, cross-sectional analysis.[17]

The results of the regression reveal striking differences between the determinants of developmental and redistributive expenditure (see table 4-2). Each type of public expenditure has its own social, economic and political determinants.

Functional theory expects developmental expenditures to be more responsive than redistributive expenditures to differentials in taxable resources. The findings are consistent with these expectations. For every unit increase in taxable resources, states spend an additional $12 per person on developmental programs but only an additional $3 on redistributive ones. It seems that citizens living in wealthier states expect their policymakers to provide more and better social and physical infrastructure.[18] Their demand for more redistributive programs for the poor is significantly less responsive to increases in wealth. Charity is apparently not as income elastic as the demand for public services that reach a broader segment of the population.[19]

Functional theory expects higher poverty rates to increase the costs of maintaining a state's social and physical infrastructure, thereby inducing an increase in developmental expenditure. The results are inconsistent with these expectations. Developmental costs do not increase with the poverty rate. Functional theory expects higher poverty rates to be associated with reductions in redistributive expenditure so as to minimize a state's chances of becoming a welfare magnet. Legislative theory expects federal mandates and political pressures

TABLE 4-2. *Determinants of State Developmental and Redistributive Expenditure*

Independent variable[a]	Developmental		Redistributive	
	b	Standard error	b	Standard error
Taxable resources	12.57	1.03***	2.96	0.45***
Poverty rate	3.32	5.27	1.80	2.46
Percent living in central cities	3.08	1.48**	2.11	0.66***
Percent minority	0.34	0.23	−2.05	0.99**
Density (distance from mean)	4.90	3.20	...	...
Population density	...	...	5.85	1.18***
Percent Democrats in state legislature	−6.17	1.25***	0.98	0.57*
Legislative salary	3.37	1.63**	5.37	0.75***
Intercept	517.94	166.62***	−103.03	73.61*
Corrected R^2	0.87	...	0.67	...
N	300	...	300	...

SOURCES: See Appendix A.
  * Significant at the .1 level.
  ** Significant at the .05 level.
  *** Significant at the .01 level.
  a. Equations also include controls for year and for state of Alaska.

from lower-income citizens to increase redistributive expenditures. The regression analysis suggests the two effects offset each other, because no statistically significant relationship between poverty rates and redistributive expenditure could be identified. I shall attempt to unravel the puzzle in chapter 5.

As both functional and legislative theory expect, both developmental and redistributive expenditures increase with the percentage of the population living in central cities. The biggest increases were for developmental expenditure. For every 1 percent increase in the percentage of the population living in central cities, developmental expenditure increased by roughly $3 per person. This is the apparent differential in the cost of providing public services in large central cities, compared with suburban and rural areas. Since the regression analysis controls for poverty rates and population density, this differential is probably due to monopoly effects and diseconomies of scale. The increase for redistributive expenditure was approximately $2 per person for every 1 percent increase in the percentage of the population living in central cities.

Legislative theory expects redistributive expenditures to be less in states with more minorities. Perceptions that minorities are undeserv-

ing of welfare, coupled with their underrepresentation in state legislatures, create a political context unfavorable to redistributive
expenditure. This hypothesis is supported by the regression analysis.
For every 1 percent increase in the minority population in a state, $2
less per person is spent on redistributive services.

Legislative theory expects developmental expenditure to increase as
population density both increases and decreases. To measure these
effects I calculated how much the density for all states differs from that
of the average state. States ranked higher on this value if they deviated
from the mean by being either more sparsely settled or more densely
populated. For every increase or decrease of ten persons per square
kilometer from the average state density, the cost of development went
up by $5 per person. However, more research is needed before these
results can be accepted; the standard error of the estimate was too
large to be sure the relationship did not occur simply by chance. According to functional theory, the effects of density on redistributive
expenditure should be positive. Increasing density increases social interdependency and therefore requires greater public expenditure to
address the problems of those in need. Findings are consistent with
these expectations. For every unit increase in the density of the population, redistributive expenditure increased by $6 per person.

Legislative theory expects partisan control of the state legislature to
have opposite effects on developmental and redistributive expenditure.
The more Republican the legislature is, the more states spend on development and the less on redistribution. The findings are consistent
with these hypotheses. For every 1 percent increase in Democratic
representation, developmental expenditure fell by $6 per person and
redistributive expenditure increased by $1.

The findings are also consistent with the professionalization hypothesis derived from legislative theory. A $1,000 increase in the annual
salary of a legislator costs the taxpayer over $3 per person in devel-
opmental expenditure and over $5 in redistributive expenditure.

Conclusions

States continue to vary substantially in their public expenditure. The
amount of variation has not declined over the past twenty-five years. In
1991 states differed from one another on most of these variables nearly
as much as they did in 1967. Despite increasing integration of the Amer-

ican economy, states remain very different from one another in many different ways.

Some differences in expenditure seem appropriate. That both sparsely inhabited and densely settled states pay more for their social and physical infrastructure seems only logical and necessary. That partisan differences should affect expenditure levels is also only to be expected. Choosing between parties that differ on the issues is one of the ways voters can influence government in a democratic society.

Federalism helps to perpetuate this variation among the states. One can scarcely deny that modern federalism has its price for those who think that public services should be more or less uniform throughout the country. The significant impact of a state's taxable resources on developmental expenditure underlines the price that federalism exacts. Those states that have more resources spend more on public services, and presumably they enjoy higher-quality public services as a result. Can aid from the national government reduce such inequity? I examine that question in chapter 6.

Also, the cost of government is higher in states dominated by professional politicians and in states where more people live in central cities. Is there a way of reducing the high cost of government in such places? The question is explored more fully in chapter 7.

Finally, the social costs of federalism seem considerable. States with higher poverty rates spend no more on redistribution than those with lower poverty rates. Apparently, redistributive expenditure is not responsive to social needs. Indeed, redistributive expenditure is actually reduced in those states where minorities are concentrated. Can such racial discrimination be avoided? To answer these questions, I shall next examine questions of poverty, race, and welfare.

5

Welfare: A Race
to the Bottom?

When poverty comes in at the door, love flies out the window.
Anonymous

In the chapter just concluded, I reported that states with higher poverty rates spent about the same on redistributive programs as did states with lower poverty rates. This finding is contrary to functional theory, which hypothesizes that states with higher levels of poverty will spend less on redistributive programs in order to avoid becoming a welfare magnet. It also is inconsistent with legislative theory, which says that mandates imposed by the national government force states with larger poor populations to spend more money on redistribution. To comply with federal mandates, states with more poor people are compelled to spend more, despite their fears of becoming a welfare magnet. Perhaps both factors are at work, producing the null finding reported in chapter 4.

In this chapter I explore the question in greater detail by examining a policy that is wholly within the discretion of state governments: the amount of the monthly benefit given to families who receive aid to families with dependent children (AFDC). Although many aspects of the AFDC program are subject to national regulations, the monthly benefit level is a matter of state discretion. A more detailed examination of changes in AFDC policy will show whether states take steps to avoid becoming a welfare magnet when they have the legal authority to do so.

In the course of exploring this issue, I shall also explain the recent propensity of state AFDC policy to race to the bottom (that is, for each state to try to have a more restrictive welfare policy than other states).

108

Under the Family Support Act of 1988, states were given the opportunity to experiment with programs of assistance to families with dependent children. Although the law seemed in principle to allow for experimentation in either a more liberal or more restrictive direction, the proposals for waiver of federal requirements approved by the Department of Health and Human Services have almost always had a conservative cast. Wisconsin and New Jersey proposed, among other things, to withhold the increase in benefits that typically came with the birth of an additional child. California's reform was decidedly more draconian in its cost-saving features. It proposed an immediate 25 percent reduction in welfare benefits, a second further reduction for all families remaining on welfare after six months, and a restriction that limited benefits to new arrivals to California to the level they were receiving in their previous state of residence.[1]

That no state requested permission to liberalize its welfare policies is in some ways surprising. States often have experimented and innovated when Washington was stultified by partisan divisions and interest group pressures. Many of the liberal policy innovations of the past were first attempted at the state level. AFDC itself grew out of mothers' pensions programs first set up in 1911 in Illinois and Missouri, long before the federal government incorporated family assistance into the Social Security Act of 1935. Wisconsin, always the great innovator, had introduced an unemployment compensation program before it was incorporated into the Social Security Act of 1935. But since 1970 states have become increasingly reluctant to liberalize their welfare systems. On the contrary, welfare policy has been moving steadily toward the bottom.

Trends in Welfare Policy

The conservative drift in state policy, culminating recently in a variety of proposed welfare demonstrations, can be observed by examining the changes in the level of welfare assistance a family received from the average state over the past fifty years (see figure 5-1). For the first thirty-three years after the establishment of AFDC as a national program in 1937, the real value of AFDC benefits steadily increased. The mean benefit paid to a family in the average state was $306 in 1940, $429 in 1950, $520 in 1960, and $605 in 1970. In retrospect, this steady increase seems to have had several causes: the steady economic growth of the immediate postwar period; the determination to show during the

FIGURE 5-1. *State Welfare Benefits,* 1940–93

1993 dollars

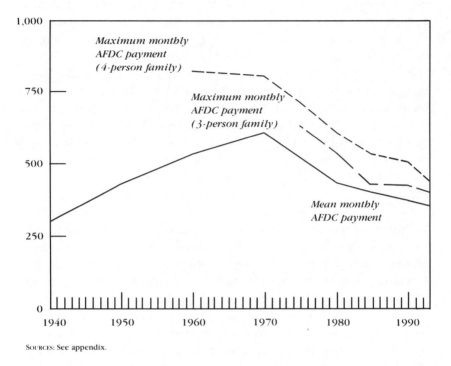

SOURCES: See appendix.

most intense years of the cold war that a democratic society with a market-based economy could care for its poor more effectively than could a communist regime; and a lingering sense left over from the depression era that poverty was as much a by-product of society's problems as a function of any individual's own personal inadequacies.

After 1970 the average cash benefit began to decline just as steadily as it had been increasing before. By 1975 in the average state it was only $512; by 1980 it had fallen to $429; by 1985 it fell even further to $393; and by 1993 it reached its postwar nadir of $349.

This measure of AFDC policy is an instructive indicator of state policy over time, because it is available for the entire fifty-three-year period between 1940 and 1993. Yet the average benefit has one characteristic that makes it less than a perfect measure of state welfare policy: it is a function of both state policy and the size of the families receiving the benefit. Since benefits typically vary with family size, and the size of the average AFDC family has declined over time, benefit levels would have fallen even without any change in state policy.

The amount a state provides an eligible four-person family that has no other income (often referred to as the maximum payment of cash assistance or the welfare guarantee) is a more direct indicator of state AFDC policy, since it is not directly influenced by characteristics of the recipient population. This measure, available since 1960, also shows steps toward the bottom have been taking place since 1970 (figure 5-1). The maximum benefit guaranteed to a four-person family by the average state fell from $802 in 1970 to $729 in 1975, $604 in 1980, $523 in 1985, and finally $469 in 1993. Over the course of the twenty-three-year period, cash benefits provided by state governments declined by 42 percent. The same pattern of declining welfare benefits applies to the maximum guarantee for a family of three.

Five potential explanations for this conservative drift in state welfare policymaking come to mind. First, the slowdown in the rate of economic growth since 1970 may have reduced the resources available for welfare. Second, AFDC recipients may be perceived as less deserving than they once were. Third, the apparently conservative trend in national politics over the past quarter of a century may have depressed welfare benefits. Fourth, an increase in federally funded welfare benefits may have decreased the perceived need for state-funded benefits. Finally, states may cut their welfare benefits because they fear that high benefits attract and retain the poor within their state. I will examine each of these explanations in turn.

Slowdown in Economic Growth

The decline in welfare benefits could well be attributed to the slow-down in the rate of growth in the U.S. economy. Suffering from low rates of growth in economic productivity and increasing competition from low-wage workers abroad, the U.S. economy over the past twenty years has yielded very few dividends for middle-income families. Welfare benefits may have fallen because middle-income Americans have been working within an increasingly constrained budget.

Economic factors help but do not fully explain the changes in state policy. Overall family income continued to grow during the 1970s and 1980s. Average family income increased by 8.7 percent between 1973 and 1989. Over this same sixteen-year period, the average income of families with children grew at the slower pace of 5.8 percent.[2] But the growth in family income took place almost exclusively among families in higher income categories. When one looks at middle America, the picture is not as rosy. The average income of all families in the middle quintile of the distribution remained stagnant, slipping slightly from $25,909 to $25,823 between 1973 and 1989. The average income of the middle quintile of families with children grew only barely, from $32,616 to $33,067.[3]

Family income remained stable only because family members in 1989 were working more hours than in 1973. Many more women entered the labor market, and, as a result, many more families were depending on the income of two wage earners. When one looks at the hourly earnings the average worker was being paid, the consequences of slow economic growth are even more apparent. In 1973 male workers were being paid an average of $10.93 in 1990 dollars. By 1991 they were being paid only $9.92, a decline of 9.2 percent.[4]

The slowdown in the rate of growth of the size and productivity of the American economy may thus be one cause of the cuts in state welfare benefit levels. Since the average American male was earning 9.2 percent less in hourly wages, the average American voter may have expected state policymakers to cut welfare benefits by at least an equivalent amount. But since welfare benefits fell by over 42 percent between 1970 and 1993, the drop in hourly compensation wages seems to be only a partial—not a complete—explanation for the conservative drift in state policymaking.

Changing Perceptions of the Poor

As discussed in the previous chapter, white Americans seem to distinguish between what they regard as the "deserving" and the "undeserving" poor. Perhaps welfare cuts are due to the fact that AFDC has become increasingly identified with the undeserving poor, who may also be perceived to be even more undeserving than they once were.

Mothers' pensions were originally established for widows of men killed in industrial accidents. Widows remained a majority of those receiving AFDC benefits as late as the 1940s. But as marriage patterns changed and welfare rolls expanded, AFDC was given mainly to families headed by women who were separated, divorced, or never married. In 1969 death was the cause of parental absence from the home in only 5.5 percent of the cases. By 1990 this percentage had fallen to 1.6 percent. Divorce and separation have become an increasingly accepted practice in American society. Yet even these more or less acceptable causes for parental absence were responsible for a declining percentage of the AFDC caseload, dropping from 43.3 percent of AFDC cases in 1969 to 32.9 percent in 1990. By contrast, the socially least legitimate cause for parental absence from the home—the parents were never married—grew from 27.9 percent in 1969 to 54.0 percent in 1990.[5] AFDC increasingly was accused of providing young men and women with an alternative to marriage.

Even as AFDC rolls were being filled by women who had never married, the larger poor population from which welfare recipients typically came was becoming femininized. During the depression years, poverty was pervasive, hitting one-parent and two-parent families, old, young, and middle-aged alike. But as the rate of poverty fell dramatically after World War II, the remaining pockets of poverty were increasingly concentrated among younger single-parent families headed by women. By 1959, 28 percent of the poor consisted of poor families headed by women. This percentage increased to 40 percent in 1967, skyrocketed to 57 percent in 1974, and continued to rise to 64 percent in 1988.[6] The employment status of women receiving AFDC also declined after 1975. In that year 10.4 percent of women receiving AFDC held a full-time job, and another 6.3 percent were employed part time. By 1990 these percentages had fallen to 2.5 and 4.2 percent, respectively.[7]

The public may also be increasingly identifying welfare policy with African Americans. This perception may have become increasingly widespread in the media and public opinion, but it has no foundation in actual welfare statistics. While the percentage of welfare recipients who were whites remained steady at about 38 percent during the two decades, the percentage who were African American declined from 45.8 to 39.7. The percentage who were Latino increased from 13.4 to 16.6.[8]

And it is not just the welfare rolls that have changed little in ethnic terms over the past twenty years. Neither has poverty changed its racial coloration to any significant degree. The percentage of African Americans who are poor has remained fairly constant at around 32 percent, while the percentage of whites who are poor has remained fairly constant at around 12 percent. Diachronic statistics on Latino poverty are notoriously unreliable, but the Census Bureau reports only a moderate increase in this group's poverty rate. The percentage of the poor population that is of a particular ethnic group has also remained much the same. The poor were 58 percent white in 1991, down somewhat from 64 percent in 1975. But the poor were only 25 percent African American in 1991, also down from 27 percent in 1975. Poverty has become more Latinized but only at a moderately faster pace than the U.S. population as a whole.[9]

If AFDC cannot be tainted as an increasingly minority program, neither can it be correctly portrayed as a program serving only the long-term poor. The percentage remaining on welfare after five years fell slightly from 26.9 percent in 1979 (the earliest figure available) to 21.7 percent in 1990.[10]

It may be that AFDC is perceived more today than ever before as a program serving the undeserving poor: an unemployed, unmarried, long-term dependent, minority population. But the actual pattern is more ambiguous. It is true that families receiving AFDC are increasingly likely to be headed by women who have never married and are currently not working. But those receiving AFDC benefits today are no more likely than recipients of ten years ago to be long-term dependent, and they are even less likely to be African American. If racism is playing an increasing role in welfare politics, it is a racism not especially well connected to reality.

But it may be incorrect to attribute the decline in state welfare benefits to intensifying racism or changing perceptions of AFDC recipients. Indeed, there is evidence that states are as prepared to cut the benefits of the deserving poor as much as those of the undeserving poor. State-determined, state-funded benefits to the blind, disabled, and aged SSI recipients also have fallen. Although a few states (California, Colorado, Michigan, Minnesota, and Oklahoma) increased the value of SSI benefits for couples between 1975 and 1990, most states did not. In the median state, benefits fell by 50 percent, a decline that was even more steep than the cuts in AFDC.[11]

Politics Turns Conservative

Drawing upon legislative theory, one might attribute the decline in welfare benefits to the increasingly conservative political climate in the United States. As of 1968, voters had elected Democrats to the presidency for twenty-eight of the thirty-six preceding years. After 1968, Republicans controlled the presidency for twenty of the next twenty-four years. During the liberal Democratic era, the welfare system steadily expanded; during the conservative Republican era, the welfare system just as steadily contracted.

There are four difficulties with this explanation. First, welfare bene-fits continued to grow during the 1950s, when the country was led by Dwight Eisenhower, a conservatively oriented president who opposed expansion of the welfare state. Second, welfare benefits declined as much or more during the years that Democrat Jimmy Carter served as president as during Republican administrations. Third, most states were under either complete or partial Democratic control. Between 1978 and 1988 Democrats controlled both the legislative and executive branch in 40 percent of the states; they controlled one or another of the two branches in another 52 percent. Republicans held complete sway at the state level only 8 percent of the time. The electoral success Republicans were enjoying in presidential politics did not spill over to lower levels of government.[12]

Finally, and most decisively, welfare benefits under the control of the national government continued to expand in the 1970s even as states were cutting the real value of their welfare benefits. During the Ken-nedy years, Congress had established a nutritional program for women, infants, and children (WIC). At the behest of the Johnson administra-tion, it had authorized medicare, medicaid, the Economic Opportunity Act of 1964, and the Housing Act of 1968. But the federal policy inno-vations after 1968 have been hardly less impressive. Although Congress did not approve the most controversial features of Richard Nixon's family assistance plan—a national minimum standard and aid to work-ing families—it passed four major programs and a plethora of minor ones that greatly expanded the size of the welfare state.

Perhaps the most important innovation was the gradual redefinition and expansion of the food stamp program. This program, initially lim-ited to a few localities, was established on a nationwide basis in 1970. Unlike the AFDC program, in which states paid up to half the program costs, the full cost of food stamps was absorbed by the federal govern-ment. Initially, recipients were asked to pay for part of the cost of food stamps, but in 1975 they were made available free of any direct cost to the recipient. Food stamp benefits also were indexed to increases in the cost of living. The definition of products that could be purchased with food stamps was very broad. Whereas food stamp's predecessor program, the commodity distribution program, had offered only basic agricultural products that were in excess supply, food stamps could be used for virtually any food product available in a grocery store—even non-nutritious soft drinks. Food stamps became virtually equivalent to dollar bills.

Food stamps also helped to reduce the variation in welfare benefits among the states. Food stamp benefits reached a maximum if the recipient had no other income. They were reduced by thirty cents for every dollar of countable income a person received from another source.[13] Because of this feature, recipients living in states where AFDC benefits were particularly low received additional food stamps. As a result, the variation among the states in the benefits received by AFDC recipients was cut in half once food stamps were included in the calculation. The inclusion of food stamps caused the coefficient of variation among states in 1975 to fall from 0.34 to 0.19.[14] By 1990 it had fallen to 0.16, further sign that conservative control of the White House was not significantly reversing egalitarian trends in welfare policy.

Changes in the social security act in 1972 created the SSI program for the blind, disabled, and the aged not eligible for the social security retirement insurance program. Previously, public assistance programs for these populations had been, like AFDC, a joint venture between the federal and state governments, each paying half the cost. By establishing a national minimum benefit, absorbing the full cost of this minimum, and indexing the minimum to changes in the cost of living, Congress raised benefits for many SSI recipients and partially protected them against the conservative trend in welfare benefits that was taking place at the state level. Not only were benefit levels indexed to increases in the cost of living, but in 1983 an additional increase was approved by Congress. As a result, the federal SSI minimum brought a single recipient's income to 71 percent of the poverty line in 1975 and 76 percent in 1985. Couples receiving the minimum had an income close to 85 percent of the poverty line in 1975, 90 percent in 1985. With the addition of food stamps and medical insurance, a couple's income would have reached 106 percent of the poverty line in 1975, 100 percent in 1985.[15] Inasmuch as SSI benefits have since kept pace with increases in the cost of living, they have continued to keep recipients near or even above the poverty line.

The third major innovation of this era was signed by Gerald Ford in 1975. It provided an earned income tax credit (EITC) for both working and nonworking low-income families. The tax credit originally equaled 10 percent of the first $9,188 in earned income. At various points over the next twenty years, the federal government increased the eligibility and grant levels. In 1990 a credit of $983 was given to families with incomes of no more than $6,810; the credit was gradually phased out as earnings increased above that level.[16] The program was further enlarged in 1993 with the passage of the Clinton administration's Economic Recovery Act.

The housing assistance program, initially established as part of the Great Society by the Housing Act of 1968, was implemented and expanded during the Nixon and Ford administrations. It had two main components. The first provided low-interest loans to developers of new housing for low- and moderate-income residents. The second, strongly backed by the Nixon administration, provided a rent supplement that paid for the cost of approved housing that exceeded 25 percent of a family's income.

Many other smaller health and welfare programs were also adopted and expanded during the Nixon and Ford administrations. In addition to the establishment of the public-sector employment program and the expansion of the supplemental food program for women, infants, and children, these programs included maternal and child health, child support, human development, immunization, the child care block grant, the juvenile justice program, and a variety of other health programs. During the Carter years, the home energy assistance program was approved and the public-sector employment program was expanded and focused to serve the long-term unemployed.

Not only was federal welfare policy liberalized in numerous ways throughout the 1970s, but these liberal innovations at the federal level remained largely intact during the 1980s, despite the Reagan administration's opposition to an expanding welfare state. Reagan attempted to turn over to the states complete responsibility for welfare. He also succeeded in getting Congress in 1981 to tighten eligibility requirements for AFDC and temporarily postponed a scheduled cost of living increase in the food stamp benefit. Yet for all of his objections to welfare, Reagan did not quash the welfare state. President Reagan's rhetorical stance against the welfare state was in fact turned against him by a Democratic Congress that accused him of trying to balance his fiscal deficit on the backs of the poor. To counter these charges, Reagan was forced to promise to keep the "safety net" for those families with children who had fallen on hard times. As a result, most welfare programs were maintained at the levels they had reached by 1980. A Democratically controlled House and a combination of Democrats and moderate Republicans in the Senate fought vigorously to sustain safety net programs, exempting most of them from the automatic cuts required by the Gramm-Rudman-Hollings Deficit Reduction Act. Inasmuch as the president was vulnerable to charges that he lacked sympathy for the

TABLE 5-1. *Social Welfare Expenditures on Programs for Poor Families, 1975–90*

Billions of 1990 dollars

Program	1975	1990
Aid to families with dependent children[a]	18.2	21.2
Food stamps[b]	8.9	16.5
Medicaid[c]	8.5	15.8
Earned income tax credit[d]	1.4	4.0
Supplemental social insurance[e]	1.2	1.7
Supplemental food program for women, infants and children (WIC)[f]	1.5	4.5
Housing assistance[g]	2.7	7.5
Home energy assistance[h]	...	0.6
Other[i]	...	15.1
Total	**42.3**	**71.9**

a. *Overview of Entitlement Programs: Background Material and Data on Programs within the Jurisdiction of the Committee on Ways and Means*, Committee Print, House Committee on Ways and Means, 102 Cong. 2 sess. (Government Printing Office, 1992), table 19, p. 654. (Hereinafter *Green Book*.)

b. *Green Book*, table 12, p. 1639; the portion of food stamp expenditures going to families with children is estimated for 1990 in *Green Book*, table 2, pp. 1582–83; the proportion going to children in 1975 is estimated by author to be the same as in 1990.

c. Cost to all AFDC recipients, whether or not they receive cash payments. *Green Book*, table 19, pp. 1660–61.

d. *Green Book*, table 18, p. 1019; the portion of EITC expenditures going to families with children is estimated for 1990 in *Green Book*, table 2, pp. 1582–83; the proportion going to children in 1975 is estimated by author to be the same as in 1990.

e. Federal and state payments reported in *Green Book*, table 25, p. 827. The portion of total state and federal SSI benefits is *Green Book* estimate for federal SSI benefits going to children in 1990, table 2, pp. 1582–83; the proportion going to children in 1975 is estimated by author to be the same as in 1990.

f. *Green Book* reports expenditures only as early as 1977, table 34, p. 1689. The 1975 estimate assumes these expenditures grew during the intervening two years at the same rate as the increase in the cost of living.

g. *Green Book*, table 2, pp. 1582–83, provides estimate for 1990. Author's estimate for 1975 based on assumption that children receive same proportion of benefit in 1975 as in 1990. Total costs are reported in *Green Book*, table 29, p. 1681. Data are available only for 1977; it was further assumed that program expanded between 1975 and 1977 at same rate as the increase in the cost of living.

h. *Green Book*, table 2, pp. 1582–83. This program did not exist until 1981.

i. Data on other programs available only for 1990; these expenditures include the proportion of total expenditures that benefit families with children in social security, veterans' compensation, child support, human development, foster care and adoption assistance, work incentives, maternal and child health, immunization, summer youth development and training, juvenile justice program, child care block grant, and other health programs. It does not include the portion of social security monies of benefit to children or a variety of educational programs, which are considered separately. *Green Book*, table 1, pp. 1582–83.

poor, he was unable to veto, or even effectively to threaten to veto, those appropriations that were keeping the safety net intact.

As a result, real expenditures on major welfare programs serving families with children continued to expand between 1975 and 1990 (see table 5-1). Two of the largest programs nearly doubled in size. The segment of the food stamp program serving families with children grew from $8.9 billion to $16.5 billion. The cost of medicaid for families with children increased from $8.5 billion to $15.8 billion. Grants under EITC grew nearly threefold, from $1.4 billion to $4.0 billion. The cost of the housing assistance program nearly tripled from $2.7 billion to $7.5 billion. Altogether, total expenditure for a wide variety of family-focused welfare programs increased from $42.3 billion to $71.9 billion between 1975 and 1990, an increase of 70 percent. Yet the cost of AFDC, a program whose benefit levels and eligibility standards are shaped by state decisions, increased during this period by only 16 percent. This increase was due entirely to a rise in the number of poor families eligible for assistance.

In sum, there is little evidence that state welfare benefit cuts were caused by the national conservative trend observable in Washington during the 1980s. Presidents were Republicans, but Congress was Democratic. In the negotiations taking place between the two branches of the federal government, poor families have done better than many might have expected. Many new programs were put in place, many other programs were expanded and indexed to changes in the cost of living, and the total social expenditure on many programs directed toward low-income citizens increased by 70 percent between 1975 and 1990.

States Offset Federal Increases

Federally funded benefit levels increased so much in the 1970s and 1980s that functional theory would expect welfare cuts at the state level as a direct consequence. As state policymakers have seen the federal government assume a greater responsibility for poor families, they have decided that poverty is a problem to which they no longer need to give much attention, especially since states are not well equipped to carry out the redistributive function. As some components of the welfare package available to low-income people are increased at the federal level, states reduce other components so that the overall package is kept more or less constant.[17]

I have already pointed out that social welfare expenditures directed toward poor families increased by 70 percent between 1975 and 1990. But the number of dollars spent on a social program, even if calculated in constant dollars, may be a misleading way to examine the effect of welfare policy over time. The social need may be greater at one time compared with another. Thus I have calculated three additional ways of estimating program effects: expenditures per poor person, expenditures per each person who would have been poor had the welfare program not been in place, and expenditures as a percentage of GNP (see table 5-2).

TABLE 5-2. *Measures of Social Welfare Expenditures on Programs for Poor Families, 1975–90*

Measure	1975	1990	Percentage increase, 1975–90
Expenditures in billions of current dollars[a]	22.0	71.9	326.8
Expenditures in billions of constant 1990 dollars[a]	42.3	71.9	70.0
Expenditures per poor person (1990 dollars)[b]	3,809	5,350	34.4
Expenditures per person who would have been poor (1990 dollars)[c]	1,759	2,696	53.2
Expenditures as percentage of GNP	1.2	1.5	25.0

a. Calculated from table 5-1.

b. *Green Book*, table 2, p. 1274.

c. Number of individuals in families with children in poverty before cash transfers, as reported in *Green Book*, table 19, p. 1306. Table provides information only as far back as 1979; I assumed that the number of pretransfer poor had declined at the same rate as the decline in the posttransfer poor between 1975 and 1979.

Each estimate has its shortcomings. Estimating expenditures as a percentage of GNP gives an indication of the percentage of societal resources the country is willing to expend for social welfare. However, it does not take into account any changes in the need for the social welfare program that may be occurring. Calculating the expenditures per poor person identifies the potential effect of these programs had they been targeted at the most needy population. But this estimation excludes from the count all those who would have been poor had the welfare program not been in place. The best approach, in my opinion, is to estimate expenditure per person who would have been poor had no welfare programs existed.[18]

No matter what estimate is used, government expenditure on programs for poor families increased between 1975 and 1990. Expenditures as a share of GNP grew from 1.2 to 1.5 percent, a 25 percent increase. Expenditures per poor person increased by 34 percent. Expenditures per person who would have been poor increased by 53.2 percent. Even after the cuts in state-determined benefits, the overall package of benefits, as a percentage of GNP, was larger in 1990 than it had been in 1975.

Some of the connections between state and federal benefits are direct. The food stamp program is designed so that it increases thirty cents for every dollar decline in cash income. Cuts in state benefits thus necessarily increase the cost of the food stamp program to the federal government. This connection also encourages state cuts in AFDC cash benefits because it gives state policymakers an incentive to find in the AFDC program any savings needed to balance state budgets. It can be argued by state policymakers that for every state tax dollar saved, the federal government will direct thirty cents more into the state economy. And it can be further argued that for every state tax dollar saved, the recipient will lose only seventy cents.

These arguments appear with some regularity in state welfare politics. For example, opponents of New York Governor Hugh Carey's effort to raise welfare benefits in 1980 claimed that even though cash benefits had declined in value in recent years, gains in food stamp and other benefits had more than compensated for this decline. The conservative argument was so compelling in New York that liberals, instead of providing a standard increase in cash benefits, gave a "special grant" to each welfare recipient to meet "non-recurring, unanticipated needs."[19]

In Texas a variety of religious organizations, social work groups, and the League of Women Voters lobbied successfully in 1978 for a special nonrecurring grant to AFDC children. The main advantage of this non-recurring grant, once again, was that it would not be regarded by the Department of Agriculture as income, which meant that the food stamp grant would not have to be reduced.[20] The device was resorted to again in 1981 and still again in 1982. That these subterfuges were thought by welfare advocates to be politically necessary reveals the appeal of the conservative argument that increases in state-funded cash benefits would only generate cuts in the federally funded food stamp program.

In sum, recent changes in welfare benefits are consistent with the expectations of functional theory. State benefits declined in part because federal welfare benefits were increasing. But to fully understand the conservative drift in state policymaking, I turn to a more detailed discussion of what has become known as the welfare magnet.

The Welfare Magnet

Functional theory says that states cut their benefits in response to increases by the federal government because states wish to minimize their attractiveness to low-income people. States that have high welfare benefits are welfare magnets, attracting poor people. The higher the benefit, the more magnetic the state—both by keeping poor people from moving elsewhere and by attracting additional poor people into the state. The lower the benefit, the more repellent the state is to poor people—both by encouraging poor residents to leave and by deterring other poor people from moving to the state.

The welfare magnet is a function of the great variation in welfare benefit levels among the states. In 1991 the maximum annual combined cash and food stamp benefits for a family of four varied between $5,952 in Mississippi and $11,898 in California.[21] The amount of variation in cash benefits was even greater in 1990 than in 1940. In 1940 the coefficient of variation for the forty-eight contiguous states and the District of Columbia was 0.33; for 1990, it was 0.35. Although the food stamp benefit reduced interstate variation considerably to 0.16 in 1990, this is still much greater than interstate variation in the cost of living (0.08).[22] With this sizable variation in benefit levels among the states, poor people, concerned about the material well-being of their families, are likely to take the benefit levels into account when making their residential choices.

Most studies based on data collected between 1950 and 1969 concluded that welfare policies had little magnetic effect. The residential choices of poor people during these decades seemed to have been little affected by state welfare policies.[23] Numerous state laws and administrative practices designed to make access to the welfare system difficult made it inadvisable to change residences merely to improve one's welfare opportunities. Among the many restrictive practices was a rule, applied by many states, that denied welfare benefits to anyone who had not lived in the state for a year. Poor families simply had to forgo public assistance for a full year if their circumstances required a move beyond state borders. Thus, before 1969 states could increase their welfare benefits without becoming a more attractive place of residence for poor people in other parts of the country.

In 1969 the Supreme Court, in *Shapiro* v. *Thompson*, ruled that for New York State to deny welfare benefits to newcomers, if it granted them to longer-term residents, was a violation of the Fourteenth Amendment's requirement that states provide citizens equal protection before the law.[24] This decision, together with the liberalization of numerous other state administrative practices, facilitated access to the welfare rolls, especially by people moving from one state to another. As a result, welfare rolls increased sharply even at a time when poverty levels in the United States were falling. The number of welfare recipients increased from just 3 million in 1960 to 7.4 million in 1970, and then to 11 million in 1975.[25] According to two policy analysts writing at the time, this was the one true moment of welfare reform in the United

States: state governments, acting under potential and actual lawsuits, finally liberalized their welfare administration so that many poor families could obtain the welfare benefits they needed.[26]

But even as state policymakers were liberalizing their administrative procedures and thus allowing poor newcomers access to AFDC benefits, they were increasingly concerned about their state's becoming a welfare magnet. Their concern seems to be well placed. Several analyses of data, using different methodologies, have reached similar conclusions: after 1969, when poor people made their residential choices, they took into account the level of benefits provided by a state.[27] In a study of the forty-eight contiguous states and the District of Columbia over three time periods (1971–75, 1976–80, and 1981–85), Mark Rom and I found that poverty increased more rapidly in states with higher benefit levels. Our study also found that states tried to avoid becoming a welfare magnet by cutting benefits whenever their poverty rates increased.[28]

One way of testing the validity of our analysis is to predict outcomes for a time period not included in the original study. To attempt such a prediction, D. Stephen Voss and I collected and analyzed data for the period 1986–90 on the same variables as used in the earlier study.

The results of our efforts to predict changes during this time period are shown in figures 5-2 and 5-3. The prediction was quite precise. It predicted that in 1990 the combined monthly cash and food stamp welfare benefit distributed to a four-person family in the average state would be $574.59. The actual average monthly benefit for such a family turned out to be $575. The prediction also survives another traditional diagnostic test. If it is reasonably accurate, 95 percent of the cases can be expected to fall within a standard estimate of error and 66 percent to fall within half of a standard estimate of error.[29] Our model was able to predict within the standard estimate of error the benefit levels of forty-six of the forty-eight contiguous states. Seventy-seven percent of the predictions fell within one-half the standard estimate of error.

The only state whose benefits were much higher than predicted (beyond the standard estimate of error) was California, whose voters two years later approved 25 percent welfare cuts. Our model predicted a $658 monthly benefit level for California. Actual monthly benefit levels in 1990 were $796, higher than in any other of the forty-eight contiguous states and 21 percent higher than predicted.

The model predicted that the poverty rate in the average state would be 13.9 percent. The actual poverty rate was 13.2 percent. Once again,

FIGURE 5-2. *Actual and Predicted Maximum State Welfare Benefit Levels, 1990*

1985 dollars

Actual benefit[a]

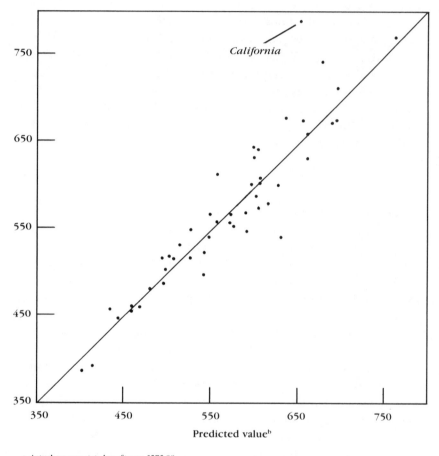

a. Actual average state benefit was $575.00.
b. Predicted average state benefit was $574.59.

the model performs well according to standard diagnostic tests. The prediction for forty-five of the forty-eight states fell within the standard estimate of error, and 69 percent of the states fell within one-half of the standard estimate of error. In short, fears of policymakers that their state's welfare policies might be attracting poor people have a basis in reality. The welfare magnet is more than a myth.

FIGURE 5-3. *Actual and Predicted State Poverty Rates, 1990*

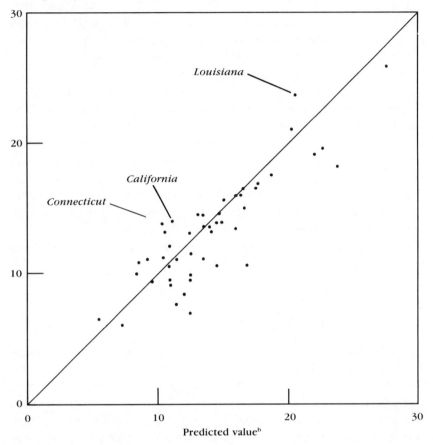

Percent

Actual poverty rate[a]

Predicted value[b]

a. Actual average state poverty rate was 13.2 percent.
b. Predicted average state poverty rate was 13.9 percent.

The poverty rate prediction for California was within the standard estimate of error, but the model nonetheless underpredicted California's poverty rate by 2.9 percent. Connecticut and Louisiana were the only two states where actual poverty rates exceeded predicted rates by a margin greater than the 2.9 percent for California. In other words, California was among the three states where poverty rates were increasing more rapidly than could be predicted by the underlying economic and policy factors we had identified. California had good reason to be especially concerned about the increasing pressure the poor population was placing on its welfare services.

The pressure to demagnetize California's welfare magnet was so great that in 1993 the state legislature passed as part of its welfare reform package a law stating that newcomers to the state could not receive benefits higher than those provided by the state from which they came for their first year of residence in California. This law is not the quite same as the New York legislation declared unconstitutional in 1969 in *Shapiro* v. *Thompson*. That legislation had denied newcomers all AFDC benefits until they had established a one-year residence in the state; the California law merely reduces benefit levels for newcomers. Yet because the new California legislation also seems to deny all residents equal protection before the law, lower courts have ruled the legislation unconstitutional. However, the Supreme Court recently decided to review a lower court decision, and *Shapiro* v. *Thompson* may be modified, although the case may be moot before the Court makes its decision.[30] Whatever happens in the courtroom, the welfare magnet is likely to remain a hot issue in state politics.[31]

The Future of State Welfare Policy

The House of Representatives approved legislation in the spring of 1995 eliminating the AFDC program, which since 1937 has required participating states to provide to all qualifying families a cash benefit and to match federally funded benefits (in most cases) with an equal amount of state-funded benefits. In place of this entitlement program, the proposed legislation gives each state a block grant equal to the amount of money the state received in the 1994 fiscal year. The terms of the block grant allow each state to set—within very limited guidelines—its own eligibility standards and benefit levels.[32]

If the legislation approved by the House is signed into law, the race to the bottom is almost certain to intensify. Some states will undoubtedly tighten eligibility standards and reduce benefit levels, and, by so doing, reduce their share of welfare costs. If this happens, some states will become more powerful welfare magnets than ever before. Poor people in low-benefit states will consider the costs and benefits of moving to a magnet state. Some will undoubtedly decide to make the move (or decide to remain in a magnet state when they might otherwise have made a move).

Under the terms of the proposed legislation, the cost of becoming a welfare magnet will be much greater than at present. The block grant is a fixed sum of money that does not change with the number of individuals in the state eligible for assistance, unlike the current federal grants, which vary according to the number of welfare recipients. If poor people move to states with more generous benefits, then those states will experience an increase in their welfare burden without any commensurate increase in federal funding. To safeguard against rapidly rising state welfare costs, the generous states will come under increasing fiscal and political pressure to reduce their benefits. Eventually, all states will be engaged in the race for the bottom, each state trying to shift the cost of welfare to its neighbors.

Since 1970 states have tried to avoid becoming welfare magnets. Cash benefits fell by 42 percent between 1970 and 1993. As sharp a decline in cash benefit levels as this represents, even more drastic declines can be expected if the proposed legislation becomes law. In the past the pressure on states to cut benefits has been mitigated by the fact that increases in the cost of welfare have been shared more or less equally between states and the national government. Under the proposed legislation, any new welfare costs caused by an increase in the poverty rate will be borne entirely by the states. Because states will bear all the additional costs themselves, they can be expected to react quickly to any sign that they are becoming a welfare magnet.

Republican leaders in the House of Representatives have also proposed to decentralize control over food stamps and medicaid policy. If these proposals become law, the race will accelerate. Until now, interstate competition to avoid becoming a magnet has been somewhat contained by the national framework within which medicaid and food stamp policy is formulated. Most medical services paid for by medicaid are mandated by federal regulations. State variation in medicaid policy is, on the whole, limited to coverage of some optional services and the amount paid providers for services. Food stamp policy is also set almost entirely at the national level.

Poor people in need of costly medical services have especially large incentives to locate in places where medical benefits are more generous. As the more generous states experience a rise in their low-income, medically needy population, they will come under increasing pressure to match cuts that have occurred elsewhere. The race to the bottom could become quite deadly.

Congress can mitigate the race to the bottom by tying federal grants to the size of the eligible population and by setting minimum eligibility and benefit-level standards for health care, nutrition, and cash benefits in any block grant it enacts. In a society in which both people and businesses are highly mobile, it makes little sense to leave the marginal cost of welfare provision to lower tiers of government. To recommend that the provision of welfare should be locally controlled and its marginal cost borne by state and local taxpayers is to recommend that the poor be all but abandoned.

6

National Grants:
Is Equity Possible?

> *[The] first and main duty [of a representative] is to get the most*
> *he can for his constituency out of the ... treasury, or by means of*
> *... legislation. No appeal to the general interest would have*
> *weight with him against the interests of that spot.*
> Lord James Bryce, *American Commonwealth*

Functional and legislative theories have different expectations about
the rules that will govern the distribution of money from the national
government to state and local governments. Functional theory expects
that monies will be distributed so as to direct national dollars to states
according to objective measures of need, including the number and
concentration of poor people living in the state, and to offset differences in state and local fiscal capacities. Legislative theory assumes that
members of Congress try to maximize benefits for their constituents.
Because of opposition by legislators from states with greater fiscal
resources, intergovernmental grants will not rectify state fiscal disparities or meet the needs of the poor. The distribution of aid will instead
be determined by election rules and the distribution of power within
Congress.

In this chapter we subject hypotheses drawn from the two theories
to an empirical test. The data will show that more developmental aid
goes to wealthier states, smaller states, rural states, states with a higher

---

Jerome Maddox is coauthor of this chapter.

percentage of minorities, states that tax their own citizens more heavily, and states well represented on the House Public Works Committee. Redistributive aid is also directed more toward wealthier states, rural states, and states with a high tax effort. But it also goes to states with higher poverty rates, states that are more densely populated, and states well represented on two House committees, Ways and Means and Education and Labor.[1]

National Determination of State Role

Analysis of the factors affecting federal grant programs poses a variety of theoretical and methodological problems. For one thing, the distribution of national grants is determined by decisions taken by Congress and the president. Yet empirical research on intergovernmental grants has shown that a number of state and local characteristics—such as poverty levels, fiscal resources, tax effort, and political centralization—influence the distribution of federal aid.[2] How do these state and local characteristics affect national policymaking?

The answers to this question are at least threefold. First, individuals with particular attributes are unevenly distributed among the states. More aid for the poor, for example, goes to those states in which the poor are concentrated. Second, federal grants are not mandatory; state sovereignty precludes the national government from ordering states to take specific actions or requiring states to accept federal dollars for a particular purpose.[3] Only if the state or locality accepts the aid, with all its attendant regulations, will the grant be made. In most instances, states and localities must promise in their grant application that they will expend the funds in ways consistent with national regulations and guidelines. Some states and localities have greater political and economic capacity and readiness to comply with national expectations. Third, and most important, many intergovernmental grants are conditioned upon the expenditure of matching state or local dollars. The mandated state share of intergovernmental aid programs varies from one program to the next, ranging from 11 percent to 75 percent.[4] By attaching matching requirements to grants, the national government devolves partial control over the distribution and level of aid to states and localities. Thus national spending becomes contingent on the actions taken by other levels of government. If a state chooses to spend little on a specific program, the national contribution will also be minimal; if the state appropriates more, the national contribution increases.

Although state and local decisions influence the distribution of grants, the role played by states and localities is itself a function of decisions taken by Congress and the president. It may be helpful in this context to think of the relationship of the national government to the states as the relationship between principals and agents. National decisionmakers are the principals who have the authority to design federal aid programs. They have chosen to ask states and localities to be their agents by giving state and local governments responsibility for applying for federal funds and matching national aid with monies from state and local sources. Except for their inability to mandate state acceptance of national funds, the principals in Washington may at any time change the rules for distributing intergovernmental grants among the states. The principals may substitute block grants with few regulations for categorical grants that include mandates designed to achieve specific purposes. They may increase, decrease, or eliminate state matching requirements. They may make it more or less difficult for any particular state or locality to become eligible for federal aid.[5] They have indeed done all of these.

If Congress and the president are able to change the rules by which national grants are distributed, then any given set of rules must reflect the distribution of power at the national level. State policies affect intergovernmental grant allocations only because national policymakers have decided that state policies are appropriate determinants of federal aid. For example, programs may contain matching requirements in order to ensure state and local commitment to program objectives. But matching requirements may also deter participation by states with fewer economic and fiscal resources. If those shaping policy in Washington feel that some states are participating at a lower level because the matching requirement is too high, then they presumably could lower—or eliminate—the matching requirement. In sum, state-level determinants of national aid should be regarded not simply as indicators of state preferences but also as indicators of the political forces shaping federal policy.

Appropriate Units of Analysis

In order to identify the congressional determinants of the distribution of national grants among the states, one needs to think carefully about the appropriate unit of analysis. If one looks at each program in every town and district, one might miss the forest for the individual trees. Two issues are particularly problematic: the fungibility of federal dollars among governmental jurisdictions, and the fungibility of federal dollars among functional programs.

Aggregating Data to the State Level

Many studies distinguish the distribution of funds granted to state governments from funds granted to local governments, implying that each can be examined without regard for the other. But states grant substantial—and widely varying—amounts of money to the subgovernments within them. Any national grant dollar given directly to a local government can be treated by the state as a substitute for state aid. Any money received by the state from the national government can be passed on to local governments within the state. Because of these interdependencies, it becomes almost impossible to decipher the real effect of federal grant programs within states.[6]

The fungibility of federal grant programs is evident in the very design of these programs. In 1984, 3.6 percent of federal aid went directly to localities; 38.8 percent of the programs gave money exclusively to the states; 10.7 percent went to some combination of states and subgovernments within them; and 47 percent of all programs aided some combination of states, localities, and other public and private organizations.[7]

The fungibility of federal grants also seems to have its political consequences. A recent study of the effect of federal spending on election outcomes indicates that members of the House of Representatives gain at least as much or even more from developmental aid allocated to other parts of their state as to their own district. Apparently there is enough fungibility in dollars allocated to a state, and enough of a spillover effect on a district's economy from development dollars invested elsewhere in the state, to make it worthwhile for representatives to bring a statewide perspective to their job.[8]

One solution to the analytic problem posed by this fungibility of funds across governmental units is to treat the state and all local jurisdictions within the state as a single unit of analysis. The state is recognized by law as the sovereign entity with complete authority over the activities of all counties, cities, towns, school districts, special districts, and other governmental units within the state. This approach unfortunately cannot identify the distributional consequences of federal programs within states, but the variability, complexity, and indeterminacy of state governmental systems leave little choice.

Using the state as the unit of analysis has a second advantage: it focuses attention on the role played by the Senate in the formation of national aid policy. Studies of Congress have tended to concentrate on the House of Representatives, both because its staff and members are more accessible and because the activities of its 435 members lend themselves more readily to quantitative analysis. This scholarly drift has been justified in part by the presumption that the House exercises more power over fiscal policy. The Constitution requires that all appropriation and taxation bills must originate in the lower chamber. Scholars have found that House subcommittees gave appropriation bills closer scrutiny than did Senate subcommittees.[9] But few would accept the proposition that senators have abdicated their fiscal authority to the other side of the Hill. Indeed, it has been argued that higher fiscal deficits result from differential partisan control of the two chambers.[10]

Aggregating Data to Broad Functional Categories

The fungibility of dollars among functional programs poses an equally nagging analytical problem. Many studies have attempted to identify the factors that affect the distribution of monies within a specific national grant program.[11] Many of these offer valuable information on the political factors that shape particular public policies. But it becomes difficult to generalize from these findings to provide a more general test of functional and legislative theories. A particular pattern of funding for one national grant program may be realized only by tacitly or explicitly agreeing to a quite different pattern of funding for another.

Not only are votes in Congress interdependent, but monies for any given national grant program may be allocated in such a way that money received for one purpose frees up money to support an altogether different functional area. More national money for schools may release state money for highways. More national money for highways may allow states and localities to cut their taxes. The actual impact of any intergovernmental grant program may be quite different from its stated purpose.

Although these considerations may suggest that intergovernmental aid should be aggregated to a unit larger than an individual program, this does not necessarily lead to the conclusion that the analyst should look at only the total amount of national aid granted to each state. If national dollars are fungible, they may not be infinitely so. One needs in particular to distinguish aid for developmental programs from redistributive ones.

Developmental aid is highly valued because it can help enhance a state's capacity to compete effectively in the national and international economy. Developmental aid is typically allocated with a minimum of national restrictions, making it highly fungible.[12] Developmental aid is also likely to be regarded as politically popular by almost all members of Congress. The battle for developmental money has thus until recently been determined by raw political power unmitigated by ideological or normative convictions.

Redistributive programs have a decidedly different quality. They are usually accompanied by tight national regulations designed to ensure that monies are not siphoned off for developmental purposes.[13] Redistributive aid is less likely to be determined by geographical interests and more likely to be affected by ideologies, general perceptions of fairness and equity, and cultural biases and prejudices. These more general considerations shape redistributive aid because its effects on state economies are ambiguous. Whereas almost all members have until recently wanted a bigger slice of the development pie, opinions can vary about the desirability of garnering a larger share of the redistributive cake. Liberal members favor redistribution in general, and many feel a special commitment to securing as large a share for their state as possible. Conservative members—and their conservative constituents—may very well want no more of the redistributive dollar than they must be forced to take. From their point of view, more money for welfare, food stamps, and medicaid attracts poor people, not resources that can enhance the local economy.

It is not just in Congress where opinions vary as to the desirability of aid for redistributive purposes. States are often required to match federal funding for distribution. Because governors and state legislatures vary in their willingness to spend redistributive dollars (see chapter 4), state willingness to match federal dollars can vary quite substantially.[14] All in all, it is necessary to analyze separately the factors affecting the allocation of developmental dollars from those influencing redistributive ones.

Factors Affecting the Distribution of Federal Grants

The following analysis of the factors affecting federal aid to states and localities groups together federal aid policies into fairly broad categories for the methodological reasons we have just elaborated. We treat all aid as grants to states, even though some go to local governments within a state. We focus on the factors that affect all developmental programs and all redistributive programs, even though there are differences among specific developmental and specific redistributive programs. This is not an exhaustive account of every detailed aspect of the intergovernmental grant program, only a portrait of its overall pattern. However, even though the data we present are subject to these methodological limitations, they reveal how functional and legislative theories together help to account for the way the intergovernmental grant program operates.

Taxable Resources

Legislative and functional theory have directly conflicting expectations with respect to the capacity of the national government to rectify fiscal disparities at state and local levels. Functional theorists expect that federal grants will help equalize state fiscal capacities. They expect intergovernmental grant programs to soften the territorial inequity in fiscal resources among states.

Legislative theory expects members to vote for programs that provide a net fiscal benefit for their constituents. Members from constituencies that pay more in taxes want to receive a share of the benefits proportionate to their contributions. These members from relatively well-off constituencies are thus unlikely to support a pattern of federal aid distribution that shifts benefits from their constituents to those living elsewhere. Legislative theory does not quite predict that the rich states will get richer, but it does expect that those states' representatives will guard against dispersing their wealth to other places.

The distribution of federal grants varies, depending on whether aid is developmental or redistributive. In both 1969 and 1991 the ten richest states got the most developmental aid, but the twenty poorest states got the most redistributive money (see figure 6-1). Wealthy states seem more willing to share money with poorer states if the money is for redistributive purposes than if the money can be used to facilitate the states' economic development.

One way Congress can design programs so as to distribute benefits disproportionately to states with higher taxable resources is to require states to pay for a share of the costs. The higher the state share (in the case of medicaid, for example, every federal dollar must be matched by a state dollar), the more likely it is that states with greater fiscal capacity will get more federal dollars—for the simple reason that these states have more resources to pay for their share.[15]

FIGURE 6-1. *State Taxable Resources and per Capita Federal Aid to State-Local Governments, 1969–91*

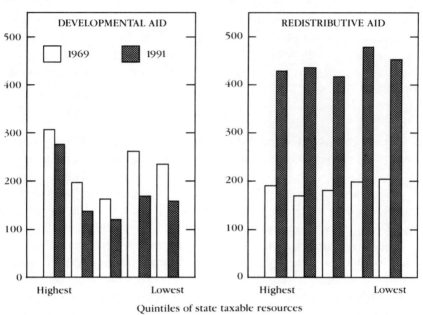

1990 dollars   1990 dollars

SOURCES: See appendix.

These conclusions are preliminary. The specific effect of a state's taxable resources on the amount of federal aid it receives will be shown in the regression analysis that concludes the chapter.

Local Demand

Legislative theory anticipates that members of Congress expect states and localities to prove they need and want national grants. Members coming from progressive parts of the country, where governmental programs are valued, will be especially insistent that state and local monies match federal dollars. These representatives win more aid for their states and localities by making the argument that matching grants are necessary in order to reduce waste and ensure state and local commitment to program objectives. Members coming from more conservative parts of the country, where governmental programs are less valued, concede to these demands for matching grants because their

FIGURE 6-2. *State Tax Effort and per Capita Federal Aid to State-Local Governments, 1969–91*

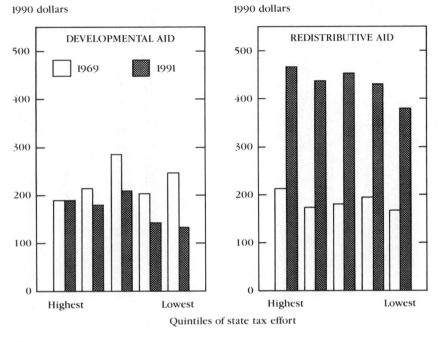

1990 dollars

1990 dollars

Quintiles of state tax effort

SOURCES: See appendix.

constituents, who place a lower value on governmental programs, will be less insistent that they receive their share of national grants.

An indicator of the constituent demand for governmental services is the level of tax effort in a state. Progressive states that impose higher taxes tend to include voters who have a greater demand for public goods and services. These progressive states are more likely than conservative states to have the political will to pay the state share of any program costs.[16] They are also likely to elect state and local officials who will make special efforts to obtain federal aid.

In both 1969 and 1991 progressive states that made a higher tax effort received more redistributive federal aid than the more conservative states (see figure 6-2). The relationship between tax effort and developmental grants was less pronounced, but there seemed to be an overall tendency, especially in 1991, for states making a higher tax effort to receive more money. The exact relationship will be reported in the regression analysis that concludes the chapter.

FIGURE 6-3. *State Poverty Rates and per Capita Federal Aid to State-Local Governments, 1969–91*

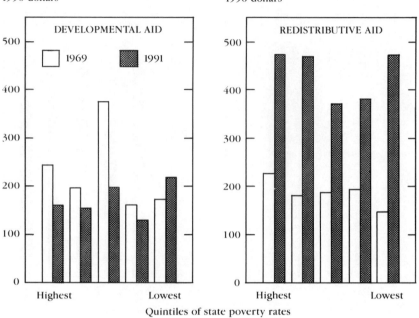

1990 dollars   1990 dollars

Quintiles of state poverty rates

SOURCES: See appendix.

Poverty

According to functional theory, those states with the highest poverty levels are likely to spend the least on welfare and other forms of redistribution.[17] If poverty levels are high, states try hard to avoid becoming a welfare magnet. To correct for this perversity, functional theory expects the national government to grant more federal redistributive aid to places that have a higher percentage of poor people. Laws providing income maintenance, medical care, and food stamps to individuals are likely to be written so as to direct more money to those states where the need is greater. Poverty is also likely to increase the cost of providing social infrastructure such as police, fire, sanitation, and educational services, and members of Congress may be willing to contribute more federal aid for such services to states with higher poverty levels.[18]

As functional theory anticipates, in 1969 the ten states with the highest poverty rates received the most redistributive assistance (see figure 6-3). In 1991 they received, on average, the same amount per person as the ten states with the lowest poverty rates, but more than any other group of states. In 1969 states with higher poverty rates received more developmental assistance than those with lower rates, but the most aid went to states that had only middling poverty rates. In 1991 the states with the lowest poverty rates actually received the most developmental aid. The regression analysis that concludes the chapter provides more precise estimates of the effects of poverty rates on the distribution of federal grants.

Representational Arrangements

Legislative theorists expect that the arrangement of the system of representation will affect the distribution of federal aid. The way representatives are elected to Congress is known to be biased in two important respects. First, the Senate overrepresents both rural areas and states with small populations. Second, the first-past-the-post electoral system, coupled with racial bloc voting, results in the underrepresentation of the interests of racial minorities.[19] From these well-known facts about the electoral system, three hypotheses about federal aid can be derived from legislative theory.

Rural states receive a disproportionate amount of aid. Rural parts of the United States are greatly overrepresented in the U.S. Senate. In addition, farm associations were among the first to be organized, and they remain inordinately active even today.[20] Because of the efforts by farm groups, agricultural interests were the first to win a cabinet department devoted exclusively to their concerns. An agricultural committee devoted exclusively to farm interests can be found in both House and Senate. The same cannot be said for either urban or suburban interests.

States with a high minority population get less aid. Legislative theory predicts that the higher the minority percentage in a state, the less redistributive aid a state receives. Because minority voters are underrepresented and because many nonminority voters believe that minorities are a disproportionate percentage of the undeserving poor,[21] members of Congress are less likely to give redistributive aid to states with a larger share of minorities.

Congress can distribute less money to states in which minorities are concentrated by requiring that states match redistributive federal grants. In states with larger minority populations, governors and legislatures are less likely to appropriate funds for redistributive programs

FIGURE 6-4. *State Population and per Capita Federal Aid to State-Local Governments, 1969–91*

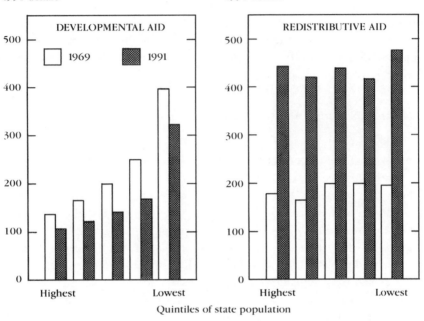

1990 dollars   1990 dollars

SOURCES: See appendix.

(see chapter 4). This reduces the amount of redistributive federal aid allocated to these states.

States with relatively small populations get more in aid. Those living in states with small populations are overrepresented in the Senate. This hypothesis is not a mere repetition of the previous hypothesis. If the Dakotas, Kansas, and Montana are large rural states, Maryland, Rhode Island, and Delaware are small urban ones. Both types of small states have the advantage over New York, California, and Florida of having a highly favorable ratio of population to Senate representation.

States with the fewest people received, on average, more aid per person in both 1969 and 1991 (see figure 6-4). They received substantially more developmental aid than any other group of states. They also received more redistributive assistance in 1991, but not in 1969. A more precise estimate of the effects of the overrepresentation of small states in the Senate on the distribution of federal grants will be made in the regression analysis below.

Population Density

The expected effects of population density on federal aid are complex. According to functional theory, the need for developmental aid increases both as a state becomes more densely populated and as it becomes more sparsely populated. If a state is sparsely populated, the cost of providing an infrastructure will be higher. Sparsely populated states will make greater efforts to match federal development dollars. They will also expect their representatives in Congress to ensure their interests are guarded in the legislative process. If a state is very densely populated, the greater social interdependency generates a greater demand for public services. Densely populated states will also expect their representatives to obtain greater federal aid. In the case of redistributive programs, a positive relationship between density and expenditure is to be expected. The social problems induced by poverty are likely to be greater in more densely populated states, creating in these states a greater demand for redistributive services. Sparsely settled states received more developmental aid in both 1969 and 1991, while densely inhabited states received more redistributive assistance in 1991 (see figure 6-5). Whether these relationships persist once other factors have been controlled will be seen in the regression analysis below.

The Organization of Congress

Functional and legislative theory differ with regard to the importance of committees for congressional decisionmaking, as discussed in chapter 2. Functional theorists think that committees must craft their legislation so as to obtain passage on the floor of Congress.[22] According to legislative theory, committees have a degree of autonomy from the floor, giving members a capacity to exercise disproportionate influence over policy.[23]

Two more specific hypotheses may be derived from the two theories. First, House committees are more likely to influence the allocation of aid than are Senate commitees. Election to the Senate is less likely to be determined by the allocation of pork, and Senate committees have less autonomy from the chamber floor than do House committees.[24] House debates are subject to tight time constraints, and votes on the House floor are subject to restrictions established by the House Rules Committee, which regularly curtails the number and kind of amendments that may be offered on the floor. The Senate floor operates under

FIGURE 6-5. *State Population Density and per Capita Federal Aid to State-Local Governments, 1969–91*

1990 dollars   1990 dollars

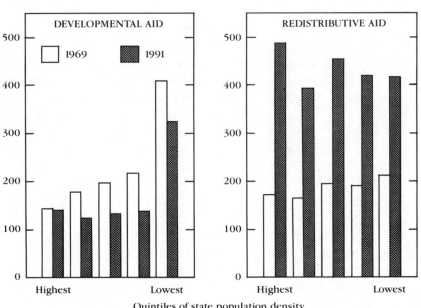

Quintiles of state population density

SOURCES: See appendix.

no such restrictions. Senators may offer on the floor as many amendments to committee recommendations as they please, and debate is unrestricted until 60 percent of the membership votes to close debate. Committees operating under these conditions are much less likely to be able to secure passage of legislation to meet the desires of their own particular constituents.

Second, House committees with responsibility for redistributive programs may be more likely to have autonomous influence than House committees with responsibility for developmental programs. Because developmental programs are more likely to be regarded by members of Congress as valuable to their constituents, members are less likely to cede control over their allocation to the committees. According to functional theory, redistributive aid is of less political value, because its effect on local communities is more ambiguous. Less pressured by constituents to secure redistributive aid for their districts, members on the chamber floor are less likely to supervise committee decisionmaking on these programs.

Less supervision on the floor may be offset by the fact that most redistributive programs are allocated according to complex formulas that seem to be universal in their application. The amount that each state receives depends on such particulars as the state's median income and the percentage of the population deemed eligible for these social programs. But the apparent objectivity of these formulas may actually enhance discretion available to committee members. Minor tinkering with these seemingly objective formulas can produce significant reallocation of funds among the states that can be quite accurately estimated in advance through computer simulation programs. There is no reason to think that committee members do not take advantage of such information when designing redistributive formulas. Because colleagues on the House floor may not insist that they receive their "fair share" of redistributive money, the apparent objectivity of these formulas may help secure their general acceptance.

A Comprehensive Explanation of Federal Aid Policy

These hypotheses taken from functional and legislative theory were tested by collecting data on the distribution of federal grants among the states for 1969, 1972, 1977, 1982, 1987, and 1991. Although the overall amount spent on federal grants varied from one year to the next (as discussed in chapter 3), the pattern of allocation among the states was relatively consistent over time. This consistency allowed us to combine the data into a pooled time-series, cross-sectional regression analysis.[25]

Taxable Resources

The regression analysis reveals that Congress is reluctant to redistribute monies from one part of the country to another. If redistribution is to occur, many members must vote to tax their constituents for the benefit of other constituents. Since such a vote violates a basic rule of thumb, a state's taxable resources strongly influence the allocation of both developmental and redistributive assistance. The effect of taxable resources on developmental aid was particularly great—for every 1 percent increase in the index of tax capacity, the state received $3.42 in additional federal aid per person (see table 6-1). The effects of

TABLE 6-1. *Determinants of the Distribution of Federal Aid among States*

Independent variable[a]	Developmental		Redistributive	
	b	Standard error	b	Standard error
Taxable resources	3.42	0.30***	0.61	0.20***
Tax effort	1.64	0.38***	2.59	0.24***
Poverty rate	2.14	1.83	7.73	1.19***
Population size	−4.33	1.65***	0.07	0.09
Percent rural	2.85	0.40***	0.78	0.24***
Percent minority	1.20	0.61**	−0.31	0.38
Population density	...	...	3.20	0.58***
Density (distance from mean)	1.71	1.14	...	...
House				
Appropriations	−0.24	0.40	−0.25	0.25
Public Works	1.02	0.42**	...	...
Energy and Commerce	−0.36	0.31	...	...
Ways and Means	0.16	0.49	0.83	0.31***
Education and Labor	...	...	0.57	0.24**
Senate				
Appropriations	−4.28	10.98	3.02	6.83
Public Works	16.89	12.75	...	...
Commerce	14.73	11.81	...	...
Finance	−11.65	12.00	−6.56	7.80
Labor and Human Resources	...	...	0.37	8.42
Intercept	−143.97	69.70**	−228.33	44.04***
Corrected R^2	0.60	...	0.70	...
N	300	...	300	...

SOURCES: See appendix.
*Significant at the .1 level.
**Significant at the .05 level.
***Significant at the .01 level.
a. Equations also include controls for year.

taxable resources on redistributive aid were also statistically significant but amounted to only $0.61 per person. Apparently members of Congress operate in a context that makes it especially difficult for them to share resources with other states if those resources might be used to enhance their economic competitiveness.

The positive correlation between state fiscal capacity and federal aid revenue raises questions for functional federalism. Congress apparently has a different definition of equity than the one many functional analysts bring to the question of territorial distribution. The congressional view seems to be that more money should go back to states that have been contributing more to the federal treasury. But this congressional definition of equity directly contradicts the usual equity case for federal aid to the states.

Local Demand

As legislative theory expects, members also design federal aid programs so that states that place a higher value on governmental programs are able to obtain more federal funds. This can be seen by the strong effect that a state's own tax effort has on its ability to get federal aid. For every 1 percent increase in the tax effort index, a state receives an additional $1.64 in developmental aid per person and $2.59 in redistributive aid (table 6-1).

Poverty

Functional theory is correct in expecting poverty to be correlated with federal aid, particularly redistributive aid. Members seem to feel that more money—especially redistributive money—should go to states with higher concentrations of poverty. For every 1 percent increase in a state's poverty rate, the state receives $7.73 in redistributive aid per person (table 6-1). The poverty rate had no measurable effect on aid for developmental purposes.

Representational Arrangements

As expected by legislative theorists, the inequalities of representation built into the design of the Senate have left their impact on public policy. Constituents living in small states get more developmental aid. For every 100,000 additional people living in a state, the state receives $4.33 less per person in developmental aid; however, the size of a state has no effect on the allocation of redistributive aid (table 6-1). Senators from small states concentrate on using their influence to get developmental dollars that help build the state's economy.

Senators from rural states seem to do much the same thing. For every 1 percent increase in the percentage of people living in a rural area, a state receives $2.85 in additional developmental aid. We found no statistically significant effects on redistributive aid. The larger effects in the developmental arena suggest, once again, that senators from rural areas use their clout more to build their economy than to help the needy within the state.

Some may argue that any overrepresentation of small, rural states is offset by the representation according to population size in the House.

However, appropriations differences between the chambers are generally split down the middle, so that the net result is still an overrepresentation of rural and small state populations.[26] Much has been said in recent years about the biases in various systems of representation. Much more might well be said about the most egregiously unrepresentative institution of all—Congress's upper chamber.

Redistributive aid is unrelated to the minority percentage living in a state. Contrary to what might be expected from legislative theory, effects of the minority rate on developmental assistance were positive (table 6-1). Congress does not seem to discriminate against minorities in the same way that state legislatures do. Although members of both Congress and state legislatures are elected by the winner-take-all electoral system, which overrepresents majorities, the negative effects on minorities of this system of representation seem to differ between Washington and state capitals. Perhaps minority interests have been better institutionalized in national politics than in state politics. Civil rights groups are better organized, obtain better press coverage, and are more legitimate political players. Policy is more closely scrutinized for any discriminatory effect it may have. States have never been known for their ability to protect the interests of the disadvantaged. For all of the modernization of state politics that has supposedly occurred, state legislatures still seem to deserve this reputation.

Density

Densely populated states secure more redistributive dollars. For every ten-person increase in the number of people per square kilometer living within a state, the state receives $3.20 more in redistributive aid (table 6-1). Developmental aid seems to go to both to the most sparsely settled and the most densely inhabited states, but the relationship is not strong enough to be statistically significant.

The Organization of Congress

Our findings provide encouragement for both legislative and functional theorists. More exactly, our findings identify the conditions under which members can win systematic allocational advantages from committee membership. In general, House committees seem to have more autonomy from the chamber floor than Senate committees and House committees have more influence on redistributive policies than on developmental policies.

TABLE 6-2. *Effect of Membership on House Appropriations Committee on Developmental Grants, Selected Years, 1969–91*

Year	Coefficient[a]	Standard error
1969	0.62	0.91
1972	−0.49	1.10
1977	0.43	0.80
1982	−0.68	1.11
1987	−1.93	1.20
1991	−1.01	1.48

a. Equations include controls for variables in table 6-1.

We were unable to detect a theoretically significant effect of membership on particular Senate committees on the allocation of either developmental or redistributive aid.[27] This finding is consistent with other studies of Congress, which have concluded that committee membership is less significant to senators than representatives.[28]

The various appropriations subcommittees in both House and Senate are often thought to have the greatest influence over developmental expenditure. Virtually all developmental expenditure must be approved annually in each chamber by one or another of these subcommittees. Yet in neither the House nor the Senate does membership on the appropriations committee give members an advantage on either developmental or redistributive policy (see table 6-1). In early studies, scholars said appropriations committee members were selected for their fairness and their ability to resist narrow constituency pressures.[29] Later studies suggested that these norms of the old Congress did not survive the more personal politics of the 1970s.[30] But we found that membership on the House Appropriations Committee had little effect on the distribution of expenditures during the 1970s, and it seems to have had a negative effect during the 1980s (see table 6-2). The power of the appropriations committees seems to have been weakened by the increasing unpopularity of pork and the enhanced power of both party leadership and the fiscally minded budget committees.[31] The appropriations committees either lost political influence, or it became politically more advantageous for members to oppose pork than to distribute special bits of bacon to their states.

We also looked at whether members of two other committees that have the capacity to influence developmental policy are able to secure a disproportionate share of the benefits for their states. In the Senate, responsibility for the largest of the developmental aid programs is shared by the Public Works and Commerce Committees. In the House, the Public Works Committee is responsible for overseeing almost all the large developmental aid programs. We also thought it possible that the Energy and Commerce Committee, headed from 1981 to 1994 by the influential representative from Michigan, John Dingell, could have influenced the allocation of these funds. But only membership on the House Public Works Committee had a discernible effect on the allocation of aid. For every 1 percent increase in a state's representation on the House Public Works Committee, the state received $1.02 in additional developmental aid per person (see table 6-1). With this exception, functional theory seems correct in expecting that the rule of universalism shapes intergovernmental developmental aid.

These results are subject to two interpretations. One might infer along lines suggested by legislative theory that logrolls in Congress are perfectly designed so that every advantage in one committee is perfectly offset by counterbalancing advantages in other committees.[32] Or one might infer along lines suggested by functional theory that committees are constrained by the floor to distribute benefits universally and without particular favor to committee members.[33] The latter is the simpler—and therefore the more persuasive—of the two inferences.

Those who doubt functional theory and the universalism rule may take the view that our evidence is inconclusive because we used the state, not the congressional district, as the unit of analysis. We doubt that our findings are an artifact of our methodology. For one thing, if committee membership significantly influenced distributions, the effects should appear in statewide aggregates, unless the influence of one member came strictly at the expense of the member's within-state peers. But other research has shown that committee members are expected to act as advocates for their states as well as their districts.[34] Second, as we shall show, the methodology did not preclude detection of a role played by committee membership in redistributive policies. Finally, we were unable to identify any effects of Senate committee membership on the distribution of aid, even though statewide aggregations of data should be ideal for identifying such effects.

Although only the House Public Works Committee could secure extra developmental dollars for home districts, two House committees— Ways and Means and Education and Labor—played an influential role in allocating redistributive aid. For every 1 percent increase in a state's representation on the Ways and Means Committee, a state received $0.83 in additional redistributive aid per person (table 6-1). This statistic can be given explained in the following way: If two states had ten representatives in Congress and one state had a member on the Ways and Means while the other did not, the first state—all other factors equal—could be expected to receive $8.30 more per person in redistributive money than the second state. Ways and Means is responsible for three of the four largest federal grant-in-aid programs: medicaid, aid to families with dependent children, and social security supplemental insurance.[35]

The impact of the Ways and Means Committee on the allocation of redistributive aid is consistent with the impression of many congressional observers that it is the one committee in Congress that comes closest to being able to dictate policy to the chamber floor. First of all, Ways and Means programs are, for the most part, entitlement programs exempt from the usual scrutiny of the appropriations committees.[36] Ways and Means in recent decades acquired additional informal advantages as well. Dan Rostenkowski, its chair from 1981 to 1994, was recognized as one of the major political forces in Congress. Its staff has consisted of sophisticated policy analysts who more than rival their counterparts in the executive agencies. Its authoritative "Green Book," issued annually, has reviewed the status of virtually all redistributive programs.[37] In recent years this publication has become the authoritative text for social policy analysts. Few other committees of Congress have accumulated such power and prestige within their policy domain. In the words of one reporter, the Ways and Means Committee "is at the center of social-welfare policy."[38]

Not only is Ways and Means the locus in the House of Representatives for designing most redistributive grant programs, but it is in general one of the most, if not the single most, powerful committees in Congress. All tax and tariff legislation passes through the committee, as does all legislation on social security, medicare, and health insurance. Bills reported out of this committee are almost always subject to a rule that precludes more than one or two floor amendments.[39] For the most part, members on the floor are confronted with a choice of voting the entire bill up or down. When a committee is this autonomous, its preferences are likely to be reflected in final legislation.[40]

Some congressional scholars have argued that the power of this committee is exaggerated. Its prestige is great and its apparent command over legislation is sweeping only because its proposed legislation quite accurately represents sentiment in the chamber as a whole. Its members are neither especially conservative Republicans nor especially liberal

Democrats but a reasonable proxy for the views of the legislative body as a whole. As Lyndon Johnson once said to one of its members, "I like you, Gibbons, because you can talk Southern and vote Northern."[41] The legislation it writes is written with a careful eye as to what can pass muster with the membership.[42]

This view may be quite accurate with regard to the broad policy questions the committee decides. However, the designers of legislation within the committee may also find it quite convenient to write the specific details of the legislation in ways that benefit disproportionately the states and localities in which committee members live.[43] The very fact that the committee is so representative of the floor on broad questions may require special attention to the electoral needs of committee members on particular matters of distribution. As one political insider has observed, "In those bills they're voting for, there's usually a lot for their district. That's the way they're able to cast those hard votes."[44] This practice has been well documented with respect to tax legislation. After broad policy questions have been decided, special transition rules are written for the benefit of cooperative committee members.[45] According to one report, "Hours before the Ways and Means Committee was to vote on tax reform legislation, [its chair] sat with a list in the committee's library and began calling other members to tell them of special tax breaks he had sneaked in the bill just for them."[46]

Most of the grants-in-aid under the jurisdiction of the Ways and Means Committee are formula grants, which appear to have no particular geographical target. But small variations in formula design can have a major impact on distribution patterns. For example, some grants are allocated according to a strict matching formula that gives states one dollar for every dollar spent by the state. This directs the money toward states with both the tax capacity and policy commitment to come up with their half of program costs. Other grants have a sliding formula that gives anywhere between 50 and 85 percent of program costs, depending on a state's economic and fiscal resources. Formula writing is arcane, but its effects are visible enough in computer printouts that members of the Ways and Means Committee can make sure their states are getting at least their fair share.

Representation on the House Education and Labor Committee also helped a state secure federal aid. For every 1 percent increase in a state's representation on the Education and Labor Committee, the state received an additional $0.57 in redistributive aid per person (table 6-1). Education and Labor is responsible for authorizing eight of the more expensive redistributive programs: compensatory education, school lunch, job training, summer work program, low-income home energy, women's, infants', and children's aid, food distribution, and rehabilitation services.

The impact of membership on Education and Labor on the allocation of redistributive aid may be a surprising finding to some observers. This committee has often been regarded as a partisan or ideological committee whose members are more interested in taking positions than getting credit for corralling federal dollars.[47] But this reputation was acquired before the growth of federal redistributive programs in the 1970s; it may well be that as more federal dollars for social programs became available, the members of this committee became less ideological and more sensitive to the political value of "social pork."[48]

It is possible that the correct causal explanation for the correlation between committee membership and the allocation of federal redistributive dollars is the reverse of that which has been inferred. It is possible that the greater flow of redistributive dollars to certain districts motivates certain members to pursue membership on both the Education and Labor and Ways and Means Committees. But we doubt that the mere desire to be on one of these two key committees is sufficient to obtain membership on them. The power of the Ways and Means Committee is such that virtually every member of the House would prefer membership on this committee to almost any other. Although the Education and Labor Committee's power and prestige is less exalted, it too is considered one of the more important committees in the House. In our view, the best explanation for the strength of the correlation between committee membership and redistributive aid is that in this policy arena there are fewer constituency pressures. Less worried about constituent criticism, members on the chamber floor seem to concede greater autonomy to the committees responsible for redistributive aid, although the Public Works Committee is also able to secure extra developmental resources for its membership.

Presidential Effects

Presidents may have a dramatic impact on the overall level of federal aid to states and localities, but they seem to have had little effect on the allocation of federal aid among the states. It might be thought that federal aid would shift toward the Rust Belt when Democrats acquired control of the presidency, then shift toward the Sun Belt when Republicans gained control of the Oval Office. In equations not reported here, we analyzed the data year by year in order to identify significant changes in the determinants of federal aid over time. But despite changes in partisan control of the presidency and major changes in the overall level of federal aid to states and localities, we could find no significant changes in the determinants of the distribution of federal aid.

Conclusions

The allocation of federal aid among the states seems to be influenced by factors identified by both functional and legislative theory. As legislative theory anticipates, Congress designs federal aid policy in such a way as to give more developmental money to states with greater fiscal capacity as well as to smaller and more rural states that are overrepresented in the Senate. As functional theory expects, more federal aid of both kinds is given to states that tax their residents at higher levels. Population density and higher poverty rates facilitate a state's ability to obtain redistributive funds.

The internal distribution of power in Congress affects the allocation of aid in complex ways. The chamber floor is more important in the Senate than in the House. On the House side of the Hill, the power of the committee depends to some extent on the nature of the policy. If the monies are for developmental purposes, the issue is of such significance to most members that the Appropriations Committee is unable to act autonomously. Only the Public Works Committee can win extra developmental dollars for its members. If the monies are for redistributive issues, which are of great interest only to the least influential constituents, the members on the chamber floor seem more willing to delegate decisionmaking responsibility to the committees. Both the Ways and Means and the House Education and Labor Committees were able to direct funds to their members' districts.

Although the level of federal aid has changed dramatically over time and from one presidency to the next, the allocation of federal aid among states remained quite constant during the period between 1969 and 1991. The stability of the allocational pattern suggests that distributive policies are a function of basic, long-term power relationships within Congress. As one careful study of federal grant formulas observed, "Nearly all matching requirements applicable in . . . 1975 were the same as those in effect when the programs were enacted."[49]

7

Big Cities: Is the Problem Financial?

The thing generally raised on city land is taxes.
George Dudley Warner, *My Summer in a Garden*

Then the Legislature goes and passes a law increasin' the liquor tax or some other tax in New York City, takes half the proceeds for the State Treasury and cuts down the farmers' taxes to suit. It's as easy as rollin' off a log—when you've got a good workin' majority and no conscience to speak of.
George Washington Plunkitt, Tammany Hall politician

Big cities are often thought to be the Achilles' heel of the federal system. Their social responsibilities are large; their taxes are high; the aid they receive from higher levels of government is declining. Their residents suffer from poor schools as well as high rates of unemployment, crime, and welfare dependency. Any calculation of the price of American federalism must take into account difficulties faced by the nation's central cities.

Analysis of big-city financial strategies can profit by distinguishing between older cities of the Rust Belt and newer cities of the Sun Belt.[1] In this chapter I shall show that big cities of the Rust Belt seem to be both profligate and unduly burdened by social responsibilities; Sun Belt cities are less so. Cities in both regions do equally well at getting national aid. Rust Belt cities get more state aid and have become increasingly capable of getting their fair share. Sun Belt cities do much more poorly.

The spending differences between Rust Belt and Sun Belt cities can be explained by functional theory. For many decades, governments in

the big cities of the Rust Belt enjoyed monopolistic control over extremely valuable land located at the conjunction of fixed water and rail
transportation systems. Their geographical advantage freed them from
some of the discipline of the marketplace. As a result, these big cities
were enticed into assuming governmental responsibilities for which
they were ill suited. In addition, the cost of supplying these services
was driven up by a large, well-organized labor force that was able to
use a combination of political and economic pressure to win relatively
high compensation packages.

The Urban Political Economy

The monopolistic position big cities of the Rust Belt enjoyed in the
late nineteenth century was gradually eroded away by technological
innovations. As trucks, automobiles, and airplanes replaced railroads,
steamships, and river barges, industrial production no longer needed
to be concentrated around those few points where land and water
transport conjoined. The telegraph and telephone reduced the importance of face-to-face interactions for commercial exchange. As economic activity decentralized, so did residential areas. As the
construction of high-speed highways facilitated movement to and from
the central business district, prosperous city dwellers moved outward
from the core of the metropolitan area toward its periphery, where
land was cheaper, lots were bigger, houses were newer, and grass was
greener. The dirty, congested inner city was left to low-income minorities who could neither find nor afford alternatives elsewhere.[2]

In many metropolitan areas, political and governmental stagnation
aggravated the problems created by these economic and social changes.
During the nineteenth century most central cities had extended their
political jurisdictions as their populations grew. Outlying areas agreed
to incorporation in order to get access to city-built sewers, roads, and
streetcar lines. But as the twentieth century progressed, these outlying
areas, now called suburbs, resisted (in state legislatures and local elections) takeover attempts by the central cities they surrounded. Almost
all cities in the Rust Belt became locked into fixed political boundaries
that usually encompassed less than half the metropolitan population.

Many of the newer cities of the Sun Belt never experienced the same
quasi-monopoly enjoyed by Rust Belt cities. From the beginning, they
were highway cities, competing with older, established cities of the
East and Midwest as well as a multitude of alternative Sun Belt locations

almost equally accessible by car and truck. Although cities of the rapidly growing Sun Belt were less constricted, by the 1990s even these cities rarely incorporated outlying areas.

With their ability to annex inhibited, central cities became increasingly distinct from their suburban hinterland. Central-city residents, instead of being financially better off, became less well off than the average American. Median family income in the big cities with more than 300,000 inhabitants was 15.2 percent higher than the national median in 1950 but 7.8 percent lower in 1990. The poverty rate of these big-city residents was 1.4 percentage points higher than the national rate in 1970, 5.9 percentage points higher in 1990. The nonwhite percentage of big-city populations was 3 percentage points above the national average in 1950; by 1990 it was 22 percentage points above.[3] Politically, central cities became heavily Democratic in their voting propensities, while suburban areas tended to be more Republican.

Central-city governmental structures were also different from those in the suburbs. Central cities established large bureaucracies with uniform policies for large, heterogeneous populations, while suburbia was divided into many small governmental units. Each town, village, or special district was responsible for governing a small and usually quite homogeneous population. Although cities had the advantage of any economies of scale that accrue to large jurisdictions, they had the fiscal disadvantage of being vulnerable to wage demands and strike threats by their large municipal work force. For all these reasons, cities began turning to the federal government for assistance.

Big cities no longer share equally in the growth of the nation's population. Although the raw numbers of people living in large central cities increased from 34 million to 42 million between 1957 and 1990, the portion of the U.S. population living in these cities declined by nearly 5 percentage points (see figure 7-1). The decline was concentrated in the Rust Belt. The number of people living in Rust Belt cities fell from 25 million to 20 million; their share of the U.S. population plummeted from 14.5 to 8.0 percent.[4] Meanwhile, the number of residents living in big cities of the Sun Belt grew from 8.5 million to 23 million. Much of this increase was due to annexation and to the fact that the number of Sun Belt cities with populations above 300,000 increased from fifteen to thirty-four.

The social composition of big cities in the two regions also differs noticeably. Median family income in the average Rust Belt city was 16.2 percent above the national median in 1950 but 11.1 percent below the

FIGURE 7-1. *Proportion of U.S. Population Living in Big Cities,*
1957–90

Percent

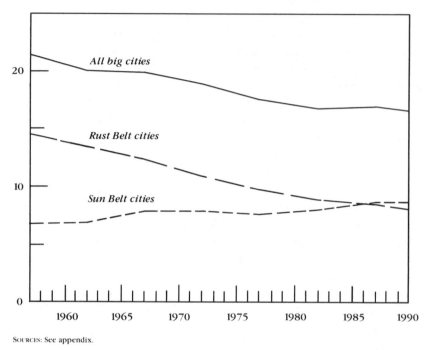

median in 1990. Changes were similar but less dramatic in the Sun Belt:
median family income went from 12.4 percent above to 4.9 percent
below the national median over this period. The percentage of the
population of European descent declined by 34.1 percent in the Rust
Belt but by only 21.5 percent in the Sun Belt.[5] Social change was occurring in all big cities, but the social and economically most challenging transformations were occurring in the older manufacturing cities
of the Northeast and Midwest.

The differences between Rust Belt and Sun Belt cities have been
intensified by their distinctive political traditions. Rust Belt cities grew
rapidly during the latter part of the nineteenth century, when political
machines dominated local politics. During the early decades of the
twentieth century, these machines responded to the rise of the labor
movement by incorporating trade unions into the machines' organiza-
tional core.[6] Public-sector unions were recognized, and city contracts

were let only to businesses with unionized workers. To forestall strikes, public-sector workers were paid the prevailing wage set by negotiations between union and management in the private sector.

Many Sun Belt cities experienced their most rapid growth after World War II. In most of these cities, reformers drove machine politicians out of office and established reform governments with close ties to the local business community. Ambitiously striving to catch up with the powerful cities of the East and the Midwest, the cities of the Sun Belt focused their attention on development. Efficient, bureaucratic administration substituted for machine-style politics. Trade unions had little influence. Most demands to provide social services to the poor and the needy were ignored.[7] As a result, Sun Belt cities would respond to the changes of the 1960s and 1970s in a manner very different from their Rust Belt cousins.

The Cost of Big-City Government

During the last third of the twentieth century, social and economic change accelerated the demand for and cost of public services in all big cities. As a result, big-city governments collected more than three times as much money in 1990 as they did in 1957 (figure 7-2). Big cities' revenues rose from $27.2 billion in 1957 to $95.9 billion in 1990.

The pattern of revenue growth varied between the Rust Belt and the Sun Belt. The revenues of Sun Belt cities increased from $570 to $1,739 per person between 1957 and 1990 (figure 7-3). The annual growth rate was fairly steep for the first twenty years but leveled off to between 1 and 3 percent after 1977. In the Rust Belt cities, the money collected increased from $865 to $2,942 per person over the course of the thirty-three years. This growth rate was not only steeper but occurred at a more uneven pace. The annual growth rate varied from a rapid increase of 6.8 percent during the prosperous 1960s to slight drops in the late 1970s to a renewed sharp rate of growth of 4.9 percent in the resurgent 1980s.

In order to see whether the growth in big-city revenues simply reflected rising economic prosperity, I calculated the amount collected by big-city governments as a percentage of GNP (see table 7-1). The differences between Rust Belt and Sun Belt cities are once again worth underlining. In the Rust Belt the percentage of GNP collected from local taxpayers by big cities declined modestly from 0.87 percent to

FIGURE 7-2. *Total Revenue Received by Big Cities, 1957–90*

Billions of 1990 dollars

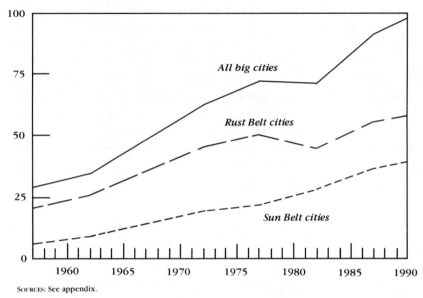

SOURCES: See appendix.

FIGURE 7-3. *Per Capita Total Revenue Received by Big Cities, 1957–90*

1990 dollars

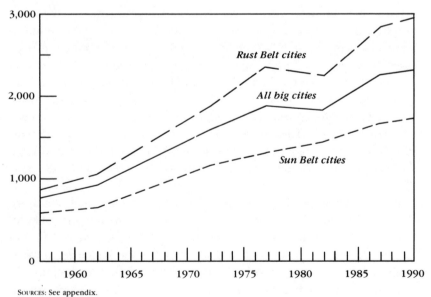

SOURCES: See appendix.

TABLE 7-1. *Percentage of Big-City Revenue from Own Fiscal Resources, Selected Years, 1957–90*

Percent

Revenue measure	Year						
	1957	1962	1972	1977	1982	1987	1990
All big cities							
Revenue as percent of GNP	1.15	1.18	1.24	1.16	1.17	1.35	1.34
Share of U.S. population	21.2	20.0	18.8	17.2	16.7	16.9	16.6
Rust Belt cities							
Revenue as percent of GNP	0.87	0.87	0.81	0.75	0.67	0.76	0.73
Share of U.S. population	14.5	13.2	11.0	9.7	8.8	8.3	8.0
Sun Belt cities							
Revenue as percent of GNP	0.28	0.31	0.43	0.42	0.51	0.59	0.61
Share of U.S. population	6.7	6.8	7.8	7.5	7.9	8.6	8.6

SOURCES: See appendix.

0.73 percent. But at the same time, the population of these cities declined dramatically—from 14.5 to 8.0 percent of the U.S. population. In other words, local government revenue as a percentage of GNP fell by only 16 percent while these cities' share of the nation's population fell by 45 percent.

The share of the nation's GNP being spent by Sun Belt cities was much less: only 0.28 percent of GNP in 1957 and 0.61 percent of GNP in 1990 (table 7-1). The increase is due in part to the 28 percent growth in the share of the nation's population living in Sun Belt cities. Sun Belt city revenues from their own fiscal resources ran ahead of increases in the Sun Belt city population, but Sun Belt cities still spent a lower proportion of GNP than Rust Belt cities.

Even these data are not conclusive evidence that Rust Belt city governments are profligate. It is possible that big-city expenditures simply reflect a nationwide increase in both the cost of and demand for local government services. To ascertain how big-city spending compared with that of the local government system in the country as a whole, I constructed an index.[8] The index takes a value of 1.0 if big cities collect the same amount of revenue per person from their own fiscal resources

FIGURE 7-4. *Big-City Spending Relative to All Local Government Spending, 1957–90*

Index

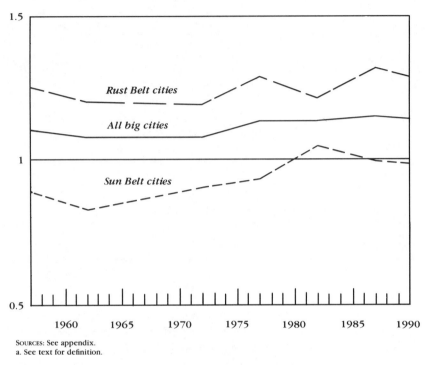

SOURCES: See appendix.
a. See text for definition.

as do local governments in general. The index is a ratio. If it assumes a value of 0.5, revenue collection is half as much as elsewhere; if it reaches 2.0, revenue collection is twice as much.

For big cities as a whole, the index climbed modestly from 1.10 in 1962 to 1.13 in 1990 (figure 7-4).[9] But the index takes dramatically different values in Rust Belt cities than in Sun Belt cities. In Rust Belt cities the index rose from an already high 1.20 in 1962 to 1.28 in 1990. This means that in 1990 Rust Belt cities spent 28 percent more per person than did the sum total of all local governments in the United States. The index for Sun Belt cities generally took a value of less than 1.0; it increased from 0.88 to 0.98 between 1972 and 1990.[10] In other words, these cities spent less than the typical local government expenditure for the country as a whole.

Some may think that these differences between the Sun Belt and the Rust Belt are perfectly understandable. Rust Belt cities suffer higher crime rates, higher poverty rates, and a greater demand for social services; they are burdened by an older infrastructure; and they may be located in states that delegate more responsibilities to local governments. Others suspect that Rust Belt cities are especially likely to suffer from diseconomies of scale. As I have pointed out, most are older cities that once exercised control over particularly valuable land. Relatively undisciplined by market forces, they adopted politically popular but inefficient governmental practices—patronage politics, bloated bureaucracies, and work-rule concessions to well-organized municipal employees.[11]

But whether the higher costs are justifiable or not, the higher spending in Rust Belt cities places them in a disadvantageous economic position. As changes in transportation and communication undermine their quasi-monopolistic position, these cities risk continuing losses in population and economic activity. Businesses and residents will continue to be inclined to locate elsewhere.

In sum, the finances of Rust Belt cities appear to be significantly different from those of Sun Belt cities. In the Rust Belt, changes in the composition of the central-city population, coupled with an overall decline in the number of residents, have been accompanied by an increasing demand for and cost of government services. The revenues of Sun Belt cities grew more in consonance with the overall growth of these cities and the local government system as a whole. By 1990 Rust Belt cities, serving a population totaling 20 million people, were spending 0.73 percent of the nation's GNP. Sun Belt city governments, with a total population of 23 million, were spending just 0.61 percent of the nation's GNP (table 7-1).

It is not possible to draw definite conclusions from these figures. It may be that in the Sun Belt states provide services that in the Rust Belt are the responsibility of municipal governments.[12] But differences in responsibilities are unlikely to account fully for the differentiated pattern of change in the two regions. The pattern of change in the Sun Belt seems to have been a fairly gradual response to population growth and increasing demand for public services. It is unlikely to culminate in a fiscal crisis. On the other hand, the demands for more government revenues in the cities of the Rust Belt seem to be placing an ever increasing strain on their economies.

The Cost of Big-City Schools

To ascertain some of the sources of the cost differences between Sun Belt and Rust Belt cities, I examined the amount cities in the two regions were spending on education. Per pupil expenditures (in constant dollars) in the twenty-five largest central cities climbed steadily throughout the postwar period; they did not miss a beat even during the 1980s, an era of federal retrenchment and fiscal restraint (table 7-2).[13] In the Rust Belt cities, average per pupil expenditures climbed from just over $1,300 in 1950 to almost $3,500 in 1970 and over $5,700 in 1992. The increase in Sun Belt cities was less, from $1,200 in 1950 to almost $4,900 in 1992.

This climb in per pupil school expenditures within the Rust Belt was not simply a matter of keeping up with trends elsewhere; instead, these cities' expenditures continued to outpace the national average. Big-city education has always been more expensive than education in other parts of the country. As early as 1950, per pupil expenditures in Rust Belt cities ran 25 percent higher than expenditures in the country as a whole, while in Sun Belt cities they were running 15 percent higher (table 7-2). Over the next four decades the price of education in Rust Belt cities relative to the national average fluctuated moderately. But by 1992 the per pupil cost of Rust Belt city schools was 13 percent higher than in the country as a whole, while costs in the Sun Belt cities had fallen to below the national average.

These regional comparisons are striking. Even the phenomenal economic growth of the Sun Belt did not create a disproportionate rise in school expenditures. Meanwhile, the Rust Belt cities, even while losing in population, employment, and overall economic activity, provided still higher financial underpinning for their educational systems. As of 1992, central-city schools of the Rust Belt had more resources per pupil in absolute terms than ever before and nearly as much as other school systems.

These increasing expenditures have not gone only to bureaucrats, bus drivers, and security guards. They have also gone to teachers, although, admittedly, teachers' salaries have fluctuated over the course of the past three decades. During the 1960s and early 1970s the salary of the average classroom teacher in the Rust Belt cities climbed steadily—along with the wages of all Americans—from $33,373 in 1961 to $40,849 in 1975 (table 7-3). But when the prosperous 1960s gave way

TABLE 7-2. *Per Pupil Education Expenditure in Twenty-five Largest Cities, Selected Years, 1950–92*
Amounts in 1992 dollars

Year	U.S. average amount	Rust Belt		Sun Belt	
		Amount per pupil	Ratio to U.S. average	Amount per pupil	Ratio to U.S. average
1950	1,077	1,351	1.25	1,240	1.15
1960	1,602	1,862	1.16	1,588	0.99
1970	2,712	3,493	1.29	2,491	0.92
1982	3,667	4,195	1.14	3,820	1.04
1992	5,058	5,729	1.13	4,852	0.96

SOURCES: U.S. Office of Education, *Biennial Survey of Education, 1948-50* (1953), chap. 3, table 3; *Current Expenditures in Large Public School Systems, 1959-60* (1962); *Statistics of Local Public School Systems, 1969-70, Finance* (1974), tables 4, 5; U.S. Bureau of the Census, *Census of Governments, 1982*, vol. 4, no. 1 (Department of Commerce, 1984), table 8; National Center for Education Statistics, *Digest of Education Statistics, 1972*, table 29, p. 32; *1987*, table 98, p. 112; *1989*, table 35, pp. 45–46; table 37, pp. 48–49; table 41, p. 55; *1990*, table 35, p. 47; *1994*, tables 92–93, pp. 98–103; and National Education Association, *Estimates of School Statistics, 1965–66*, p. 10; *1992-93*, p. 25.

TABLE 7-3. *Average Classroom Teacher's Salaries in Twenty-five Largest Cities, Selected Years, 1961–93*
Salaries in 1993 dollars

Year	U.S. average salary	Rust Belt		Sun Belt	
		Average salary	Ratio to U.S. average	Average salary	Ratio to U.S. average
1961	25,201	33,373	1.32	29,797	1.18
1971	33,069	38,672	1.17	35,498	1.07
1975	31,395	40,849	1.30	34,215	1.09
1980	28,003	34,276	1.22	31,328	1.12
1985	31,684	37,811	1.19	35,645	1.13
1990	34,607	40,656	1.17	37,566	1.08
1993	34,777	41,097	1.18	37,804	1.09

SOURCES: National Education Association Research Division, *Salaries Paid Classroom Teachers, Principals, and Certain Others, 1960–61, Urban Districts 100,000 and Over in Population; 1970–71*; Educational Research Service, *Salaries Paid Professional Personnel in Public Schools, 1974–75; 1979–80; 1984–85; 1989–90; 1992–93*, table 27; National Education Association, *Estimates of School Statistics, 1960–61*, p. 13; *1989–90*, p. 19; *1992-93*, p. 19; and National Center for Education Statistics, *Digest of Education Statistics, 1988*, table 57, p. 72.

to the low-growth, low-productivity, high-inflation years of the late 1970s, central-city teachers' salaries fell sharply. Neither unionization nor the formation of a new national Department of Education stemmed the tide. But, surprisingly, this downward trend reversed itself after 1980. Despite harsh criticisms of public schools by William Bennett, then secretary of education, and despite federal deficits and cutbacks in domestic spending, central-city teachers' salaries in the Rust Belt climbed to $41,097 in 1993. Salaries of teachers in the Sun Belt fluctuated up and down in roughly the same manner, though they generally lagged behind their Rust Belt peers by roughly 10 percent.

Trends in central-city teachers' salaries have been fairly consistent with national trends. Teachers throughout the United States enjoyed salary increases in the 1960s, suffered cuts in the 1970s, and had raises in the 1980s. Admittedly, the 32 percent cost of living differential that Rust Belt central-city teachers had received in 1961 (table 7-3) declined over the decades (perhaps because the cost of living outside the central cities became more similar to that within the city center), but in 1993 Rust Belt city teachers were still paid 18 percent more than the average teacher nationwide while their Sun Belt counterparts received only 9 percent more.

Despite the higher expenditure on education within central cities, there is little evidence that the result was better education for the minority students who live there. Drawing upon previously unpublished data from the National Assessment of Educational Progress (NAEP), the most careful national survey of what students are learning in school, Lyle Jones has provided information on the educational progress of African Americans in public schools in three types of communities—rural, central-city and suburban.[14] According to his report, reading scores within central cities improved as much as they did nationally for the elementary years. But at the high school level, blacks in central cities, though making some gains, improved at only one-fourth to one-half the rate blacks were gaining nationally. The same pattern emerges when white-black comparisons are made. Blacks' scores have improved relative to those of whites in nearly all circumstances. In suburban areas they have improved during the high school years by as much as sixteen and seventeen points. But apart from an improvement by black nine-year-olds, no closing of the racial gap has taken place within central cities. In other words, African Americans attending central-city public schools do not seem to have been making the same kind of educational progress they have been making in other parts of the country.

Federalism and Big Cities

Mayors of Rust Belt cities regularly blame national and state governments for their financial predicaments. To see whether the fact that citizens of Rust Belt cities have to pay more for their services is due to unfair treatment by higher levels of government, I shall examine the success that big cities have had in the competition for national and state aid. Functional theory expects big cities to do as well as any other type of locality in the competition for grants from higher levels of government. Legislative theory is less sure. It is possible that rural and suburban members of legislatures are able to control the committees that distribute intergovernmental grants and use this power to deny aid to big cities.

National aid can be given either directly to cities or to states, which can then allocate it either for the states' own purposes or among local governments. Big cities prefer direct aid from the national government, because they have more influence in Congress than they do in most state legislatures.

National Aid to Cities

Congress has seldom, if ever, enacted a major policy devoted exclusively to the problems of big cities. Most programs affecting cities are simply the urban component of policies legislated for the country as a whole. Legislation designed specifically for cities has typically been small, experimental, and short term.

The structure of Congress militates against the passage of programs aimed solely at urban areas. Because Congress includes representatives from all states and congressional districts, it is reluctant to exclude more than a very few places from the legislation it approves. Because broad coalitions are necessary to pass legislation, benefits usually need to be distributed over a wide geographic reach.

This political inhibition on urban-focused policymaking was reinforced in the nineteenth century by Supreme Court interpretations of Congress's constitutional powers. Since local governments were considered creatures of the state, policies affecting specific geographic areas within states were considered outside the congressional domain.[15]

Despite these political and constitutional inhibitions, the changes in cities wrought by industrialization and immigration began to place urban problems on the congressional agenda toward the end of the nineteenth century. Spurred by Jacob Riis's 1890 book, *How the Other Half Lives*, Congress in 1892 asked the commissioner of labor to conduct a study of big-city slums. The commissioner's report, submitted two years later by the Grover Cleveland administration, made no recommendations. It simply reported that residents of slums were more likely than other urban residents to be foreign born, illiterate, crowded in tenement housing, and living in close proximity to a saloon. A Democratic administration sensitive to the rights of states was not about to take responsibility for social problems in the inner city.

Official investigation of urban problems took place again in 1908, when a presidential commission appointed by Theodore Roosevelt reviewed slum conditions in Washington, D.C. While this commission made numerous recommendations with respect to social conditions in the nation's capital, it studiously avoided mention of any urban problem elsewhere. Republicans were no more willing than Democrats to encroach upon state sovereignty.

This narrow conception of the appropriate federal role was initially challenged by Franklin Roosevelt's New Deal. But the great expansion in national aid given directly to big cities came during the period of cooperative, or "marble-cake," federalism.[16] Between 1957 and 1977 direct national aid to big cities increased in real dollar terms from $0.3 billion to $9.3 billion. On a per capita basis, it climbed from $10 to $244 (figure 7-5).[17]

In the mid-1970s, the mood changed. Implementation studies were showing that federalism was not quite as cooperative as earlier theorists had suggested. The 1975 New York fiscal crisis prompted the most financial relief ever given to a big city. Congress authorized $2.3 billion in loan guarantees for New York on the condition that the city institute a more disciplined budgeting system. But it also helped induce the backlash against big cities. New York became a symbol of urban profligacy that, along with a new conservatism and burgeoning federal deficits, would undermine pro-urban forces in Congress. National aid to big cities fell from $9.3 billion in 1977 to $4.5 billion in 1990. Per capita aid fell from $244 to $109 (figure 7-5). Sun Belt and Rust Belt cities enjoyed roughly parallel increases in national aid during the era of cooperative federalism. The period of retrenchment also hit cities in both regions in much the same way.

In order to see how well big cities did in comparison with other local governments, I calculated an index of national aid. The index (constructed along the same lines as the big-city spending index) identifies the extent to which big cities received more or less than their per capita share of national aid dollars.

Big cities did particularly well during the halcyon days of the Great Society. The index of national aid climbed from 1.45 to 1.92 between 1957 and 1972 (see figure 7-6). This means that by 1972 cities were

FIGURE 7-5. *Per Capita National Aid to Big Cities, 1957–90*

1990 dollars

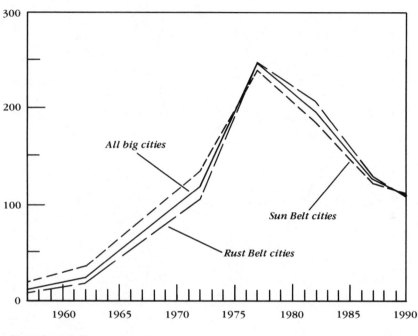

SOURCES: See appendix.

doing about twice as well as the typical local government. Richard Nixon and Gerald Ford sought to reduce this bias in favor of the cities by introducing revenue sharing and block grant programs that would distribute monies more widely among local governments. As these programs expanded in the mid-1970s, the index of aid to cities fell to 1.66 and eventually to 1.49 by 1990. Still, even after a decade of Republican rule inside the White House, big cities received nearly 50 percent more money than could be accounted for on a strictly per capita basis.

Residents of Rust Belt cities may think these extra federal dollars are no more and probably even less than what these cities deserve. Rust Belt cities endure a higher crime rate, an older infrastructure to maintain, greater exposure to the hazards of fire, more citizens in need of social services, and young people who arrive at school with greater educational deficiencies. The costs of public services are necessarily greater, if for no other reason than the higher cost of land in densely populated areas. City mice simply need more money than their country

FIGURE 7-6. *National Aid to Big Cities Relative to National Aid to All Local Governments, 1957–90*

Index[a]

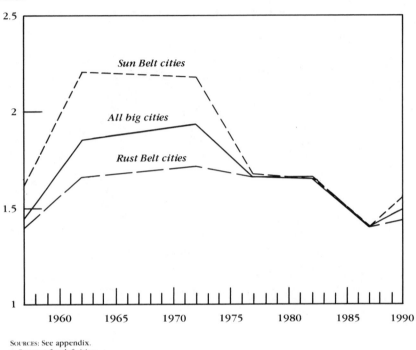

SOURCES: See appendix.
a. See text for definition.

cousins. Why should they not get at least 50 percent more in federal dollars?

Residents of small towns and suburbs may have exactly the opposite view. Big cities still enjoy control over some of the most valuable land in the region. They should be able to generate ample revenue from the property taxes they levy on expensive central business district properties, commuter taxes, and tourist taxes levied on the small town mice enticed by the entertainments provided by the big city. Rural areas with large concentrations of poor people have no comparable sources of revenue. Cities should receive less than the national per capita average.

Only the most foolhardy—or those with a clear vested interest—should attempt to adjudicate this debate over the appropriate allocation of federal dollars among cities, suburbs, and rural communities. However, any local government jurisdiction that receives more than the national per capita average will find it difficult to win the political argument that it should receive still more. As long as the system of representation in Congress weights votes equally, the allocation of funds among jurisdictions is not likely to be based on formulas that depart too dramatically from the per capita average. States with small populations, who are overrepresented in the Senate, may be able to do better than average. But because cities were not given any such protection in the Constitution, they are probably fortunate to be doing as well as they are.[18]

If the fiscal crisis of Rust Belt cities cannot be clearly attributed to "unfair" treatment by the national government, the problem may lie elsewhere in the federal system. Big cities have historically been more dependent upon fiscal assistance from the states than from the national government. Perhaps recent trends in state grants to big cities help to account for the fiscal problems of Rust Belt cities.

State Aid to Cities

In 1957 big cities received more than ten times as much state aid as national aid. During the era of cooperative federalism, states greatly expanded the size of their urban assistance programs. Although state expansion did not take place at the same rate as national expansion, in 1977 states still provided cities with nearly twice as much money as did the national government (see figures 7-5 and 7-7). State grants to cities jumped from $112 per person in 1957 to $442 in 1977 (figure 7-7). Nor did states follow the national government in retrenching their urban assistance programs after 1977. As the national government cut deeply into its urban assistance programs, state aid remained relatively constant, falling only slightly to $430 per person by 1990.

Regional differences in state aid are striking. Historically, the level of state aid to Rust Belt cities has been much higher than to Sun Belt cities. This historical difference may be due in part to the fact that some services provided by cities in the Northeast and Midwest are provided by state governments in the South and the West. The historical differences between the two parts of the country were greatly magnified during the era of cooperative federalism. State aid to cities climbed sharply in the Rust Belt during the 1960s and 1970s, while it remained relatively flat in the Sun Belt (figure 7-7). During the early 1980s state aid to Rust Belt cities declined sharply, but in the latter part of the decade it regained its former level and then surpassed it. In the Sun Belt the level of state aid remained fairly constant.

FIGURE 7-7. *Per Capita State Aid to Big Cities, 1957–90*

1990 dollars

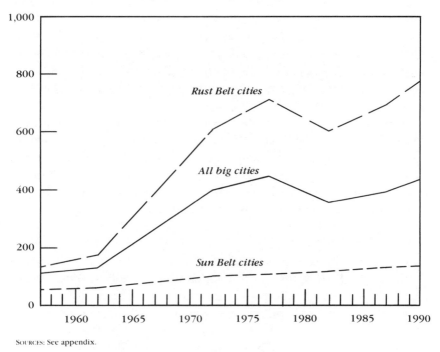

SOURCES: See appendix.

To ascertain how well cities were doing relative to other local governments, I constructed an index of state aid along the same lines as
the index of national aid discussed previously. Big cities in general have
done poorly in the competition for state aid. At no point between 1957
and 1990 did big cities achieve their "fair share" of state aid (see figure
7-8). The closest they came was during the mid-1970s, when the country seemed most sensitive to urban problems. After 1977 big cities
began to lose considerable ground within state legislatures; by 1990
they got less than two-thirds of what may have been justified on a per
capita basis.

The ups and downs of state aid affected Rust Belt cities more than
Sun Belt cities, simply because Rust Belt cities have historically been
more dependent on state aid. In 1977, when cities were doing comparatively well within state legislatures, Rust Belt cities received about a
third more than what might have been justified on a per capita basis.
But by 1990 they were able to secure only about 10 percent more than

FIGURE 7-8. *State Aid to Big Cities Relative to State Aid to All Local Governments, 1957–90*

Index[a]

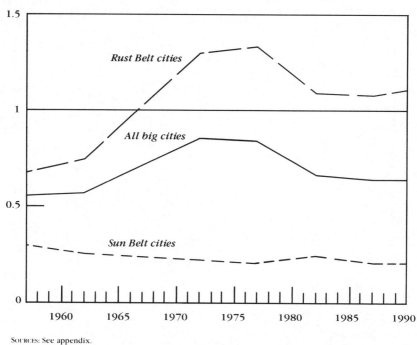

SOURCES: See appendix.
a. See text for definition.

the typical local government. Meanwhile, the share of money going to Sun Belt cities remained very small, usually only about a fifth of what their numbers would seem to have justified. Sun Belt cities do not receive much state aid either in absolute terms or relative to other local governments.

One must be cautious in making these regional comparisons. It may well be that Sun Belt cities were not being treated as unfairly as the data suggest. It may be that their states assumed responsibility for public services that were being provided at the local level in the Rust Belt. Even so, it is quite remarkable that Sun Belt cities enjoyed only a pale reflection of the steep increases in state aid going to Rust Belt cities. In 1990 Sun Belt cities were digging into their own pockets for 84 percent of the costs of city government, but Rust Belt cities needed to obtain only 69 percent of their revenue from local sources (figure 7-9). If Rust Belt cities are in financial difficulty, the problem does not

FIGURE 7-9. *Big Cities' General Revenue from Local Sources,*
1957–90

Percent

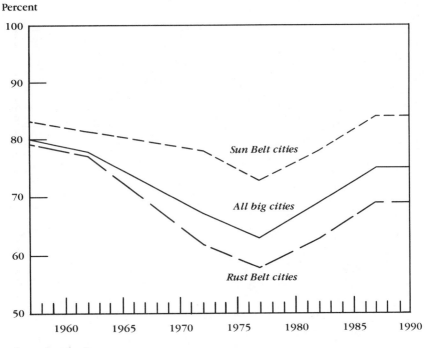

SOURCES: See appendix.

seem to lie in the amount of aid they have received from higher levels
of government. By comparison with Sun Belt cities, they have done
reasonably well.

National Politics and the Fiscal Future of Big Cities

Much has been written about the competition among regions, states,
and communities for national resources. It is often claimed that the
Democratic party, with its roots in cities of the Rust Belt, skews the
distribution of federal funds to the big cities of the Northeast and
Midwest. Conversely, it is claimed that Republicans distribute federal
dollars to the suburbs and small towns of the South and West in order
to solidify their hold on these parts of the country. It is further con-
tended that the flow of federal dollars is significantly affected by the
decennial changes in the system of representation in the House of
Representatives. As regions and types of communities gain in popula-

tion, they gain power on Capitol Hill. As a result, they gain better access to federal dollars.

There are reasons to doubt these claims. First, power in Washington was divided between the two political parties for twenty-four of the thirty-six years between 1956 and 1992. Even when the Democratic party controlled the executive and legislative branches, a conservative coalition of Republicans and southern Democrats exercised considerable influence on Capitol Hill. Legislative compromise—not naked, unconstrained pursuit of narrow partisan objectives—has generally constrained both presidential initiatives and congressional responses.

More important, the distribution of national aid seems to be strongly influenced by a rule of universalism that requires a broad distribution of funds among states and localities. To win the large, stable coalitions necessary to pass legislation through a bicameral legislature divided into many competing jurisdictions, and to win the president's signature on the legislation, it is essential that the legislation be perceived to be equitable among regions, states, and localities.

The universalism rule is not so powerful that all regional distinctions are eliminated. There is some evidence in my data that the Rust Belt does better when Democrats are in power and that the Sun Belt does better when Republicans are in power. For example, the Rust Belt seems to have been helped disproportionately by the initial construction of cooperative federalism between 1957 and 1972, when Democrats controlled Congress for all fifteen years and the presidency for eight of them. Yet this gain in the Rust Belt simply reduced an original bias of federal aid formulas in favor of the Sun Belt. By 1972 Sun Belt cities were still receiving $29 more federal aid per person than Rust Belt cities.

Ironically, it was while Richard Nixon and Gerald Ford held the presidency that Rust Belt cities finally reached a level playing field with Sun Belt cities. Despite the talk of Richard Nixon's southern strategy, aid to the Rust Belt continued to increase more rapidly than did aid to the Sun Belt. By 1977 the Rust Belt cities were receiving virtually the same amount of direct federal aid per person as their counterparts in the Sun Belt (figure 7-6).[19]

Divided government probably explains these Rust Belt gains during a Republican presidency. In order to win congressional support for his revenue sharing and block grant programs, President Nixon was forced to accept a distribution formula that favored a part of the country that was only a peripheral part of the emerging Republican majority. The

pattern continued under his successor, Gerald Ford, who not only pre-
sided over the largest increment in federal aid to American cities passed
by a Democratic Congress but acquiesced in a continuing shift in federal aid to the Rust Belt. In retrospect, President Ford hardly seems to
have deserved the "Drop Dead" headline accorded to him by the *New
York Daily News*.

Not only were big cities of the two regions treated in much the same
way after 1977, but big cities have fared better than other local governments in the federal system. During the construction of cooperative
federalism between 1957 and 1972, an increasingly disproportionate
share of national aid directed to local governments went to big cities.
There seems to be some—but only some—truth to the conventional
wisdom that John Kennedy and Lyndon Johnson paid their debt to
Chicago's Mayor Richard Daley and other big-city politicians by giving
them special favors.

Later, when cuts in direct federal aid to localities were promulgated,
all local governments suffered the consequences. Between 1977 and
1990 direct federal aid was reduced by 43 percent. Cities were hit
somewhat more severely. There is thus some truth to the conventional
belief that Carter, Reagan, and Bush turned their backs on big cities in
particular. But even in 1990 big cities received 42 percent more than
their "fair share" of national aid. More important than the petty politics
of partisan shifting of funds to one part of the country or another are
the tides in ideological opinion about the proper role to be played by
the federal government in addressing the country's social problems.
The enormous increments in federal dollars that came to the cities
during the 1960s and early 1970s were rooted in a belief in cooperative
federalism. Public officials were committed to the principle that all
governments, working together, could ameliorate the country's social
ills. In more recent years expectations that governments could solve
social problems have been sharply dampened. As a result, federal aid
to states and localities has been cut back to levels not much higher—
as a percentage of GNP—than those prevailing when Dwight Eisenhower held the presidency. Big cities must turn increasingly to their
own resources, not because of shifts in regional balances of power, but
because of shifting ideological opinion about the appropriate role of
government.

8

Reducing the Price
of Federalism

*The problem which all federalized nations have to solve is how
to secure an efficient central government and preserve national
unity, while allowing free scope for the diversities, and free play
to the ... members of the federation. It is ... to keep the
centrifugal and centripetal forces in equilibrium, so that neither
the planet States shall fly off into space, nor the sun of the
Central government draw them into its consuming fires.*
Lord James Bryce, *American Commonwealth*

President-elect Bill Clinton recruited to his administration two scholars who had contrasting views of the appropriate policy responsibilities
of the national government. In the words of Tammany Hall politician
George Washington Plunkitt, one scholar was a "mornin' glory," who
"looked lovely in the mornin'" of the Clinton administration but "with-
ered up in a short time." The other scholar was like a "fine old oak"
that "went on flourishin' forever."[1] The story of their fate in the early
years of the Clinton administration says much about the direction in
which the federal system is moving.

Bill Clinton's Investment Strategy

The new secretary of labor, Robert Reich of Harvard's John F. Kennedy School of Government and a friend of the president since their
years together at Oxford, was the mornin' glory. He advocated renewed
national investments in economic development. In his book *The Work
of Nations*, Reich called for more public investment in education and

175

job training and more federal dollars to improve systems of transportation and communication. The country's key resources, Reich said, consisted of the human capital embedded in the American people and the physical capital fixed in its landscape.[2] His writings greatly influenced a key document of the Clinton presidential campaign, *Putting People First*, which called for $35 billion a year in new public investments.

Trim, diminutive Alice Rivlin did not look like the fine old oak she would turn out to be. She barely knew Bill Clinton, and her involvement in his presidential campaign had been marginal at best. Appointed deputy director of the Office of Management and Budget (OMB), she was an experienced Washington hand who knew well the plethora of programs for which the national government was responsible.[3] Her book, *Reviving the American Dream*, had a quite different message than the one Reich was delivering. The national government was taking on too many responsibilities, she said. Too many jobs were being shared by national, state, and local officials, making it difficult for each level of government to do its work cleanly and efficiently. Although the national government had to take on certain essential responsibilities, including social security, management of the health care system, and other social programs, it should turn over much of what it was doing to state and local governments. Job training, road improvements, and other public works programs were the province of state and local governments, not that of the government in Washington.[4]

Although both scholars were appointed to top-level positions, there was little doubt in the opening days of the Clinton administration as to which one had the presidential ear. Even though Reich's post as secretary of labor had been of secondary significance in prior Republican administrations, Reich had unimpeded access to the president. Rivlin's appointment as deputy director of OMB was a disappointment. She had every reason to expect to be named director, arguably the highest ranking domestic policy position in the government, but she apparently failed to impress the president when he first met her. Despite the fact that he was eager to appoint women to high-level positions, he passed over Rivlin for the top job—in part, it was said, because she was not as friendly and chummy as Leon Panetta, the able chair of the House Budget Committee, to whom Clinton eventually turned.

It may have all been a matter of personality, but Rivlin's book did not help her cause either. The president-elect was not at all convinced that the national government should do less; he in fact had been saying throughout his campaign that it needed to do more to promote the country's economic development. Rivlin quietly accepted the position of deputy director of OMB, a post of substantial responsibility but lacking the visibility and cachet of a cabinet-level appointment. No one thought she had special access to the Oval Office. On the contrary, the president was reported to have reprimanded her early on. At a meeting on the new Clinton budget, Rivlin expressed enthusiasm for cuts in farm supports. She reportedly said, "Mr. President, I've got a slogan for your reelection. 'I'm going to end welfare as we know it for farmers.' " "Spoken like a true city dweller," the former governor of Arkansas chided, adding, "Farmers are good people. . . . We're going to make these cuts. But we don't have to feel good about it."[5] One member of the Clinton inner club revealed confidentially that Rivlin was among "the living dead" and that "no one listens to her advice anymore." He thought she would "be gone from the Cabinet by the end of the year."[6]

It was not only in news leaks and gossip columns where Reich had the early advantage. His impact could also be seen in the substantive budget Clinton sent to Congress in February 1993. Clinton called for the immediate passage of a $19.5 billion stimulus package that was to get a floundering economy going again.[7] The package contained one redistributive program, $4 billion in unemployment benefits. Otherwise, it was chock-full of job training, transportation, and other developmental programs that seemed to be the beginnings of Reich's investment plan.

The stimulus package was only a warm-up for the main event. In the long-term economic plan sent to Congress, Clinton proposed an additional $160 billion in new spending over the next four years, much of it for transportation facilities, including highway construction, mass transit, high-speed rail links, and improvements at aging airports.[8] To Reich and others who had helped write *Putting People First*, these proposals constituted the core of the Clinton administration's economic philosophy. Clinton himself was reported as saying, "If I do too little investment, then some other candidate won the election, not me."[9]

Reich had every reason to expect that Clinton's stimulus and investment proposals would sail through Congress. They had none of the political costs associated with the president's proposed tax increases. The monies could be ladled out as pork by senators and representatives eager to get credit for new projects. Both Republican and Democratic constituencies would benefit from the dollars to be spent.

No one outside the administration knew Rivlin's opinions on these matters (unless they had read her book). Even Robert Woodward's inside account of the early days of the Clinton administration was unable to tease them out.[10] She seemed to have swallowed both her ideas and pride—or else had the political acumen to keep her mouth shut.

Reich's influence peaked with the February 1993 economic message to Congress. In the months to come, his ideas were reduced from the flagship of the Clinton economic package to a tiny tugboat. The stimulus package was the first to go. Data released soon after Clinton's budgetary address indicated that the economy in the fourth quarter of 1992 was growing at an astounding 4.2 percent rate. Why was a further stimulus needed? Congressional hearings on the stimulus package revealed that some of the so-called investment money was to go for line drawings of historic buildings, grandstands for the canoeing course at the 1996 summer Olympics, warming huts at skating rinks, and gambling casinos on Indian reservations.[11] In what way were these projects an investment in the country's future?

Declaring the stimulus package to be nothing more than a vast new pork barrel scheme, Senate Republicans united in opposition. Knowing that the Democrats did not have the sixty votes needed to shut off Senate debate, Republicans felt they had a good enough argument to justify a filibuster that could put the new administration's entire legislative agenda off schedule. After a couple of futile attempts to shut off debate, the Senate leadership abandoned its efforts to pass the bill. Only the stimulus package's most prominent redistributive component—the $4 billion in unemployment benefits—was voted into law.

No sooner did Congress dismiss the stimulus package than it gutted half of the investment program in Clinton's main budget. The squeeze on investments came from the administration's commitment to cutting the nation's budget deficit by $500 billion over the next five years. This commitment was strongly recommended by Panetta, Rivlin, and officials at the Federal Reserve, all of whom thought that the best stimulus for the economy was a reduction in long-term interest rates (which a deficit reduction was expected to help bring about). To reduce the deficit, taxes were to be increased and existing programs cut. If the $160 billion investment package was enacted at the same time the deficit was being reduced, still more new taxes would have to be levied or still other programs would have to be cut. Balking at deep cuts in existing programs and hesitant to pass a new tax on energy, Congress decided the $500 billion deficit reduction could be achieved only by dropping most of the investment strategy.

If Reich was disappointed, OMB officials Panetta and Rivlin could hardly have been more pleased. The president's pledge to cut the deficit by $500 billion over the next five years survived months of congressional maneuvering (which ended with passage by a single vote in both the House and Senate). Interest rates fell. The economy recovered. In the first year the deficit fell by $50 billion more than projected.[12] A few months later, Panetta was asked to become the chief of staff of the White House. Rivlin was promoted to Panetta's job as OMB director, the very position for which she had been passed over eighteen months earlier. Reich concentrated on his work in the Department of Labor. Fine oaks replaced mornin' glories.

One can see this as a story of personal and political intrigue within an administration committed to diverse, inconsistent goals. Or one can see the story as an illustration of the way the logic of functional federalism currently shapes American public policy, even to the point of affecting the roles played by particular individuals espousing contrasting policy alternatives. Constrained by fiscal and economic realities, and facing aggressive partisan opposition, the Clinton administration was forced to sort through its priorities until it found a policy choice that was politically and economically satisfying. When push came to shove, the public investment strategy highly touted in Clinton's political campaign simply could not be sustained. As a consequence, the national government did not get involved in activities that functional federalism says are more properly carried out at the state and local level.

The Future of Redistributive Policy

The Clinton administration is not the first to feel the logic of functional federalism. Just as President Clinton discovered he could not pursue a national development strategy, so President Reagan found out that he could not shift redistributive policy to state and local governments. In 1982 the Reagan administration proposed handing over to the states complete fiscal responsibility for welfare policy (in exchange for national fiscal control over medicaid policy). When that proposal failed to win either congressional or gubernatorial support, the administration issued a report in 1986 that urged greater state control of welfare policy, arguing that "our centralized welfare system contribute[s] significantly to the persistence of poverty in America." It specifically recommended "legislation that would waive federal welfare rules in order to allow states and communities to experiment."[13] But within two years President Reagan signed a law that further centralized the welfare system. Although the Family Support Act of 1988 allowed states to engage in some experimentation (see chapter 5), it also imposed new requirements on states, telling them for the first time that they must withhold court-ordered child support payments from the wages of absent parents, provide benefits to needy two-person families for at least six months a year, establish work and training programs, and provide financial assistance to ease the transition to work.[14] Just as Bill Clinton was unable to force the national government to assume additional developmental responsibilities, Ronald Reagan was unable to shift redistributive responsibilities downward to states and localities.

In 1995, the country is witnessing still another attempt to defy the logic of functional federalism. A Republican majority controls both houses of Congress, and Republican legislative leaders are proposing a broad range of policy initiatives that, if enacted, could significantly change the structure of American federalism. Some Republican proposals—to give back to the states responsibility for transportation, job training, education, crime control, and other development policies—are quite consistent with the recommendations I make in the pages below. Many of these proposals are winning support within the Clinton administration. If partisan bickering can be put to one side, it is entirely possible that some version of these proposals will be enacted and American federalism will continue to shift in the functional direction it has been moving in the last couple of decades.

But in addition to decentralizing development policy, Republican leaders have also proposed delegating to the states responsibility for a broad range of redistributive policies. The House approved legislation in the spring of 1995 eliminating AFDC entitlements and a number of other programs for low-income groups. In their place, legislation gives each state a block grant equal to the amount of money the state received in the 1994 fiscal year. The terms of the block grant allow each state to set—within certain guidelines—its own eligibility standards and benefit levels.[15] The amount of money a state will receive under the legislation is fixed. It will not, as at present, increase or decrease, depending on the number of welfare recipients.

From the perspective of legislative theory, such policy proposals make political sense. National politicians can get credit for cutting government expenditure and avoid being blamed for ineffective poverty programs that help those who seem undeserving. The problems of meeting the genuine needs of the poor and unfortunate are left to governors, mayors, and other state and local officials. Legislative theory predicted accurately the rapid growth of national developmental programs at a time when the political costs to fiscal expansion were relatively small (see chapter 3). Legislative theory may now help to explain an equally dramatic change in the opposite direction: a shift of redistributive responsibilities from national to local governments.

Two inexorable forces are currently creating powerful political pressures to reduce the size of almost all national programs, whether developmental or redistributive, and whatever their quality or worth. First, tax indexation enacted in 1981 eliminated the possibility of invisible tax increases. Yet national politicians periodically need to appease voters by enacting highly visible tax cuts. In the 1950s and 1960s the tax cuts were more symbolic than real, because they simply offset invisible tax increases.[16] But the tax cuts of the 1980s and 1990s have been and will continue to be real cuts, not the figurative ones of yesteryear. Second, the costs of social security and medicare have continued to mount because more people are entering their retirement years, senior citizens are living longer, and real benefits have continued to rise. Despite rising costs, the political support for these programs is so widespread among retirees (and the soon-to-be-retired) that neither party is willing to propose more than token modifications. In his 1995 call for new spending cuts, for example, President Clinton explicitly ruled out making any changes in medicare or social security. The Republican Contract with America actually favors their expansion.

Tax cuts and the rising costs of senior citizen entitlements have up until very recently been financed in three different ways, none of which is likely to be politically viable in the foreseeable future. First, they were financed by increasing the federal deficit. Following the tax cut of 1981, deficits rose from less than 2 percent to over 5 percent of GNP. But as deficit spending sailed through the roof, driving up private-sector interest rates, Bush and Clinton signed into law politically costly tax increases that brought fiscal deficits down to a manageable size. Both President Clinton and Senate Republican leaders have expressed strong opposition to deficit spending on the scale reached during the 1980s. An amendment to the Constitution requiring a balanced budget passed the House and came within a single vote of passing the Senate in early 1995. Major increases in the size of the deficit no longer seem politically viable.

Second, defense spending was cut from nearly 7 percent of GNP in 1986 to less than 4 percent of GNP in 1994. By making deep cuts in defense, the Clinton administration was able to reduce the deficit while keeping intact social security, medicare, and most other domestic programs. But the easy cuts in defense have now been made; further reductions will be small. If Republicans in Congress have their way, defense spending is slated to increase.

Third, developmental programs have been sharply curtailed. Targets of these cuts have included programs operated directly by the national government and those funded by intergovernmental grants. Carter began the pruning, Reagan slashed more deeply, and Clinton has said he wants to carve even more. Applauding Clinton's new proposals, the new Republican leadership in Congress wishes to go even further. With bipartisan support ensured, further diminution of the national government's role in the making of development policy has become virtually certain.

Many of these reductions in developmental programs are exactly what functional theory recommends. But however desirable they remain, they cannot generate the additional savings needed to finance anything more than token tax cuts. Developmental programs have already been slashed almost to the bone. Not enough money is left to cover the seemingly insatiable demand for both tax cuts and senior citizen entitlement programs.

With all other options disappearing, it is politically tempting to finance tax cuts by turning over to the states many of the social programs (other than senior citizen entitlements) that have become the responsibility of the national government. If legislative theory is once again becoming applicable to national politics, that is what can be expected in the next few years. To win reelection, members of Congress will try to shift blame by giving states the job of helping the poor. But if functional theory is correct, such blame shifting will be limited in scale and difficult to enact. Interest groups defending the poor and the needy will accuse Republicans of destroying the nation's safety net. States and local officials will fight hard against unfunded mandates. Democrats will delay and filibuster Republican proposals. President Clinton can be expected both to threaten and, perhaps, to employ, his veto power. All in all, it is my (perhaps reckless) prediction that any legislation that dramatically shifts the responsibility for welfare downward to states, cities, and towns will prove unworkable and short-lived, simply because such shifts run at odds with the underlying structure of the federal system. If I am wrong and welfare policy is permanently turned over to the states, the well-being of the most marginal members of society, including large numbers of children living in poverty, will be adversely affected in serious ways.

Stability and Change in American Federalism

Unless Republican leaders prove more successful in pursuing their plan for turning social policy over to the states than past experience leads one to anticipate, American federalism will continue to evolve in the direction expected by functional theory. The national government will continue to assume custody for the country's redistributive efforts, and state and local governments will continue to shoulder the burden of facilitating economic development. Efforts to shift burdens or to invade the area of competence by either side will encounter strong resistance.

This does not mean that the national government will no longer concoct new ways of distributing pork. Political storms can readily produce strange policies. Senator Edward Kennedy, facing a serious reelection challenge in 1994, told his Massachusetts constituents that, as a consequence of his intervention with administration officials, an air force laboratory scheduled for closure would be kept in the budget for the 1996 fiscal year.[17] Earlier that fall, a majority of Congress voted for a crime bill that gave federal dollars to state and local governments to help pay policemen, build prisons, run recreational programs, and do many other things that can be accomplished more readily by lower tiers of government. The temptation to pass popular legislation, no matter how inappropriate and unnecessary, will remain a basic feature of American politics.

But if the political weather varies from day to day, a climatic shift has been slowly occurring in American federalism. It is more difficult for members of Congress to find things for which they can claim credit, and pork-laden crime bills now only squeak by an increasingly budget-minded Congress. Daniel Patrick Moynihan, the powerful head of the Senate Finance Committee until 1995, has also found it difficult to capture pork in recent years. Committed to building a new Pennsylvania Railroad station in New York City, he was able to get money authorized for this purpose slipped into irrelevant legislation providing relief for those suffering from the Los Angeles earthquake. But the House of Representatives failed to appropriate a dime for the station. Said a Republican representative from Virginia, "We know this is wrong, and we know what's happening." A Democrat from New York City admitted that the odds in the House were overwhelmingly against him: "Pork has a bad name."[18] Even the pork-laden crime bill did not survive intact. No sooner did the Republicans capture control of Congress than leaders vowed to cut back a sizable chunk of the appropriations authorized under the crime bill.

The climatic alteration has not altogether transformed the federalist terrain, however. Mountains and valleys can remain in place long after the glaciers have receded. Many of the remnants of an older system of federalism remain well entrenched.

Many of the stable elements in the federal system are clearly identified by legislative theory. Legislators in a federal system seldom use their authority to shift resources from rich places to poor ones. Such reallocations of wealth fail to pass Congress or state legislatures because legislators from the better-off places cannot justify taxing their own constituents for the benefit of those living elsewhere. To secure reelection, they must do what is best for their own constituents, however mean-spirited this may seem. Geographic inequities will not disappear as the result of actions taken by legislators at higher levels of government.

Legislative theory also helps to explain why big cities of the Rust Belt suffer fiscal deficits, population losses, and economic decline. These cities once controlled the most valuable land in their regions. They enjoyed a quasi-monopoly, which gave them taxable resources greater than those available to more economically constrained local governments. It was in these places that politics was first professionalized. The Tammany Hall that produced the insightful wit of machine politician George Washington Plunkitt was but one of dozens of political alliances that turned a natural monopoly into a political treasure.

Most of these machines were built in the nineteenth century, but a style of politics in which political leaders are responsive to well-organized groups and special interests has continued into the late twentieth. Political responsiveness to group pressures remains the norm even when traditional sources of patronage have disappeared. In place of the ward heeler, one finds the union boss and the municipal employee's representative. In place of graft and corruption, one finds cumbersome, inefficient bureaucracies. In place of the need to find jobs for aunts and cousins, there are demands to hire still more police and fire officers. In place of handouts to the poor, there are demands to preserve community hospitals, AIDS programs, drug abuse centers, and shelters for the homeless. Since politics remains professionalized, leaders do their best to accommodate many of these and other demands placed upon them.

Legislative theory also helps to account for some of the short-term fluctuations in the shape of American federalism. It explains the rapid rise of developmental spending in the 1970s, and it may be successful in predicting a round of redistributive burden shifting that could take place in the late 1990s.

If legislative theory identifies forces that produce short-term fluctuations in the federal system, functional theory does a better job of explaining longer-term changes in the general climate. According to this theory, the federal system has evolved in response to changes in the nation's economy. Each level of government has assumed a distinctive set of responsibilities. The economic changes that created these distinctions are likely to perpetuate them. Capital and labor are more mobile now than ever before. Migration and immigration are spiraling. Competition is intensifying. Quasi-monopolies are eroding. Traditional ways of doing things are necessarily called into question.

The results of these changes are threefold. First, state and local governments are becoming ever more reluctant to provide for the needy within their ranks. These governments' idea of welfare reform is to eliminate benefits and impose new requirements. Second, the national government is becoming increasingly reluctant to distribute pork, bail state and local governments out of their fiscal difficulties, or take charge of tasks that are a local obligation. During the heyday of cooperative federalism, policymakers deluded themselves into thinking that any and all levels of government could address any and all problems. Since bracket creep gave the national government extra dollars to spend, it was easy to pass the money along to state and local officials. But with tax indexation and the rising cost of services for senior citizens, the national government has enough difficulty financing just those burdens for which it must bear the cost. The extra dollars are much harder to find. Third, without federal largesse to help them out, big cities, especially the older cities of the Rust Belt, are increasingly under pressure to reorganize their services to become more cost effective. They are losing the quasi-monopoly they once enjoyed. Business activity is relocating to the suburbs, the Sun Belt, and Latin America. Whether the cities can adapt to the new realities quickly enough remains to be seen.

The shift in the climate of American federalism is likely to continue. President Nixon proposed simplification of federal programs but endorsed sharing national revenues with state and local governments. The

National Governors Association called for a reduction in national mandates. Of all the proposals, the most thoughtful was made in 1986 by the Committee on Federalism and National Purpose, chaired by two former governors, former Republican Senator Daniel Evans of Washington and Democratic Senator Charles Robb of Virginia. They called for a simplification of the federal system by working toward "a greater separation of responsibilities" among governments. They recommended that the national government should assume greater responsibility for health care and welfare policy while disengaging its involvement in most other policy arenas.[19]

In making policy recommendations, the first rule must be to strive vigorously not to do harm. Much in the existing federal system deserves respect. The path the federal system is taking is basically sound. It is not a matter of overhauling or reversing the fundamental direction in which the system is moving. The system only needs to be updated and fine-tuned. The second rule is to recognize underlying political realities that preclude certain kinds of changes, however desirable these changes may be. These political realities require that the country pay a certain price for the federal system it has inherited. One may regret the price without feeling compelled to try to avoid the charge. After all, the price paid may be less than the cost of any likely alternative. But if there are many things that should not be changed, and many other things that cannot be changed, there are still some things that might well be changed in due course. If the task is approached intelligently, it may be possible to continue to reduce the price of federalism.

Things That Should Not Be Changed

The contemporary shape of American federalism conforms in most respects to functional theory's normative prescriptions. The national government assumes the bulk of the responsibility for income redistribution through pensions, welfare, health care, and other programs aimed at the needy, the sick, the disabled, and the disadvantaged. The national government's role in redistribution has become increasingly prominent, though it is possible that this general direction could be reversed by the new Republican Congress. If Congress succeeds in decentralizing control over AFDC, food stamps, and other social programs, it will redirect American federalism away from the path that it has long been following.

Although proposals for dramatic change have been included in the Republican "Contract with America," it is by no means certain that the contract will be signed, sealed, and delivered, if for no other reason than the increasing reluctance of state and local officials to pay for the cost of social policy. Welfare benefits have been cut. AFDC benefits have been reduced. State general assistance programs have all but disappeared. State supplementary benefits to the long-term unemployed and to disabled persons have been virtually eliminated (even while federal benefits have kept pace with increases in the cost of living).[20]

Intensified state and local opposition to redistribution is understandable in an economy that has become increasingly integrated and a society that has become ever more mobile. States and localities can no longer make policy choices as if they were living in isolation from other parts of the country. The decisions they take are noticed by people elsewhere, and the impact on their economic and fiscal situation will be felt sooner rather than later. One may regret that states and localities no longer seem capable of caring for their sick and needy, but it is a price a federal system must pay in an ever more integrated society.

Because states and localities are unequipped to finance social welfare programs, they should not be given the job of welfare reform. Those trying to defend welfare cuts from budget slashers in Washington may be tempted to accept state control of welfare policy in exchange for smaller cuts in expenditure. However sensible this may seem in the short run, serious long-term costs are likely to accompany any shift in the responsibility for welfare policy to state governments. The more states talk about reforming welfare, the more cuts they make. The fear of becoming a welfare magnet is accelerating. One fears a race to the bottom as each state tries to become the least attractive place for poor people to live. Massachusetts has reported that welfare recipients are already leaving the state in response to cuts enacted in the spring of 1995.[21] The state of Wisconsin reported in the summer of 1994 that about 20 percent of new AFDC applicants in Milwaukee County were new residents, many arriving from Illinois, a state with lower welfare benefits. To respond to these pressures, Wisconsin asked the national government for permission to try an experiment in which recent migrants would, for six months only, receive a level of benefits equal to that of the state from which they were migrating. In the past the courts have declared such discriminatory treatment of newcomers as unconstitutional, but the Supreme Court announced in the fall of 1994 that it would be willing to revisit this issue (though the case under consideration may become moot).[22] If discrimination against newcomers to a state is given constitutional blessing, a new round of state welfare cuts can be anticipated.

Functional theory recommends a modest role for the national government in the making of developmental policy.[23] The national government has few market signals to help it choose among alternative developmental proposals. Without these market signals, development policy readily degenerates into pork. State and local governments have more direct ways of gauging the effects of their policy choices. If states and localities err, their choices will not be copied by competitors. If they choose developmental policies wisely, their selections will be observed by other state and local officials and will disseminate throughout the federal system.

This does not mean that the national government should play no role in developmental policy. Some developmental policies (such as investment in scientific research) have such broad and far-reaching consequences that they must be carried out by the national government. Other developmental policies (such as the design of certain components of the communication and transportation system) must be coordinated at the national level in order to achieve a desired degree of national integration. Still other developmental aid to states and localities is desirable insofar as it enables the national government to ameliorate the adverse environmental effects of economic development. But if the national role in economic development should not be eliminated altogether, neither should it be unduly expanded. If anything, it should be allowed to dwindle, much as both President Clinton and Republican leaders recommended in early 1995.

Clinton's proposals only extend a trend that has become increasingly well established. Under the pressure of fiscal deficits, antitax pressures, and senior citizen entitlements, the national government has pulled back from the financing of developmental projects. Although President-elect Clinton promised to reverse that trend, President-in-office Clinton has wisely chosen to subordinate this goal to other, more worthwhile objectives.

Although developmental programs should be trimmed, care should be taken before accompanying national mandates are stripped from remaining grants. In early 1995 Congress passed a law banning the imposition of any additional unfunded federal mandates on state and local authorities. The long-term effect of this legislation remains unclear, but if interpreted strictly it could cause considerable mischief. If national mandates are deleted from developmental grants, then (unless they reduce fiscal disparities) there is hardly any justification for a national grant. Put more strongly: a national grant should be made only when it is necessary to encourage state and local governments to co-operate in order to achieve some broader national objective, such as the reduction of environmental pollution or the achievement of a more coordinated transportation system. There is no reason why Congress should not fund mandates it thinks necessary, but a law banning any and all unfunded federal mandates could limit Congress's capacity to coordinate policy among the states.

Things That Cannot Be Changed

Even if the national government concentrates on redistribution while state and local governments provide the physical and social infrastructure necessary for economic development, federalism commands a certain price. The most obvious price has to do with the fiscal inequalities among states and localities. People have segregated themselves into towns, cities, and neighborhoods according to their income, and, as a result, these places differ in their taxable resources, their tax effort, and the amount they spend on both economic development and redistribution.

One should not exaggerate the extent of fiscal disparity among state and local governments. Geographical stratification by income is much lower than racial and ethnic segregation. Indices of racial isolation in metropolitan areas vary between 60 and 80 (on a 100-point scale), depending on the size and age of the city. Indices of income segregation are about half as large.[24] Still, the taxable resources of cities, towns, and states vary considerably, and the degree of variation has not diminished much over time (see chapter 4). The federal system is going to suffer from fiscal disparities for decades to come.

Placing a normative price on fiscal disparity is more easily said than done. Some have argued that every state and local governmental jurisdiction should have the same taxable resources and the same tax effort so that all citizens may have equal access to all public goods, whether these be schools, roads, sanitation facilities, or police and fire protection. This argument is made by those who are quite willing to accept considerable inequality in the private sector, permitting great variation in access to food, shelter, clothing, and many other essentials. This demand for equality in the provision of public services (while accepting extreme variation in access to the private marketplace) is more often assumed than justified.

Another way of thinking about the issue is to say that any modern industrial society will wish to provide for at least some redistribution among social groups. The exact degree of redistribution depends on a country's level of economic development and the cost of further redistribution to both individual liberties and continued economic development. There is no single best solution. The choices are best made at the national level through a political process in which all citizens have an opportunity to influence policy choices. If the national government addresses the question of redistribution, then fiscal disparities in public services will be roughly proportionate to other inequalities. By not insisting on uniform public services, a society can preserve the efficiency that comes from a multiplicity of state and local decisionmakers.

A society may decide that it wishes to achieve more equality in the public sector than the private sector. It may think that it is more important that citizens have equal access to schools, police security, fire protection, and other public services than equal access to food, clothes, housing, and other goals ordinarily provided by the marketplace. Alice Rivlin, for example, accepts as inevitable the inequality generated by the market. Yet she recommends that nationally collected revenues be used to reduce fiscal disparities among states and localities by targeting such revenues toward those state and local governments with the fewest resources.[25]

The case for public-sector equality is the most persuasive when it comes to education. The United States has long prided itself on providing its citizens equality of opportunity, if not equality of result. Disparities of income and wealth in the United States have frequently been justified on the grounds that the country at least ensures equality of opportunity. But if all people are to have the same opportunities for economic success, then they must be given the wherewithal in early life to make the best use of their abilities. Differences in family resources should not be translated into differences in access to good schools. Every local district should have the same fiscal resources so as to be able to provide all students with the same learning opportunities. Not surprisingly, this issue has been subject to a great deal of litigation. The Supreme Court rejected the argument that equal educational expenditure within a state was required to provide citizens with equal protection before the law, as required by the Fourteenth Amendment.[26] But many state courts have found in state constitutions a rule demanding equality of per pupil expenditure among the communities within the state. However, despite some progress toward equity in some states, it has usually been difficult to get state legislatures to implement court decisions or to otherwise reduce fiscal disparity among their states' towns and cities.[27] In Massachusetts, for example, no sooner did the state pass a fiscal reform bill helping poor school districts than leaders from wealthy suburban communities tried to revise it once again. The leader of the interest group formed to promote their cause pointed out that suburban school officials "feel they are sliding toward a level of education that is way below the expectation of their own communities because of the funding formulas."[28]

Court-mandated equalization of local fiscal resources might be one way of reducing the price of federalism. But courts have become increasingly reluctant to accept new social burdens. In the meantime, both members of Congress and members of state legislatures will find it difficult to vote for laws that shift resources from one geographical area to the next. Legislators are elected to bring home their fair share of the bacon. Asking legislators to give up pork for themselves while giving it to competing states and localities is asking them to commit political suicide. Because of these kinds of electoral constraints, Congress has not concentrated its funding on needy states and localities. On the contrary, states with higher tax capacity receive more national dollars. The pattern is unlikely to change in any substantial way as long as Congress allocates grants, parties are decentralized, and members of Congress seek to represent the constituencies that elect them.

Things That Can and Should Be Changed

If some warts on the American federal system cannot be wished away, others deserve treatment. Indeed, under certain political circumstances, changes could well be introduced. This is not the place to discuss in detail major policy initiatives. I shall only mention briefly the aspects of the federal system where reform efforts should be concentrated.

The national government should continue to assume increasing responsibility for financing and setting the standards for redistributive policy. Efforts to redress inequities in the provision of medical services should continue. Any effective national health policy needs to be designed so as to limit state discretion and thus ensure essentially equivalent programs throughout the country. Otherwise, states will be tempted to shift their health costs to competing jurisdictions.

Welfare policy, too, needs to be determined at the national level. The best welfare program would include substantial child allowances and tax credits for all low- and moderate-income families so that families no longer need to be asked to make the choice between work and welfare. As the number of single-parent families continues to rise and as more women enter the labor force, often at poverty-level wages, the need for supplemental family allowances continues to rise. As a first step toward this goal, Congress, at the prompting of the Clinton administration, enacted in 1993 a substantial expansion of the earned income tax credit that provides significant new monies to the working poor. Clinton moved further in this direction in 1995 with his recommendation to give a $500 tax credit to every moderate-income family with a child under the age of twelve. Further steps along these lines need to be far-reaching enough to substitute entirely for the existing program of aid to families with dependent children. If this goal cannot be achieved, then expansions of welfare assistance at the national level need to be accompanied by tightened federal control over AFDC so that states do not continue to cut welfare benefits.

These changes in health and welfare policy may or may not be politically feasible in the mid-1990s. But nothing in the constitutional design of the federal system precludes their enactment at any time political forces are appropriately aligned. Since many other industrial democracies have both national health insurance and a national system of family allowances, it can still be hoped that the United States will eventually move in this direction.

The national government should also continue to wind down its allocation of developmental pork among states and localities. Pressures to expand the amount of developmental pork beyond what is reasonable are omnipresent. Whenever a national problem arises, presidents are expected to respond, and the easiest way to do so is to propose a new round of grants to state and local governments. If student test scores decline, the president asks for more money for schools. If crime rates (or television reports of crime) rise, then the president asks for more money for police and prisons. If drug use becomes prevalent, a national war on drugs is declared. If roadways or airports become congested, the transportation budget is enlarged.

Some may think that developmental pork is one of those aspects of American federalism that cannot be changed. Presidents need to propose solutions to real or imagined problems. Members of Congress have every incentive to go along with popular presidential proposals. But as the story of the Clinton stimulus package illustrates, the day of developmental pork may have passed. Congress can no longer allocate more pork without increasing taxes, hiking the deficit, or cutting other popular governmental programs. Developmental pork, instead of being a congressional staple, may well become an increasingly rare delicacy.

The greatest challenge to American federalism is posed by the social, economic, and political decline of big central cities in the northeastern and midwestern Rust Belt. It may be that this decline is one of the costs of American federalism that must simply be accepted. Technological innovation will continue to undermine the monopoly older central cities traditionally enjoyed over crucial nodes in the transportation and communication system. As new businesses and prosperous residents continue to migrate to the fringes of metropolitan areas and new parts of the country, older cities, stuck with decaying infrastructure, inevitably stagnate and decline. As long as the United States is a large, thinly populated country, land values will be low enough to entice economic activity away from places suffering from congestion and diseconomies of scale.

The propensity of poor minorities to concentrate in central cities may also be an inevitable part of the American federal system—at least as long as poverty persists and remains disproportionately concentrated among people of color. As the housing stock ages, it declines in value, making it available to people of lower income. Since central cities have a disproportionate share of older, lower-priced housing stock, they necessarily attract low-income tenants. This propensity is aggravated by suburban restrictions on land use that ensure that most new housing stock is directed toward the middle and upper ends of the housing market. Federal programs that require racial and economic integration of suburban areas have been notoriously unsuccessful in achieving their objectives.[29]

The fiscal problems of older central cities of the Rust Belt may also be unavoidable. When these cities enjoyed a quasi-monopoly over valuable land, they took on a broader range of social responsibilities than other local governments. They also conceded benefits to their municipal employees that are difficult to retract. As a result, big cities of the Rust Belt provide public services less efficiently than do other local governments. Such public-sector inefficiency further contributes to central-city decline.

Neither the states nor the national government is likely to assume the fiscal burdens central cities in the Rust Belt have acquired. When allocating aid, states in the Rust Belt no longer systematically discriminate against central cities. Neither does the national government. But neither level of government is likely to take on major new fiscal responsibilities. Big cities must solve their own fiscal problems. They cannot expect another level of government to do the job for them.[30]

The most viable, if still extremely controversial, alternative still available to cities is for them to give the private sector as much responsibility as possible for the delivery of central-city services. Public-sector delivery has become burdened by political and contractual obligations to organized groups. Threats of strikes in big cities are particularly effective because of the large-scale disruption that can occur and the near impossibility of finding replacement workers. Older big cities need to take strong steps to realize the efficiencies necessary to make them competitive with suburbs, towns, and newer cities. The solution may well require private-sector delivery of publicly financed services.

Education is the area in which such a solution offers the greatest promise. For most cities, education constitutes at least a third of the municipal budget. Over the past decade per pupil expenditures have been steadily rising, yet the quality of services provided to students may well have deteriorated. Big-city school bureaucracies are notoriously cumbersome and inefficient. Teacher organizations are extremely well organized. They drive up labor costs and complicate the introduction of innovative approaches. As middle-class white families have left central-city schools for the suburbs or for the private sector, central-city schools have becoming increasingly segregated.[31]

Despite the extraordinarily desperate state of big-city schools, they, too, may have to be accepted as simply another particularly large and ugly stain on American federalism. Teacher organizations, eager to protect the privileges they have won for their members, are unequivocally opposed to proposals that would give families a voucher that they could use to pay for their child's education in any public or private school the family chooses. Public school officials argue that tuition vouchers would divide the nation into competing religious, racial, and ethnic cliques, intensifying racial segregation. They claim it would limit access of low-income children to good schools, aggravating educational inequality. They denounce such plans as schemes to destroy publicly financed education altogether. Public school advocates even refuse to subject their propositions to an empirical test by opposing any pilot tuition voucher plan.

Up until now, most black leaders and most civil rights organizations have agreed with teacher organizations that tuition voucher plans would have these deleterious consequences. But this unity may not prevail over the long run. If big-city school systems continue to decline, new leaders may begin to propose alternatives to the urban public school system. Already, central-city minority families are more likely than any other group to favor a plan that would allow them to choose between public and private schools.[32] Despite the opposition of well-financed, entrenched interests, minority leaders may eventually be tempted to capitalize on the widespread discontent with education in the big cities.

On the whole, the problems of American federalism have been greatly exaggerated. The state and local fiscal crises caused by the 1991 recession now seem to be temporary phenomena, not a harbinger of a torturous future. The national government is at least for the moment concentrating more on what it does best: caring for the sick, the poor, and the needy. State and local governments continue to foster the country's economic development. National and state aid programs could be designed more equitably, but the inequity cannot be erased without undermining local governments' capacity to foster economic development.

Were it not for two considerations, my story of modern federalism would have a quite satisfactory conclusion. First, there is a new threat to the national redistributive role. Some national political leaders may have discovered a political advantage to sloughing off the responsibility for unpopular redistribution to state and local governments. It remains to be seen how ominous and enduring this threat will prove to be. Second, and just as serious, is the inability of most big-city governments to find a way to provide efficient, humane public services for their residents. It is the lives of the minority poor isolated in our central cities that haunt the ending of this otherwise happy tale.

Appendix

Expenditures

The expenditures that I show for each level of government are only those expenditures paid for from their own fiscal resources. To calculate government expenditures in this way, I followed a complex set of procedures to avoid including officially reported expenditures by states and localities of monies provided them by higher levels of government. These procedures were, with minor exceptions, the same as those followed in Peterson (1979). Redistributive expenditures are the same here as the expenditures classified as redistributive in that study. Because redistributive and developmental are treated here as mutually exclusive and exhaustive categories of domestic expenditure, my definition of development is more inclusive in this book than in the prior study. Expenditures classified as developmental include those classified in the prior study as housekeeping, development, education, and other.

I used the following equation to calculate state government expenditures from their own fiscal resources: $EOR_s = TE_s - FIT_s - LIT_s$, where TE_s equals total state expenditure, FIT_s equals federal intergovernmental transfers to states, and LIT_s equals local intergovernmental transfers to states. I assume that all state intergovernmental transfers for housekeeping were spent by localities, and that all federal intergovernmental transfers for housekeeping were spent by the states. Similarly, $EOR_l = TE_l - FIT_l - SIT_l$, where TE_l equals total local expenditure, FIT_l equals federal intergovernmental transfers to localities, and SIT_l equals state intergovernmental transfers to localities. I assume that federal spending from own resources (EOR_f) is equal to total federal expenditure minus defense spending, space research, and interest on the debt. General local support was treated as a state transfer to local government and included in all categories of state expenditure proportionately.

197

Note that the state data used in chapter 4 do not include utility expenditures. There is one minor difference between the procedures used in my prior study and those used here to calculate sources of revenue for each level of government. The "other" category in the earlier study was added to the "user and miscellaneous taxes" category in table 2-1. Also, "other business taxes" includes severance taxes.

All data reported in figures come from U.S. Bureau of the Census, U.S. Census of Governments, *Compendium of Government Finances* (Department of Commerce, various years); and U.S. Bureau of the Census, *Government Finances in 1990–91*, series GF/90-5 (Department of Commerce, 1993).

Federal Aid Programs

The sources for all intergovernmental grant data were two Department of Commerce compilations of federal aid, *Federal Aid to the States* and *Federal Expenditures by States for Fiscal Year...* These sources listed all federal aid programs and the quantity of aid received by each state. The following list includes all programs I coded as either developmental or redistributive. Defense spending was omitted from the data set. Not all programs listed existed in each year in the data set.

Developmental Programs

Department of Agriculture: Agricultural Marketing Service; basic scientific research grants; Consumer and Marketing Service; cooperative agricultural extension work; cooperative projects in marketing; Cooperative State Research Service; Extension Service; Food Safety and Inspection Service; forest protection, utilization, and restoration; national forest and school funds; national grasslands; price support donations; removal of surplus agricultural commodities; resource conservation and development; rural community fire protection; rural development; rural water and waste disposal grants; state and private forestry; watershed protection.

Department of Commerce: development facilities grant; economic development center and community assistance; National Telecommunications and Information Administration; payments to states under Federal Power Act; planning and research; state technical services.

Environmental Protection Agency: construction of waste water treatment works.

Federal Emergency Management Agency: emergency planning, preparedness, and mitigation.

Funds appropriated to the president: accelerated public works program; Appalachian regional development program.

Department of Health, Education, and Welfare/Department of Health and Human Services/Department of Education: art, humanities, and educational broadcasting activities; colleges of agricultural and the mechanical arts; elementary and secondary educational activities; educational research and improvement; higher educational facilities; libraries and community services; Office of Post Secondary Education; school improvement programs; school assistance in federally affected areas; Teacher Corps; air pollution; hospital, health, education and health research facilities.

Department of Housing and Urban Development: metropolitan development; urban planning assistance; urban renewal; urban transportation; water and sewer facilities.

Department of the Interior: abandoned mine reclamation; certain special funds; commercial fisheries research and development; fish and wildlife restoration; land and water conservation fund; Mineral Leasing Act payments; national wildlife refuge fund; payments in lieu of taxes; preservation of historic properties; regulation and technology; waste treatment works construction; water supply and pollution control; water resources research.

Department of Justice: federal prison system; law enforcement assistance; legal services-assets forfeiture fund; Office of Justice Assistance.

Department of Labor: classroom instruction; Mine Safety and Health Administration; Occupational Safety and Health Administration; training allowances.

National Foundation on the Arts and Humanities

Tennessee Valley Authority: shared revenues.

Department of Transportation: Coast Guard; federal airport program; airport and airway trust fund; Federal Highway Administration; Federal Railroad Administration; forest and public land highways; highway safety; highway trust fund; interstate transfer grants; landscaping and scenic enhancement; motor carrier safety grants; National Highway Traffic Safety Administration; Urban Mass Transportation Administration; Water Resources Council.

Department of the Treasury: Customs Bureau and IRS refunds.

Redistributive Programs

Department of Agriculture: child nutrition programs; child distributions; community distributions; food donations; food stamp program;

mutual and self-help housing; school milk program; special milk program; special supplemental food program (WIC); temporary emergency food assistance.

Department of Commerce: job opportunities program.

Funds appropriated to the president: disaster relief; adult work training and development; community action programs; neighborhood youth corps; work experience and training.

Department of Education: bilingual education and minority language affairs; compensatory education for disadvantaged; Indian education; special programs and populations; Office of Special Education and Rehabilitative Services.

Equal Employment Opportunity Commission

Federal Emergency Management Agency: disaster relief.

Department of Health, Education, and Welfare/Department of Health and Human Services: Administration on Aging; aid for dependent children; alcohol, drug abuse, and mental health; American Printing House for the Blind; assistance to public schools; cooperative vocational education; educational improvement for the handicapped; chronic disease; communicable disease activities; community health services; community service block grant; comprehensive health planning services; control of tuberculosis and venereal diseases; dental and nursing resources and services; health manpower education and utilization; health resources and services administration; human development services; low-income home energy assistance; medicaid; mental health research and services; maintenance payment grants; maternal and child health and welfare services; medical assistance grants; mental retardation; miscellaneous HEW programs; public assistance grants; refugee assistance; regional medical programs; rehabilitation services; schools in federally affected areas; social services block grant; social services training and demonstration projects; supplemental security income; urban, industrial, and radiological health; work incentive activities.

Department of Housing and Urban Development: fair housing assistance; housing payments (Section 8); low-income housing demonstration projects; low-rent housing operating assistance; low-rent public housing; model cities program; neighborhood facilities; open space land grants; public housing; rental housing rehabilitation and development; urban development action grants.

Department of the Interior: Bureau of Indian Affairs.

Department of Labor: Unemployment compensation.

Department of Treasury: general revenue sharing.
Veterans Administration

Description and Source of Variables

Density: State population divided by area, in tens of persons per square kilometer. U.S. Bureau of the Census, *Statistical Abstract of the United States*, various years.

Developmental aid: State per capita aid revenue for developmental programs (see above for list of programs). Department of the Treasury, *Federal Aid to States*, various years; U.S. Bureau of the Census, *Federal Expenditures by State for Fiscal Year. . .*, various years.

House committees: percentage of state delegation serving on committee. U.S. Congress, Joint Committee on Printing, *Congressional Directory*, various years.

Mean density: Each state's deviation from the mean density for all states for that year.

Population: State population, in hundreds of thousands. *Statistical Abstract*, various years.

Legislative salary: Annual salary of representatives elected to state legislature, in thousands of dollars. Council of State Governments, *The Book of the States* (Lexington, Ky.: Council of State Governments, various years).

Percent living in central cities: Percentage of state population residing in cities with populations over 100,000. U.S. Bureau of the Census, *City Government Finances*, GF Series, various years.

Percent Democrats in state legislature: Percentage of state legislature that is Democratic. Nebraska legislators are elected without party designation. Unofficial records of Nebraska legislators' affiliation were obtained from Professor Robert F. Sittig, University of Nebraska at Lincoln. Minnesota elected legislators without party designation in 1966 and 1968. For those years, Minnesota was set to the mean value of all states. *Statistical Abstract*, various years.

Percent minority: Nonwhite percentage of state population. *Statistical Abstract*, various years.

Poverty rate: *Statistical Abstract*, various years.

Redistributive aid: State per capita aid revenue for redistributive programs (see above for list of programs). *Federal Aid to States*; *Federal Expenditures by State for Fiscal Year. . .*, various years.

Rural: Percentage of state population residing outside 264 metropolitan statistical areas and 20 consolidated metropolitan statistical areas. *Statistical Abstract*, various years.

Senate committees: Number of members of state delegation serving on committee. *Congressional Directory*, various years.

Tax effort: Indexed measure of state rate of taxation. Tax effort is defined as the ratio of actual tax collection to a state's tax capacity. The index is the ratio between the state's tax effort and the average for all states. Advisory Commission on Intergovernmental Relations, *Significant Features of Fiscal Federalism* (Washington: ACIR, 1990).

Taxable resources: Indexed measure of state wealth. The index is the per capita tax capacity divided by the per capita average for all states. Per capita tax capacity is the amount of revenue a state would raise if it used a national average set of tax rates. *Significant Features of Fiscal Federalism*. Also see Advisory Commission on Intergovernmental Relations, *Tax Capacity of the 50 States: Methodology and Estimates* (Washington: ACIR, 1982).

Notes

Chapter 1

1. Bartlett (1980, p. 538).
2. Hayward (1993, p. 42).
3. Bartlett (1980, p. 698).
4. Robert Reinhold, "Nation's Land of Promise Enters an Era of Limits," *New York Times,* August 23, 1993, p. A12.
5. Paulson and others (1992, p. 426).
6. Hayward (1993, p. 42).
7. Richard D. Hylton, "It Will Get Worse in California" *Fortune*, April 19, 1993, pp. 71–81.
8. Robert Reinhold, "California's Fiscal Crisis Tests Government's Role," *New York Times,* April 3, 1991, p. A12.
9. Tax Foundation (1969, 1973, 1983, 1992); U.S. Bureau of the Census (1992, 1993b); Advisory Commission on Intergovernmental Relations (1992a, 1993).
10. Sam Howe Verhovek, "Growing Economy Produces Surplus in State Governments," *New York Times,* September 6, 1994, pp. A1, A15.
11. *Federalist* 51 (1951, p. 323).
12. Commager (1958, pp. 176–77).
13. Bailey (1956, p. 177).
14. Historians have focused on the personalities and political controversies surrounding the election of 1800 to the exclusion of a consideration of the military balance of power. Not much attention is given to what might have happened had the Federalists been able to establish the national army that Alexander Hamilton promoted. The absence of this army seems to me to be something like the "dog not barking in the night." Since the Federalists lacked the military power to prevent a Jeffersonian takeover, they never seriously considered doing so, despite deep misgivings. For a discussion of the debate over the national army, see Elkins and McKitrick (1993, pp. 714–19).
15. Greenstone (1993, chap. 3).
16. Bailey (1956, p. 261).
17. Skocpol (1992).
18. *United States* v. *E. C. Knight Co.*, 156 U.S. 1 (1895).
19. *Schechter Poultry Corp.* v. *United States*, 295 U.S. 495 (1935).

20. *Carter* v. *Carter Coal Co.*, 298 U.S. 238, 308 (1936).
21. *NLRB* v. *Jones & Laughlin Steel Co.*, 301 U.S. 1, 41 (1937).
22. *Wickard* v. *Filburn*, 317 U.S. 111 (1942).
23. *Massachusetts* v. *Mellon*, 262 U.S. 447 (1923).
24. *Hilvering* v. *Davis*, 301 U.S. 548, 599 (1937).
25. *South Dakota* v. *Dole*, 438 U.S. 203 (1987).
26. See table 3-1 in chapter 3.

Chapter 2

1. See, especially, Bartik (1991); Bish (1971); Brace (1993); Brown and Oates (1986); Burns (1994); Dye (1990); Ladd and Doolittle (1982); Miller (1981); Oates (1972); Peterson (1981); Peterson, Rabe, and Wong (1986); Peterson and Rom (1990); Rivlin (1992); Rose-Ackerman (1983); Stein (1990); Tiebout (1956).

The theories of federalism discussed here focus on domestic policy. I do not apply them to defense expenditure, mainly because national defense has been considered the sole responsibility of the national government since the Civil War. Whether national defense policy is better explained by legislative or functional theory depends on what one is trying to explain. The overall level of spending on national defense has probably varied more directly with the ups and downs of the cold war than with changes in legislative politics or the lobbying efforts of the defense industry. When the cold war was most intense, the United States spent well over 10 percent of GNP on defense (even during the period between the Korean and Vietnam Wars). After the end of the Vietnam War and the Helsinki agreement in 1975, defense expenditures fell to close to 5 percent of GNP, only to rise (beginning under Carter) after the Soviet invasion of Afghanistan to about 7 percent of GNP. After that invasion stagnated in the early 1980s, defense expenditure (as a percentage of GNP) fell once again—even under Reagan. In the 1990s, defense expenditures as a percentage of GNP continued to fall toward 3 percent, accounting for much of the decline in the size of the federal deficit. Peterson (forthcoming).

The location of defense facilities may be more significantly affected by congressional influence. Congress seems to be especially active in keeping military sites open after their useful life may have expired. But the location of defense facilities also depends on the physical attributes of geographical sites. Nuclear weapons test sites and intercontinental missiles must be placed far from population centers; navies must be located in coastal areas; fighters, bombers, and space research need dependable weather; and defense research is better located where highly educated personnel are available.

2. In a prior study I distinguished among three types of government policy: developmental, allocational, and redistributive. Peterson (1981). Developmental policy was limited to those policies that were self-consciously designed to enhance the economic well-being of a particular locality. Basic public services were regarded as allocational—neither developmental nor redistributive but somewhere in between.

I now find the simpler classification proposed here both more elegant and more satisfying. First, it takes into account the profound developmental consequences of the quality of basic services provided by state and local governments. A city without good schools, police, fire protection, and sanitation facilities has limited economic prospects, no matter how many tax concessions it may propose to potential business firms. Second, it makes clear my belief that residential amenities—parks, schools, recreational facilities—can be at least as important to the economic development of an area as industrial parks and shopping centers. Third, the empirical analyses that form the basis for the findings reported in chapters 4 and 6 found no important distinction between the determinants of developmental and allocational expenditure. Empirically as well as theoretically, the tripartite classification system seemed to have been drawing a distinction where there was little difference.

It has been argued that regulatory policy deserves to be classified as a separate category. In my view, this confuses a governmental tool or technique with a governmental purpose. Just as the purpose of fiscal policy may be either developmental or redistributive, so may the purpose of regulation fall into either of these two arenas. The purpose of regulation may be redistributive—to facilitate equal access for the disabled, affirmative action for minorities, or reduction of occupational hazards for employees. Or it may be developmental—to prevent monopolies, eliminate price fixing, guarantee truth in advertising, or require prices to include such externalities as water and air pollution. The blending of objectives may complicate the classification of any particular regulation, but this difficulty does not justify setting up a new category. This study focuses on the use of the fiscal tool in a federal system. A quite distinct study to examine the use of the regulatory tool is badly needed. A strong case can be made that an increasingly integrated society needs a common regulatory framework, yet a common framework may not be sufficiently responsive to the specific needs and circumstances of particular localities.

3. Rawls (1971).

4. Bryce (1921, vol. 1, p. 132).

5. *Statistical Abstract of the United States,* 1992, p. 20, table 22.

6. Bryce (1921, vol. 1, pp. 132–33).

7. When power was decentralized in China, experimentation at local levels facilitated the country's rapid economic growth. Montinola, Qian, and Weingast (1994, p. 20) report that "as the results of the divergent policies [among local governments] became known, policies evolved. Failed experiments were discarded. Successful ones were expanded and imitated."

8. Advisory Commission on Intergovernmental Relations (1992b, p. 76).

9. Ostrom and Whitaker (1974); see also Ostrom and Parks (1973); Ostrom (1983); Rogers and Lipsey (1975).

10. Advisory Commission on Intergovernmental Relations (1992b, p. 76).

11. Schneider (1986, pp. 255–63).

12. Advisory Commission on Intergovernmental Relations (1992b, p. 62).

13. Alonso (1971); Edel (1980).

14. Conlan (1988); Musgrave (1959); Oates (1972); Reagan and Sanzone (1981).

15. Although virtually all block grants are readily identifiable as developmental programs, one can find examples of redistributive programs funded by so-called block grants. The welfare block grant approved by the House in 1995 is the most well known recent example. But even this block grant contains restrictions, such as denial of benefits to immigrants, making it by my definition a categorical grant (however convenient it may be for some politicians to refer to it as a block grant).

16. Peterson, Rabe, and Wong (1986, chap. 3). For a comprehensive examination of one of the largest block grant programs, see Rich (1993).

17. Oates (1972).

18. Rivlin (1992).

19. Oates (1972).

20. Yin (1980).

21. Netherlands Scientific Council for Government Policy (1990, p. 148).

22. Parkinson (1992, pp. 63–81). It may be objected that neither the Netherlands nor Great Britain is a federal system. But that is the point that is being made here. When the national government assumes a large share of the fiscal responsibility, local governments do not have sufficient incentives or enough autonomy to pursue their developmental objectives.

23. On ways to overcome these problems, see Rabe (1994).

24. Bryce (1921, vol. 2, p. 437).

25. Teaford (1984).

26. The course of the debate during the 1980s is thoughtfully reviewed in Graham (1992).

27. Eisinger (1988).

28. Geeta Anand, "Circling of the Welcome Wagons: Selectman Candidates Rip Social Programs," *Boston Globe*, West Weekly Section, March 19, 1995, pp. 1, 8.

29. DeLeon (1992, pp. 2, 171). In 1994, "while the country lurched right, San Francisco's eleven-member board . . . tilted further and further left, with voters booting out the board's sole Republican. Now, an unabashedly radical majority finds itself in the position to override the vetoes of the city's moderate mayor, Frank Jordan." G. Pascal Zachary, "Who Needs Oprah? San Francisco Has Board of Supervisors," *Wall Street Journal*, February 2, 1995, p. A1.

30. *Statistical Abstract of the United States*, 1992, p. 20, table 22.

31. *Shapiro v. Thompson*, 394 U.S. 618 (1969).

32. Reischauer (1971); Steiner (1971).

33. Peterson and Rom (1990, pp. 18–19).

34. Organization for Economic Cooperation and Development (1980).

35. Peterson, Rabe, and Wong (1986).

36. Caro (1974); Hayes (1972); Wolfinger (1974).

37. See, especially, Rivlin (1992).

38. Peterson (1981).

39. Mollenkopf (1983); Stone (1989); Wong (1990).

40. For an analysis of legislative politics consistent with functional theory, see Arnold (1990).

41. Alford and Lee (1968, p. 803); Eulau and Prewitt (1973, p. 380).

42. Thomas and Hrebenar (1992, p. 166). I develop this argument in more detail in Peterson (1981, chap. 6).

43. Vogel (1989, p. 297).

44. Zeigler (1965).

45. Plotke (1992).

46. Cox and McCubbins (1993); Krehbiel (1991); Krehbiel, Shepsle, and Weingast (1987); Smith (1989).

47. Barry (1965, pp. 255–56); Mayhew (1974, p. 88).

48. Markusen, Saxenian, and Weiss (1981a, 1981b).

49. Patterson (1988, p. 31).

50. Henning (1992, p. 212).

51. Peterson (1990, p. 157).

52. Peterson and Greene (1994).

53. The major contributions to this theory have been made by scholars not interested in federalism per se. For the best of a vast literature, see Arnold (1981, pp. 250–87); Ferejohn (1974); Fiorina (1989, 1994); Jacobson (1990); Mayhew (1974); and Shepsle (1978). Legislative theory has given very little explicit attention to the workings of a federal system. The most important work includes Chubb (1985a, 1985b); and Gramlich (1977).

54. Henning (1992, p. 7).

55. Henning (1992, p. 208).

56. Henning (1992, p. 208).

57. James M. Perry, "GOP Congressman Shows How to Keep Power, Even While under Indictment for Corruption," *Wall Street Journal,* June 14, 1994, p. A16.

58. Bach and Smith (1988); Fenno (1973); Fiorina (1989).

59. Peter J. Howe, "State's Share of Federal Dollars Drops," *Boston Globe,* July 2, 1994, p. 17.

60. Plotnick and Winters (1985).

61. Chubb (1985a, 1985b); Ferejohn (1974); Rundquist and Ferejohn (1975); Shepsle and Weingast (1987); Stein and Bickers (1994); Weingast and Marshall (1988).

62. Peltzman (1980).

63. Levitt and Snyder (1995, table 3). The findings reported suggest members actually lose votes. For every additional $20 in redistributive aid a House member's district receives, the member seems to lose one vote. The finding is plausible if it is thought that redistributive money has a negative effect on local economies. (I interpret the categories labeled "low variation" and "high variation" in the Levitt-Snyder study as proxies for redistributive and developmental.)

64. Weaver (1986).

65. Peterson and Rom (1990, pp. 109–10).

66. Coughlin, Ku, and Holahan (1994); Grogan (1994); Holahan and others (1993).

67. On the costs of environmental mandates, see Feiock (1994).

68. Gregory S. Lashutka, "A Mayor's Plea: Mandate No More," *Wall Street Journal,* December 1, 1994, p. A18.
69. Clark and others (1994).
70. Lashutka (1994). See also Conlan (1991); Grogan (1994).
71. Fenno (1966, 1973); Matthews (1960).
72. See the illuminating essays in King (1978).
73. Makin and Ornstein (1993); Schick (1980).
74. Sundquist (1992).

Chapter 3

1. Although I focus on the changing nature of American federalism, I also describe the system's stable features and characterize its overall state. When I emphasize that each level of government is increasingly concentrating on its arena of competence, I also imply and show that each level has already substantially moved in that direction. In other words, it would be wrong to conclude that each level is far from where it should be but is finally beginning to move in the right direction. Instead, each level has come a long way, has been moving in the right direction (at least up until the end of 1994), but has some distance to go.
2. Calculated from data in Fuchs (1992, p. 210).
3. Grodzins (1966). See also Elazar (1962).
4. The expansion of federal programs is discussed in Walker (1995, chaps. 4, 5).
5. Commission on Behavioral and Social Sciences (1985); Levin (1977).
6. Greenstone and Peterson (1973).
7. Birman and others (1987, p. 17).
8. Peterson (1983).
9. Lord (1977, p. 13).
10. Telephone conversation, Department of Housing and Urban Development, Office of Research, August 1992.
11. U.S. Bureau of the Census (1961, vol. 1, table 216, p. 576).
12. U.S. Bureau of the Census (1983, vol. 1, table 101, p. 70).
13. Peterson, Rabe, and Wong (1986, chap. 4).
14. Conlan (1988, p. 175).
15. Bardach (1982); Derthick (1972); Kirp and Jensen (1986); Nakamura and Smallwood (1980); Neustadt and Fineburg (1978); Pressman and Wildavsky (1984); Williams (1980). For a critique of implementation studies, see Anton (1984).
16. Derthick (1972).
17. Peterson, Rabe, and Wong (1986); Pressman and Wildavsky (1984).
18. McKay (1989); Walker (1995).
19. For expenditure data, see sources given in the appendix. Housing information obtained in telephone conversation, Department of Housing and Urban Development, Office of Research, August 1992.
20. See sources given in the appendix.
21. Some may think that intergovernmental grants should be counted as part of the expenditures of the government that actually carries out the

governmental task. The national aid is simply given as an inducement to encourage the state or locality to do something that will benefit itself and its neighbors. The primary consequences are local. For some purposes, such a classification might be appropriate, but my purpose in this book is to provide a political explanation for why each level of government does what it does. To fulfill this purpose, I needed to charge the grant to the account of the government that made the political decision to finance the undertaking.

22. The social security and medicare programs in the United States are sometimes thought to have few redistributive consequences, because they are called insurance programs to which all workers contribute and from which many nonpoor citizens receive benefits. But social security and medicare programs have several redistributive features: the programs do not operate in any way similar to private pension or insurance programs, in which individuals receive benefits proportionate to contributions made or are insured at a rate proportionate to their risk of illness; lower-income workers can expect to receive a much higher rate of return on their contributions to the cost of social security and medicare; those at risk of high medical costs pay no more for medicare benefits and can receive medical benefits at an earlier age than those not at risk; and higher-income recipients must pay a tax on benefits received, while lower-income recipients do not. Poverty rates among the elderly declined from 25 percent in 1970 to 11 percent in 1989, largely because of rising social security and medicare benefits. See Peterson (1992a, pp. 152–53). It is true that social security and medicare, unlike food stamps, medicaid, and other redistributive programs, are not directed solely at individuals of very low income. Although universal coverage helps to sustain political support for the programs, they remain substantially redistributive in character. See Greenstein (1991); Skocpol (1991); Wilson (1991). On the design of social security and medicare programs, see Derthick (1979); Light (1985); Weaver (1988).

23. On the effects of families and schools on student achievement, see Chubb and Moe (1990); Coleman and others (1966); Coleman and Hoffer (1987); Jencks (1979); Jencks and others (1972). On the consequences of compensatory educational programs, see Congressional Budget Office (1987); McLaughlin (1977). The common school has always been more myth than reality. See Glenn (1988).

24. Although the social security program was established in 1935, its initial outlays were very modest. Retirement benefits were established at low levels and were not indexed to inflation, and substantial numbers of workers (including agricultural and domestic workers) were excluded from the program. Medical benefits were not included. Benefits were calculated in proportion to tax contributions, and early contributors had not worked enough years to be eligible for significant benefit levels. Although these limitations on the program were gradually whittled away, the biggest policy changes occurred during the Johnson and Nixon administrations. More workers were covered. Medical insurance was added. Benefits were indexed to inflation in two different ways, allowing them to grow even faster than the increase in the cost of living.

25. The best summary and analysis of these and other changes is to be found in Weaver (1988).

26. Fiorina (1992).

27. Tate (1993, pp. 1–2); Williams (1987).

28. Similar conclusions are reached in Berkman (1993, chap. 5).

29. Fiorina (1994).

30. Bachrach and Baratz (1962).

31. Peterson (1985a).

32. Calculated from data in table 3-5.

33. Weaver (1988, pp. 198–99).

34. Light (1985).

35. Levitt and Snyder (1995, table 4).

36. Bach and Smith (1988); Davidson (1992); Peterson (1992b); Shepsle (1989); Smith (1989).

37. Jorgensen (1995).

38. Bob Hohler, "Mass. Delegation Copes with Diminishing Clout," *Boston Globe,* August 30, 1994, pp. 1, 16.

39. Christopher Georges, "Playing to Growing Antigovernment Sentiment, Many Candidates Criticize Pork-Barrel Projects," *Wall Street Journal,* October 31, 1994, p. A16.

40. Calculated from data in table 3-6.

41. Anton (1989, p. 71).

Chapter 4

1. All propositions concerning expenditure advanced in this chapter and in chapter 6 are to be understood to refer to per capita expenditures, whether or not this is explicitly stated in the text.

2. Thompson (1965).

3. I assume that all variables discussed in this chapter have a normal distribution.

4. See discussion in chapter 3, p. 64.

5. A recent study comparing California with other states uses a similar approach for much the same reasons: "Wherever possible, this report examines revenues and expenditures for state and local governments combined.... The division of responsibilities between state and local governments varies widely from state to state, and it can change within a state over time. As a result, the combined figures for state and local governments provide the best measure of fiscal activity within a state over time and are the most appropriate measures for comparisons across states." Lav, Lazere, and St. George (1994, p. 118).

6. Although Congress was passing Great Society legislation in the mid-1960s, most programs had yet to be implemented at the state and local levels by 1967.

7. Cnudde and McCrone (1969); Dawson and Robinson (1963); Dye (1966); Fry and Winters (1970); Hofferbert (1966); Jennings (1979); Plotnick and Winters (1985, 1990); Winters (1976).

8. Inman (1978).

9. Peltzman (1980). I attribute this position to legislative theory in general even though several studies have identified a negative relationship between poverty rates and redistributive policies. Dawson and Robinson (1963); Peterson (1981); Plotnick and Winters (1985). Despite these findings, I have yet to come across any work by a prominent legislative theorist who incorporates into his or her model the assumption that poverty rates negatively affect redistributive spending. To make such an assumption, the legislative theorist would need to assume that poor people do not vote, that the election prospects of legislators depend significantly on the size of campaign finances (to which the poor can be assumed to contribute little), or that the presence of the poor stimulates the nonpoor to higher rates of political activity. I am unaware of any legislative theorist who uses one or another of these assumptions to predict a negative relationship between poverty and redistributive expenditure.

10. Grogan (1994).

11. Katz (1986).

12. Peterson (1992a).

13. Grofman, Handley, and Niemi (1992); Guinier (1994); Lublin (1994).

14. Erikson, Wright, and McIver (1989); Plotnick and Winters (1990). This result is quite consistent with median-voter models of public decisionmaking. Since both parties are seeking the support of a majority of voters, they both must appeal to the person standing in the middle of the distribution of opinion. If this model works perfectly, one would find no partisan effects on public expenditure. Although some find median voter models of decisionmaking intuitively satisfying, others think policy models need to take into account the influence of party activists, who are often more liberal (in the case of Democrats) or more conservative (in the case of Republicans) than the voter at the median of the opinion distribution. To appeal to these core party supporters, who provide the money and personnel necessary to run a political campaign, legislators from the two parties must differentiate themselves from one another. Alesina and Rosenthal (1995); Alt and Lowry (1994); Hibbs (1987). The results reported below are consistent with this view.

15. Prewitt (1970).

16. Fiorina (1994).

17. Separate equations were run for each year. No statistically significant relationships among variables were observed from one year to the next. Year-by-year dummies were included in the equations presented in table 4-2. They are not reported in the table, because they simply show changes in expenditure over time, as discussed in chapter 3.

18. Citizens in less wealthy states might well desire public services of similar quality, but because they have fewer resources they could afford them only by paying a higher percentage of their income, thereby forgoing other goods and services that they value even more.

19. Similarly, survey research has revealed that political contributions are much more income elastic than are charitable contributions. Verba, Schlozman, and Brady (1995).

Chapter 5

1. Wiseman (1993).
2. U.S. House of Representatives. Committee on Ways and Means (1992, table 45, p. 1371). (Hereinafter *Green Book.*) This report has been issued annually since 1981 and has become one of the most comprehensive sources of information on U.S. social policy.
3. *Green Book,* table 45, p. 1371.
4. *Green Book,* table 37, p. 585.
5. *Green Book,* table 22, pp. 669–70.
6. Jencks (1991, p. 33).
7. *Green Book,* table 24, p. 580; table 30, p. 671.
8. *Green Book,* table 29, pp. 669–70.
9. U.S. Bureau of the Census (1993c). See also Robert Pear, "Ranks of U.S. Poor Reach 35.7 million, the Most since '64," *New York Times,* September 4, 1992, p. A14.
10. *Green Book,,* table 30, p. 671.
11. Peterson and Rom (1990, pp. 146–47).
12. Fiorina (1992, p. 27).
13. Before counting other income, deductions were made, including a standard deduction and, if applicable, a child care deduction, an excess housing cost deduction, and a transportation cost deduction.
14. Peterson and Rom (1990, p. 8).
15. Peterson and Rom (1990, p. 146).
16. *Green Book,* pp. 1013–15.
17. Moffitt (1988).
18. Yet even this best way of estimating policy effects has some disadvantages: it ignores the fact that many welfare programs are not narrowly targeted at the almost poor or the fact that many of those who would have been poor would have found alternative sources of income (such as working or saving) had the program not been in place.
19. Robin Herman, "15% Welfare Grant Wins Passage in Albany," *New York Times,* May 12, 1981, p. B1.
20. Champagne and Harpham (1987, p. 287).
21. *Green Book,* table 11, p. 1209.
22. Peterson and Rom (1990, pp. 8, 12).
23. Fields (1979); Glantz (1973); Lansing and Mueller (1967); Long (1974); Reischauer (1971); Schlottmann and Herzog (1981); Sommers and Suits (1973); Steiner (1971).
24. *Shapiro* v. *Thompson,* 349 U.S. 618 (1969).
25. Peterson and Rom (1990, p. 115).
26. Piven and Cloward (1971). I am not arguing that increasing migration added new recipients to the national welfare rolls. I am only suggesting that access to the rolls was eased for newcomers to states, thereby adding to the total number. This reform, together with numerous other legal and administrative changes, lowered barriers to welfare, accounting for much of the observed increase in welfare use. See Moffitt (1983).

27. In addition to Peterson and Rom (1990), see Blank (1985); Clark (1990); Gramlich and Laren (1984); and Southwick (1981).

28. Peterson and Rom (1990, pp. 78–79).

29. The standard estimate of error is equal to two standard deviations from the mean.

30. *Anderson* v. *Green,* No. 94-97, case pending (1995). See also Linda Greenhouse, "Justices Take On Welfare Benefits Case," *New York Times,* October 8, 1994, p. 10.

31. Wiseman (1993, pp. 49–58).

32. Robert Pear, "House Committee Completes Plan to Overhaul Welfare," *New York Times,* March 4, 1995, p. A9.

Chapter 6

1. In 1995 the House Public Works Committee was renamed Transportation and Infrastructure, and the Education and Labor Committee was renamed Economic Opportunity. Since our analysis covers the period from 1969 to 1991, we shall use the former names.

2. Greenstone and Peterson (1968); Markusen, Saxenian, and Weiss (1981a, 1981b).

3. *New York* v. *U. S.,* 112 S.Ct. 2408 (1992).

4. Advisory Commission on Intergovernmental Relations (1984, pp. 16–48).

5. Anton (1983); Stein (1981); Yin (1980).

6. Markusen, Saxenian, and Weiss (1981b, pp. 6–7).

7. Advisory Commission on Intergovernmental Relations (1984, table 3).

8. Levitt and Snyder (1995, table 3). We interpret their categories of "low variation" and "high variation" as proxies for redistributive and developmental spending.

9. Fenno (1973); Wildavsky (1964).

10. Cox and McCubbins (1991); McCubbins (1991).

11. Arnold (1979); Caraley (1976); Chubb (1985b); DeLeon and LeGates (1976); Dommel (1974); Ferejohn (1974); Friedland and Wong (1983); Goss (1972); Nathan and others (1975); Nathan, Adams, and Associates (1977); Rundquist and Ferejohn (1975).

12. Peterson, Rabe, and Wong (1986).

13. Peterson, Rabe, and Wong (1986).

14. Peterson and Rom (1990).

15. Plotnick and Winters (1985).

16. Peterson and Rom (1990).

17. See chapter 4, pp. 91–93.

18. Markusen, Saxenian, and Weiss (1981b).

19. Grofman, Handley, and Niemi (1992).

20. Hansen (1985); McConnell (1953); Moe (1980).

21. Katz (1986).

22. Barry (1965, pp. 255–56); Cox and McCubbins (1993); Krehbiel (1991); Krehbiel, Shepsle, and Weingast (1987); Mayhew (1974, p. 88); Smith

(1989). If each level of government is to focus on its level of competence, committees of Congress must be controlled by floor majorities to keep them from pursuing biased, inappropriate policies.

23. Chubb (1985a, 1985b); Ferejohn (1974); Hall and Wayman (1990); Rundquist and Ferejohn (1975); Shepsle and Weingast (1987); Stanfield (1985); Stein and Bickers (1994); Weingast and Marshall (1988).

24. Bach and Smith (1988); Fenno (1973); Fiorina (1989).

25. Developmental and redistributive aid were regressed on independent variables in an ordinary least squares equation. To control for overall changes in the level of aid from one year to the next, we included dummy variables for each fiscal year in all equations. (See the appendix for a description of the variables and the sources from which their values were obtained.)

26. Wildavsky (1964).

27. In an analysis not reported in the text, we found that membership on the Senate Public Works and Commerce Committees had a positive effect on the distribution of redistributive assistance, but these committees are not responsible for any significant redistributive programs. Since membership on these committees did not have any discernible effect on the distribution of developmental money, we interpret this result as further evidence that committees do not play an independent role in the Senate.

28. Fenno (1973); Fiorina (1989); Smith and Deering (1984).

29. Fenno (1966); Wildavsky (1964).

30. Fiorina (1989).

31. Davidson (1992); Peterson (1992b); Shepsle (1989).

32. Weingast and Marshall (1988).

33. Krehbiel (1991).

34. Deckard (1973); Fenno (1966, pp. 87–88; 1973, pp. 272–73); Kingdon (1981); Murphy (1968, p. 8).

35. U.S. House of Representatives. Committee on Ways and Means (1990).

36. Weaver (1988).

37. Weaver (1988).

38. Robin Toner, "Health Care Tests Mettle of Ways and Means Panel," *New York Times,* May 8, 1994, p. A1.

39. Smith (1989).

40. Shepsle and Weingast (1987).

41. Katherine Q. Seelye, "Inheriting the Helm of a Vital Panel," *New York Times,* June 1, 1994, p. B7.

42. Fenno (1973); Manley (1969).

43. Alvarez and Saving (1994).

44. Toner, "Health Care Tests Mettle of Ways and Means Panel," p. 22.

45. Birnbaum and Murray (1987).

46. David Rosenbaum, "A Giant Void in Congress," *New York Times,* June 1, 1994, p. A1.

47. Fenno (1973); Smith and Deering (1984).

48. Chubb (1985b) also found that membership on the Education and Labor Committee affected the allocation of education dollars among school districts.

49. Advisory Commission on Intergovernmental Relations (1978, p. 114).

Chapter 7

1. The definition of the Rust Belt used in this chapter includes the cities and states of the Northeast, Mideast, and border-state regions, together with Washington, D.C.; Sun Belt cities are located in the states that are west of the Mississippi or were part of the Old Confederacy.

2. Bradbury, Downs, and Small (1982); Downs (1981); Peterson (1985b).

3. U.S. Bureau of the Census (1953, table 86, pp. 138–40; table 92, pp. 156–58; table 71, pp. 122–23); U.S. Bureau of the Census (1973, table 371, pp. 1694–95); U.S. Bureau of the Census (1993a, table 170, pp. 336–42; table 171, pp. 343–50). I define big cities throughout this chapter as those of more than 300,000 in population.

4. Approximately 20 percent of this decline was due to the fact that the population of four Rust Belt cities fell below 300,000, thereby no longer meeting my definition of what constitutes a big city. The remaining 80 percent of the population decline occurred in the seventeen Rust Belt cities that continued to have populations above 300,000 in 1990.

5. U.S. Bureau of the Census (1953, table 86, pp. 138–40; table 92, pp. 156–58; table 71, pp. 122–23); U.S. Bureau of the Census (1993a, table 170, pp. 336–42; table 171, pp. 343–50).

6. Greenstone (1969).

7. Bridges (1994); Wolfinger and Field (1966).

8. Money given to all local governments includes money given to counties, municipalities, villages, townships, school districts, special districts, and all other local governmental jurisdictions. It is the total amount of money given to all local governments within each region. By comparing monies given to big cities to monies given to all local governments, I am assigning to big-city governments the full set of local government responsibilities. Although many big-city municipalities have responsibility for the full range of local government services, this is not always the case, and to the extent that it is not the case I am underestimating the relative size of big-city revenues and grants.

9. The index was actually the highest in 1957, but this could well be an artifact of the poorer quality of the underlying data in 1957, the first year the Bureau of the Census collected financial data from local governments.

10. I am unable to interpret the widely fluctuating value of the index for 1957 and 1962. I suspect that the quality of the data is much poorer for these years (see note 9).

11. Brecher and Horton (1993) examine in detail the efficiency (or, more exactly, the lack thereof) with which services are provided by New York City's local government. Mollenkopf (1992) describes the politics that perpetuated patterns of inefficient, ineffective government in New York City even under a mayor supposedly committed to rooting them out. Since these are only case studies, they do not by themselves "prove" that the largest Rust Belt city is any less efficient than other local governments. But the material they present is certainly consistent with such a hypothesis.

12. It is for this reason that I have not attempted a regression analysis of the determinants of big-city expenditure. Because the legal responsibilities

of big cities (relative to that of state governments) vary from state to state, an examination of big-city finances that does not take into account these differences in legal responsibilities is subject to serious omitted-variable bias.

13. These twenty-five cities are a subset of the cities discussed elsewhere in this chapter. See data sources cited in the note to table 7-2 for details.

14. Jones (1987). The NAEP study classifies communities into rural, disadvantaged urban areas, and advantaged urban areas. I have relabeled the categories rural, central-city, and suburban areas.

15. Dillon (1911).

16. Elazar (1962); Grodzins (1966).

17. Since my data are taken, for the most part, from the five-year U.S. census of governments, my figures report the fiscal situation for every fifth year beginning in 1957. Although straight lines connect the data points, the actual fiscal trend during the intervening period could well be bumpier, inasmuch as the years for which information was available do not always coincide with the watershed political events that are discussed in the text.

18. Some may think that a better standard of evaluation is to see whether residents of central cities receive back from the national government the same proportion of tax dollars they contribute to national coffers as do suburban and rural residents. As interesting as such an analysis might prove to be, the data were not available.

19. It should be emphasized at this point that my analysis is limited to an examination of intergovernmental grants. It does not include direct national spending for defense, space research, or other programs operated directly by the national government.

Chapter 8

1. Riordon (1963, p. 17).

2. Reich (1991).

3. Rivlin once headed the influential Congressional Budget Office and had served for many years as a senior fellow at the Brookings Institution.

4. Rivlin (1992).

5. Woodward (1994, pp. 127–28).

6. Quoted from a May 1993 issue of *Newsweek* in William F. Powers, "Alice Rivlin's Apolitical Pitch," *Washington Post,* August 9, 1994, p. C6.

7. Adam Clymer, "G.O.P. Senators Prevail, Sinking Clinton's Economic Stimulus Bill," *New York Times,* April 22, 1993, p. A1; Jon Healey, "Rushed Stimulus Package Held Pending Spending Cuts Bill," *Congressional Quarterly Report,* February 27, 1993, pp. 447–49.

8. R.W. Apple, Jr., "Clinton Plan to Remake the Economy Seeks to Tax Energy and Big Incomes," *New York Times,* February 18, 1993, p. A16.

9. Woodward (1994, p. 124).

10. Woodward (1994).

11. Michael Wines, "Job Plan Sounding Less Monumental," *New York Times,* March 26, 1993, p. A16.

12. *Budget of the United States Government, Fiscal Year 1994*; Congressional Budget Office (1994).

13. Domestic Policy Council (1986, p. 3).

14. Peterson and Rom (1990, p. 6).

15. Robert Pear, "House Committee Completes Plan to Overhaul Welfare," *New York Times,* March 4, 1995, p. 9.

16. See discussion in chapter 3, pp. 77–80.

17. Scott Lehigh, "Kennedy Gets a Save at Hanscom," *Boston Globe,* September 8, 1994, p. 25.

18. Todd S. Perdum, "A Rough Stretch of Track for a New Penn Station," *New York Times,* September 21, 1994, p. B1.

19. Anton (1989, p. 226).

20. Peterson and Rom (1990, pp. 146–47).

21. "Welfare Exodus?" *USA Today*, March 15, 1995, p. 3A.

22. *Anderson* v. *Green*, No. 94-97, case pending (1995). See also Linda Greenhouse, "Justices Take On Welfare Benefits Case," *New York Times*, October 8, 1994, p. 10.

23. Some may think that the national government should assume responsibility for more development simply in order to enhance the prestige of the national government at a time when voters have become increasingly distrustful and cynical about government. But if the national government is less capable than local governments of managing development efficiently and effectively, it can hardly win popular respect over the long run by concentrating on its arena of incompetence.

24. Farley (1991, p. 289); see also Farley and Frey (1994). These data are based on trends as of 1980. Farley reported to me in a personal conversation (November 4, 1994) that his preliminary assessment of the 1990 census data reveals no clear reversal—and perhaps a continuation—of the trends throughout the 1980s.

25. Rivlin (1992, pp. 142–52).

26. *San Antonio School District* v. *Rodriguez,* 411 U.S. 1 (1973).

27. Brown and others (1978); Carroll (1979); Odden, Berne, and Stiefel (1979); Underwood and Verstegen (1990).

28. Laura Pappano, "Richer Towns Feel Pinch of School Reform: State Aid Reallocation Targeted," *Boston Globe*, West Weekly Section, March 19, 1995, p.1.

29. Derthick (1972); Downs (1973, 1981); Elmore and McLaughlin (1982); Hochschild (1984).

30. Peirce (1993).

31. Peterson (1993).

32. Lee, Croninger, and Smith (1994).

References

Advisory Commission on Intergovernmental Relations. 1978. *Categorical Grants: Their Role and Design.*

———. 1982. *Tax Capacity of the 50 States: Methodology and Estimates.*

———. 1984. *A Catalog of Federal Grant-In-Aid Programs to State and Local Governments: Grants Funded FY 1984.*

———. 1992a, 1993. *Significant Features of Fiscal Federalism.* Vol. 2.

———. 1992b. *Metropolitan Organization: The Allegheny County Case.*

Alesina, Albert, and Howard Rosenthal. 1995. *Partisan Politics, Divided Government, and the Economy.* Cambridge University Press.

Alford, Robert R., and Eugene C. Lee. 1968. "Voting Turnout in American Cities." *American Political Science Review* 62 (September): 796–813.

Alonso, William. 1971. "Equity and its Relation to Efficiency in Urbanization." In *Essays in Regional Economics,* edited by John F. Kain and John R. Meyer, 40–57. Harvard University Press.

Alt, James E., and Robert C. Lowry. 1994. "Divided Government, Fiscal Institutions, and Budget Deficits: Evidence from the States." *American Political Science Review* 88 (December): 811–28.

Alvarez, R. Michael, and Jason Saving. 1994. "Feeding at the Trough: Committees and the Political Economy of Federal Outlays to Congressional Districts." California Institute of Technology, Division of Social Sciences.

Anton, Thomas J. 1983. "The Regional Distribution of Federal Expenditures, 1971–1980." *National Tax Journal* 36 (December):429–42.

———. 1984. "Intergovernmental Change in the United States: An Assessment of the Literature." In *Public Sector Performance: A Conceptual Turning Point,* edited by Trudi C. Miller, 15–64. Johns Hopkins University Press.

———. 1989. *American Federalism and Public Policy: How the System Works.* Random House.

Arnold, R. Douglas. 1979. *Congress and the Bureaucracy: A Theory of Influence.* Yale University Press.

———. 1981. "The Local Roots of Domestic Policy." In *The New Congress,* edited by Thomas E. Mann and Norman J. Ornstein, 250–87. American Enterprise Institute.

———. 1990. *The Logic of Congressional Action.* Yale University Press.

Bach, Stanley, and Steven S. Smith. 1988. *Managing Uncertainty in the House of Representatives: Adaptation and Innovation in Special Rules.* Brookings.

Bachrach, Peter, and Morton S. Baratz. 1962. "Two Faces of Power." *American Political Science Review* 56 (December): 947–52.

219

Bailey, Thomas A. 1956. *The American Pageant: A History of the Republic.* Little, Brown.

Bardach, Eugene. 1982. *The Implementation Game,* 4th ed. MIT Press.

Barry, Brian M. 1965. *Political Argument.* London: Routledge and Kegan Paul.

Bartik, Timothy J. 1991. *Who Benefits from State and Local Economic Development Policies?* Kalamazoo, Mich.: W. E. Upjohn Institute for Employment Research.

Bartlett, John. 1980. *Bartlett's Familiar Quotations, Revised and Enlarged.* Little, Brown.

Berkman, Michael B. 1993. *The State Roots of National Politics: Congress and the Tax Agenda, 1978–1986.* University of Pittsburgh Press.

Birman, Beatrice F., and others. 1987. *The Current Operation of the Chapter I Program: Final Report from the National Assessment of Chapter I.* U.S. Department of Education, Office of Research, Office of Educational Research and Improvement.

Birnbaum, Jeffrey H., and Alan S. Murray. 1987. *Showdown at Gucci Gulch: Lawmakers, Lobbyists, and the Unlikely Triumph of Tax Reform.* Random House.

Bish, Robert L. 1971. *The Public Economy of Metropolitan Areas.* Chicago: Markham.

Blank, Rebecca M. 1985. "The Impact of State Economic Differentials on Household Welfare and Labor Force Behavior." *Journal of Public Economics* 28 (October): 25–58.

Brace, Paul. 1993. *State Government and Economic Performance.* Johns Hopkins University Press.

Bradbury, Katherine L., Anthony Downs, and Kenneth A. Small. 1982. *Urban Decline and the Future of American Cities.* Brookings.

Brecher, Charles, and Raymond D. Horton with Robert A. Cropf and Dean Michael Mead. 1993. *Power Failure: New York City Politics and Policy since 1960.* Oxford University Press.

Bridges, Amy. 1994. "Morning Glories: The Urban Southwest and the Course of Reform." University of California at San Diego, Department of Political Science.

Brown, Charles C., and Oates, Wallace E. 1986. "Assistance to the Poor in a Federal System." University of Maryland, Department of Economics.

Brown, Lawrence, and others. 1978. "School Finance Reform in the Seventies: Achievements and Failures." *Journal of Education Finance* 4 (Fall): 195–212.

Bryce, James. 1921. *Modern Democracies.* Vols. 1, 2. Macmillan.

Burns, Nancy. 1994. *The Formation of American Local Governments: Private Values in Public Institutions.* Oxford University Press.

Caraley, Demetrios. 1976. "Congressional Politics and Urban Aid." *Political Science Quarterly* 91 (Spring): 19–45.

Caro, Robert A. 1974. *The Power Broker: Robert Moses and the Fall of New York.* Knopf.

Carroll, Stephen J. 1979. *The Search for Equity in School Finance: Results from Five States.* Santa Monica, Calif.: Rand Corporation.

Champagne, Anthony, and Edward J. Harpham, eds. 1987. *Texas at the Crossroads: People, Politics, and Policy.* Texas A & M Press.

Chubb, John E. 1985a. "Federalism and the Bias for Centralization." In *The New Direction in American Politics,* edited by John E. Chubb and Paul E. Peterson, 273–306. Brookings.

———. 1985b. "The Political Economy of Federalism." *American Political Science Review* 79 (December):994–1015.

Chubb, John E., and Terry M. Moe. 1990. *Politics, Markets, and America's Schools.* Brookings.

Clark, Rebecca L. 1990. "Does Welfare Affect Migration?" Discussion Paper. Washington: Urban Institute, Population Studies Center.

Clark, Rebecca, and others. 1994. "The Fiscal Impacts of Illegal Immigration: Selected Evidence from Seven States." Washington: Urban Institute.

Cnudde, Charles F., and Donald J. McCrone. 1969. "Party Competition and Welfare Policies in the American States." *American Political Science Review* 63 (September): 858–66.

Coleman, James S., and others. 1966. *Equality of Educational Opportunity.* U.S. Office of Education.

Coleman, James S., and Thomas Hoffer. 1987. *Public and Private High Schools: The Impact of Communities.* Basic Books.

Commager, Henry Steele, ed. 1958. *Documents of American History.* New York: Appleton-Century-Crofts.

Commission on Behavioral and Social Sciences. National Research Council. 1985. *Youth Employment and Training Programs.* Washington: National Academy Press.

Congressional Budget Office. 1987. *Educational Achievement: Explanations and Implications of Recent Trends.*

———. 1994. *The Economic and Budget Outlook: An Update.*

Conlan, Timothy. 1988. *New Federalism: Intergovernmental Reform from Nixon to Reagan.* Brookings.

———. 1991. "And the Beat Goes On: Intergovernmental Mandates and Preemption in an Era of Deregulation." *Publius* 21(Summer):43–57.

Coughlin, Teresa, Leighton Ku, and John Holahan. 1994. *Medicaid since 1980.* Washington: Urban Institute.

Cox, Gary W., and Mathew D. McCubbins. 1991. "Divided Control of Fiscal Policy." In *The Politics of Divided Government,* edited by Gary W. Cox and Samuel Kernell, 155–75. Westview.

———. 1993. *Legislative Leviathan: Party Government in the House.* University of California Press.

Davidson, Roger H. 1992. "The Emergence of the Postreform Congress." In *The Postreform Congress,* edited by Roger H. Davidson, 3–23. St. Martin's Press.

Dawson, Richard E., and James A. Robinson. 1963. "Inter-party Competition, Economic Variables, and Welfare Policies in the American States." *Journal of Politics* 25 (May):265–89.

Deckard, Barbara. 1973. "State Party Delegations in the United States House of Representatives—An Analysis of Group Action." *Polity* 5 (Spring): 311–34.

DeLeon, Richard, and Richard LeGates. 1976. *Redistribution Effects of Special Revenue Sharing for Community Development.* University of California, Institute of Governmental Studies.

DeLeon, Richard Edward. 1992. *Left Coast City: Progressive Politics in San Francisco, 1975–1991.* University Press of Kansas.

Derthick, Martha. 1972. *New Towns in Town: Why a Federal Program Failed.* Washington: Urban Institute.

———. 1979. *Policymaking for Social Security.* Brookings.

Dillon, John F. 1911. *Commentaries on the Law of Municipal Corporations,* 5th ed. Vol. 1. Little, Brown.

Domestic Policy Council. Low Income Opportunity Working Group. 1986. *Up from Dependency: A New National Assistance Strategy.* Government Printing Office.

Dommel, Paul R. 1974. *The Politics of Revenue Sharing.* Indiana University Press.

Downs, Anthony. 1973. *Opening Up the Suburbs: An Urban Strategy for America.* Yale University Press.

———. 1981. *Neighborhoods and Urban Development.* Brookings.

Dye, Thomas R. 1966. *Politics, Economics and the Public: Policy Outcomes in the American States.* Chicago: Rand McNally.

———. 1990. *American Federalism: Competition among Governments.* Lexington, Mass.: D. C. Heath.

Edel, Matthew. 1980. "People vs. Places in Urban Impact Analysis." In *The Urban Impacts of Federal Policies,* edited by Norman J. Glickman, 175–91. Johns Hopkins University Press.

Eisinger, Peter K. 1988. *The Rise of the Entrepreneurial State: States and Local Economic Development Policy in the United States.* University of Wisconsin Press.

Elazar, Daniel J. 1962. *The American Partnership: Intergovernmental Competition in the Nineteenth-Century United States.* University of Chicago Press.

Elkins, Stanley, and Eric McKitrick. 1993. *The Age of Federalism.* Oxford University Press.

Elmore, Richard F., and Milbrey Wallin McLaughlin. 1982. *Reform and Retrenchment: The Politics of California School Finance Reform.* Cambridge, Mass.: Ballinger.

Erikson, Robert S., Gerald C. Wright, and John P. McIver. 1989. "Political Parties, Public Opinion, and State Policy in the United States." *American Political Science Review* 83 (September): 729–50.

Eulau, Heinz, and Kenneth Prewitt. 1973. *Labyrinths of Democracy.* Indianapolis: Bobbs-Merrill.

Farley, Reynolds. 1991. "Residential Segregation of Social and Economic Groups among Blacks, 1970–1980." In *The Urban Underclass,* edited by Christopher Jencks and Paul E. Peterson, 274–98. Brookings.

Farley, Reynolds, and William H. Frey. 1994. "Changes in the Segregation of Whites from Blacks during the 1980s: Small Steps Toward a More Integrated Society." *American Sociological Review* 59 (February): 23–45.

Federalist, The. 1951. New York: New American Library of World Literature.

Feiock, Richard C. 1994. "Estimating Political, Fiscal and Economic Impacts of State Mandates: A Pooled Time Series Analysis of Local Planning and Growth Policy in Florida." Paper prepared for the annual meeting of the American Political Science Association.

Fenno, Jr., Richard F. 1966. *The Power of the Purse: Appropriations Politics in Congress*. Little, Brown.

————. 1973. *Congressmen in Committees*. Little, Brown.

Ferejohn, John A. 1974. *Pork Barrel Politics*. Stanford University Press.

Fields, Gary S. 1979. "Place-to-Place Migration: Some New Evidence." *Review of Economics and Statistics* 61 (February): 21–32.

Fiorina, Morris. 1989. *Congress: Keystone of the Washington Establishment*, 2d ed. Yale University Press.

————. 1992. *Divided Government*. Macmillan.

————. 1994. "Divided Government in the American States: A Byproduct of Legislative Professionalism?" *American Political Science Review* 88 (June): 304–26.

Friedland, Roger, and Herbert Wong. 1983. "Congressional Politics, Federal Grants and Local Needs: Who Gets What and Why?" In *The Municipal Money Chase: The Politics of Local Government Finance*, edited by Alberta M. Sbragia, 213–44. Westview.

Fry, Brian R., and Richard F. Winters. 1970. "The Politics of Redistribution." *American Political Science Review* 64 (June): 508–22.

Fuchs, Ester. 1992. *Mayors and Money*. University of Chicago Press.

Glantz, Frederic B. 1973. "The Determinants of the Interregional Migration of the Economically Disadvantaged." Research Report 52. Federal Reserve Bank of Boston.

Glenn, Charles Leslie, Jr. 1988. *The Myth of the Common School*. University of Massachusetts Press.

Goss, Carol F. 1972. "Military Committee Membership and Defense-Related Benefits in the House of Representatives." *Western Political Quarterly* 25 (June):215–33.

Graham, Otis L., Jr. 1992. *Losing Time: The Industrial Policy Debate*. Harvard University Press.

Gramlich, Edward M. 1977. "Intergovernmental Grants: A Review of the Empirical Literature." In *The Political Economy of Fiscal Federalism*, edited by Wallace E. Oates, 219–41. Lexington, Mass.: Lexington Books.

Gramlich, Edward M., and Deborah S. Laren. 1984. "Migration and Income Redistribution Responsibilities." *Journal of Human Resources* 19 (Fall): 489–511.

Greenstein, Robert. 1991. "Universal and Targeted Approaches to Relieving Poverty: An Alternative View." In *The Urban Underclass*, edited by Christopher Jencks and Paul E. Peterson, 437–59. Brookings.

Greenstone, J. David. 1969. *Labor in American Politics*. Knopf.

————. 1993. *The Lincoln Persuasion: Remaking American Liberalism*. Princeton University Press.

Greenstone, J. David, and Paul E. Peterson. 1968. "Reformers, Machines, and the War on Poverty." In *City Politics and Public Policy*, edited by James Q. Wilson, 267–92. Wiley.

————. 1973. *Race and Authority in Urban Politics: Community Participation and the War on Poverty*. New York: Russell Sage.

Grodzins, Morton. 1966. *The American System: A New View of Government in the United States*, edited by Daniel J. Elazar. Chicago: Rand McNally.

Grofman, Bernard, Lisa Handley, and Richard G. Niemi. 1992. *Minority Representation and the Quest for Voting Equality*. Cambridge University Press.

Grogan, Colleen M. 1994. "The Influence of Federal Mandates on State Policy Decision-Making." Paper prepared for the annual meeting of the American Political Science Association.

Guinier, Lani. 1994. *The Tyranny of the Majority: Fundamental Fairness in Representative Democracy*. Free Press.

Hall, Richard L., and Frank W. Wayman. 1990. "Buying Time: Moneyed Interests and the Mobilization of Bias in Congressional Committees." *American Political Science Review* 84 (September): 797–820.

Hansen, John Mark. 1985. "The Political Economy of Group Membership." *American Political Science Review* 79 (March): 79–96.

Hayes, Edward C. 1972. *Power Structure and Urban Policy: Who Rules in Oakland?* McGraw-Hill.

Hayward, Steven. 1993. "West of Eden: California's Economic Fall." *Policy Review* 65 (Summer):42–47.

Henning, Chuck, comp. 1992. *The Wit and Wisdom of Politics: Expanded Edition*. Golden, Colo.: Fulcrum.

Hibbs, Douglas A., Jr. 1987. *The American Political Economy*. Harvard University Press.

Hochschild, Jennifer L. 1984. *The New American Dilemma: Liberal Democracy and School Desegregation*. Yale University Press.

Hofferbert, Richard I. 1966. "The Relation between Public Policy and Some Structural and Environmental Variables in the American States." *American Political Science Review* 60 (March):73–82.

Holahan, John, and others. 1993. "Explaining the Recent Growth in Medicaid Spending." *Health Affairs* 12 (Fall):177–93.

Inman, Robert P. 1978. "Testing Political Economy's 'As if' Proposition: Is the Median Income Voter Really Decisive?" *Public Choice* 33(4): 45–65.

Jacobson, Gary C. 1990. *The Electoral Origins of Divided Government: Competition in U. S Elections, 1946—88*. Westview.

Jencks, Christopher. 1979. *Who Gets Ahead? The Determinants of Economic Success in America*. Basic Books.

———. 1991. "Is the American Underclass Growing?" In *The Urban Underclass*, edited by Christopher Jencks and Paul E. Peterson, 28–102. Brookings.

Jencks, Christopher, and others. 1972. *Inequality: A Reassessment of the Effect of Family and Schooling in America*. Basic Books.

Jennings, Edward T., Jr. 1979. "Competition, Constituencies, and Welfare Policies in American States." *American Political Science Review* 73 (June):414–29.

Jones, Lyle V. 1987. "Achievement Trends for Black School Children, 1970 to 1984." University of North Carolina, Chapel Hill.

Jorgensen, Miriam. 1995. "The Changing Popularity of Congressional Committees." Occasional Paper. Harvard University, Department of Government, Center for American Political Studies.

Katz, Michael B. 1986. *In the Shadow of the Poorhouse: A Social History of Welfare in America*. Basic Books.

King, Anthony, ed. 1978. *The New American Political System*. American Enterprise Institute.

Kingdon, John. 1981. *Congressmen's Voting Decisions*. Harper and Row.

Kirp, David L., and Donald N. Jensen, eds. 1986. *School Days, Rule Days: The Legislation and Regulation of Education*. Philadelphia: Falmer.

Krehbiel, Keith. 1991. *Information and Legislative Organization*. University of Michigan Press.

Krehbiel, Keith, Kenneth A. Shepsle, and Barry Weingast. 1987. "Controversy: Why Are Congressional Committees Powerful?" *American Political Science Review* 81(September): 929–45.

Ladd, Helen F., and Fred C. Doolittle. 1982. "Which Level of Government Should Assist the Poor?" *National Tax Journal* 35 (September):323–36.

Lansing, John B., and Eva Mueller. 1967. *The Geographic Mobility of Labor*. University of Michigan, Survey Research Center.

Lashutka, Gregory S. 1994. "Local Rebellion: How Cities Are Rising Up against Unfunded Mandates." *Commonsense* 1 (Summer):66–72.

Lav, Iris J., Edward B. Lazere, and Jim St. George. 1994. *A Tale of Two Futures: Restructuring California's Finances to Boost Economic Growth*. Washington: Center on Budget and Policy Priorities.

Lee, Valerie, Robert Croninger, and Julia Smith. 1994. "Parental Choice of Schools and Social Stratification in Education: The Paradox of Detroit." *Educational Evaluation and Policy Analysis* 16 (Winter): 434–57.

Levin, Henry M. 1977. "A Decade of Policy Developments in Improving Education and Training." In *A Decade of Federal Anti-Poverty Policy*, edited by Robert Haveman, 123–88. New York: Academic Press.

Levitt, Steven D., and James M. Snyder, Jr. 1995. "The Impact of Federal Spending on House Election Outcomes." Working Paper 5002. National Bureau of Economic Research (September).

Light, Paul. 1985. *Artful Work: The Politics of Social Security Reform*. Random House.

Long, Larry H. 1974. "Poverty Status and Receipt of Welfare among Migrants and Nonmigrants in Large Cities." *American Sociological Review* 39 (February):46–56.

Lord, Tom. 1977. *Decent Housing: A Promise to Keep*. Cambridge, Mass.: Schenkman.

Lublin, David. 1994. "Gerrymander for Justice? Racial Redistricting and Black and Latino Representation." Ph.D. dissertation, Harvard University.

McConnell, Grant. 1953. *The Decline of Agrarian Democracy*. University of California Press.

McCubbins, Mathew D. 1991. "Government on Lay-Away: Federal Spending and Deficits under Divided Party Control." In *The Politics of Divided Government*. edited by Gary W. Cox and Samuel Kernell, 113–53. Westview.

McKay, David. 1989. *Domestic Policy and Ideology: Presidents and the American State, 1964–1987*. Cambridge University Press.

McLaughlin, Donald H. 1977. *Title I, 1965–1975: A Synthesis of the Findings of Federal Studies*. Palo Alto, Calif.: American Institutes for Research in the Behaviorial Sciences.

Makin, John H., and Norman J. Ornstein. 1993. *Debt and Taxes: Politics and Fiscal Policy in America*. American Enterprise Institute.

Manley, John F. 1969. "Wilbur D. Mills: A Study in Congressional Influence." *American Political Science Review* 63 (June):442–64.

Markusen, Ann R., Annalee Saxenian, and Marc A. Weiss. 1981a. "Who Benefits from Intergovernmental Transfers?" In *Cities under Stress: The Fiscal Crises of Urban America,* edited by Robert Burchell and David Listokin, 617–64. Rutgers University Press.

———. 1981b. "Who Benefits from Intergovernmental Transfers?" *Publius* (Winter):5–35.

Matthews, Donald R. 1960. *U.S. Senators and Their World.* University of North Carolina Press.

Mayhew, David R. 1974. *The Electoral Connection.* Yale University Press.

Miller, Gary. 1981. *Cities by Contract: The Politics of Municipal Incorporation.* MIT Press.

Moe, Terry M. 1980. *The Organization of Interests: Incentives and the Internal Dynamics of Political Interest Groups.* University of Chicago Press.

Moffitt, Robert. 1983. "An Economic Model of Welfare Stigma." *American Economic Review* 73 (December):1023–35.

———. 1988. "Has State Redistribution Policy Grown More Conservative?" Working Paper 88-5. Brown University and National Bureau of Economic Research.

Mollenkopf, John H. 1983. *The Contested City.* Princeton University Press.

———. 1992. *A Phoenix in the Ashes: The Rise and Fall of the Koch Coalitions in New York City Politics.* Princeton University Press.

Montinola, Gabriella, Yingyi Qian, and Barry R. Weingast. 1994. "Federalism, Chinese Style: The Political Basis for Economic Success in China." Stanford University, Department of Political Science.

Murphy, James T. 1968. "Partisanship and the House Public Works Committee." Paper prepared for the annual meeting of the American Political Science Association.

Musgrave, Richard A. 1959. *The Theory of Public Finance.* McGraw-Hill.

Nakamura, Robert T., and Frank Smallwood. 1980. *The Politics of Policy Implementation.* St. Martin's Press.

Nathan, Richard P., and others. 1975. *Monitoring Revenue Sharing.* Brookings.

Nathan, Richard P., Charles F. Adams, and Associates. 1977. *Revenue Sharing: The Second Round.* Brookings.

Netherlands Scientific Council for Government Policy. 1990. *Institutions and Cities: The Dutch Experience.* Report to the Government 37. The Hague, Netherlands.

Neustadt, Richard E., and Harvey V. Fineburg. 1978. *The Swine Flu Affair: Decision-making on a Slippery Disease.* U.S. Department of Health, Education and Welfare.

Oates, Wallace E. 1972. *Fiscal Federalism.* Harcourt, Brace, Jovanovich.

Odden, Allan, Robert Berne, and Leanna Stiefel. 1979. *Equity in School Finance.* Denver, Colo.: Education Finance Center, Education Commission of the States.

Organization for Economic Cooperation and Development. Committee on Fiscal Affairs. 1980. *The Tax/Benefit Position of Selected Income Groups in OECD Member Countries, 1974–1978.*

Ostrom, Elinor. 1983. "Equity in Police Services." In *Evaluating Performance of Criminal Justice Agencies,* edited by Gordon P. Whitaker and Charles David Philips, 99–125. Beverly Hills, Calif.: Sage.

Ostrom, Elinor, and Roger B. Parks. 1973. "Suburban Police Departments: Too Many and Too Small?" In *The Urbanization of the Suburbs,* edited by L. H. Masotti and J. K. Hadden, 367–402. Urban Affairs Annual Review 7. Beverly Hills, Calif.: Sage.

Ostrom, Elinor, and Gordon P. Whitaker. 1974. "Community Control and Governmental Responsiveness: The Case of Police in Black Neighborhoods." In *Improving the Quality of Urban Management,* edited by David A. Rogers and Willis Hawley, 303–34. Urban Affairs Annual Review 8. Beverly Hills, Calif.: Sage.

Parkinson, M. 1992. "Leadership and Urban Regeneration: Britain and the Rise of the 'Entrepreneurial' European City." In *Debating Institutions and Cities: Proceedings of the Anglo-Dutch Conference on Urban Regeneration,* edited by A. J. J. Kruekels and W. G. M. Salet, 63–81. Preliminary and Background Studies 76. The Hague, Netherlands: Netherlands Scientific Council for Government Policy.

Patterson, Bradley H., Jr. 1988. *The Ring of Power: The White House Staff and Its Expanding Role in Government.* Basic Books.

Paulson, Linda Dailey, and others. 1992. "Blundering Toward a Budget." *California Journal* 23 (September):425–30.

Peirce, Neal R., with Curtis W. Johnson and John Stuart Hall. 1993. *Citistates: How Urban America Can Prosper in a Competitive World.* Washington: Seven Locks Press.

Peltzman, Sam. 1980. "The Growth of Government." *Journal of Law and Economics* 23 (October):209–87.

Peterson, Mark A. 1990. *Legislating Together: The White House and Capitol Hill from Eisenhower to Reagan.* Harvard University Press.

Peterson, Paul E. 1979. "A Unitary Model of Local Taxation and Expenditure Policies in the United States." *British Journal of Political Science* 9 (September): 281–314.

———. 1981. *City Limits.* University of Chicago Press.

———. 1983. "Background Paper." In Twentieth Century Fund Task Force on Federal Elementary and Secondary Education Policy, *Making the Grade.* New York: Twentieth Century Fund.

———. 1985a. "The Politics of Deficits." In *The New Direction in American Politics,* edited by John E. Chubb and Paul E. Peterson, 365–98. Brookings.

———, ed. 1985b. *The New Urban Reality.* Brookings.

———. 1992a. "An Immodest Proposal." *Daedalus* 121 (Fall): 151–74.

———. 1992b. "The Rise and Fall of Special Interest Politics." In *The Politics of Interests: Interest Groups Transformed,* edited by Mark P. Petracca, 326–42. Westview.

———. 1993. "Are Big City Schools Holding Their Own?" In *Seeds of Crisis: Public Schooling in Milwaukee since 1920,* edited by John L. Rury and Frank A. Cassell, 269–301. University of Wisconsin Press.

———. Forthcoming. "The Domestic and International Sources of U.S. Deficits." In *The United States after the Cold War,* edited by Herbert Dittgen and Michael Minkenberg. University of Pittsburgh Press.

Peterson, Paul E., and Jay P. Greene. 1994. "Why Executive-Legislative Conflict in the United States Is Dwindling." *British Journal of Political Science* 24 (January):33–56.

Peterson, Paul E., Barry G. Rabe, and Kenneth K. Wong. 1986. *When Federalism Works.* Brookings.

Peterson, Paul E., and Mark C. Rom. 1990. *Welfare Magnets: A New Case for a National Standard.* Brookings.

Piven, Frances Fox, and Richard A. Cloward. 1971. *Regulating the Poor: The Functions of Public Welfare.* New York: Pantheon.

Plotke, David. 1992. "The Political Mobilization of Business." In *The Politics of Interests: Interest Groups Transformed,* edited by Mark P. Petracca, 175–98. Westview.

Plotnick, Robert D., and Richard F. Winters. 1985. "A Politico-Economic Theory of Income Redistribution." *American Political Science Review* 70 (June):458–73.

———. 1990. "Party, Political Liberalism, and Redistribution: An Application to the American States." *American Politics Quarterly* 18 (October):430–58.

Pressman, Jeffrey L., and Aaron Wildavsky. 1984. *Implementation,* 3d ed. University of California Press.

Prewitt, Kenneth. 1970. "Political Ambition, Volunteerism, and Electoral Accountability." *American Political Science Review* 64 (March):5–17.

Rabe, Barry G. 1994. *Beyond NIMBY: Hazardous Waste Siting in Canada and the United States.* Brookings.

Rawls, John. 1971. *A Theory of Justice.* Harvard University Press.

Reagan, Michael E., and John G. Sanzone. 1981. *The New Federalism,* 2d ed. Oxford University Press.

Reich, Robert B. 1991. *The Work of Nations: Preparing Ourselves for Twentieth Century Capitalism.* Knopf.

Reischauer, Robert D. 1971. "The Impact of the Welfare System on Black Migration and Marital Stability." Ph.D. dissertation, Columbia University.

Rich, Michael J. 1993. *Federal Policy-making and the Poor: National Goals, Local Choices, and Distributional Outcomes.* Princeton University Press.

Riordon, William L. 1963. *Plunkitt of Tammany Hall.* New York: E. P. Dutton.

Rivlin, Alice M. 1992. *Reviving the American Dream: The Economy, the States, and the Federal Government.* Brookings.

Rogers, Bruce D., and C. McCurdy Lipsey. 1975. "Metropolitan Reform: Citizen Evaluations of Performances in Nashville-Davidson County, Tennessee." *Publius* 4 (Fall): 19–34.

Rose-Ackerman, Susan. 1983. "Tiebout Models and the Competitive Ideal: An Essay on the Political Economy of Local Government." In *Perspectives on Local Public Finance and Public Policy,* edited by John Quigley, 23–46. Vol. 1. Greenwich, Conn.: JAI Press.

Rundquist, Barry S., and John A. Ferejohn. 1975. "Observations on a Distributive Theory of Policy-Making: Two American Expenditure Programs Compared."

In *Comparative Public Policy: Issues, Theories, and Methods,* edited by Craig Liske, William Loehr, and John McCamant, 87–108. Wiley.

Schick, Allen. 1980. *Congress and Money: Budgeting, Spending, and Taxing.* Washington: Urban Institute.

Schlottmann, Alan M., and Henry W. Herzog, Jr. 1981. "Employment Status and the Decision to Migrate." *Review of Economics and Statistics* 63 (November):590–98.

Schneider, Mark. 1986. "Fragmentation and the Growth of Government." *Public Choice* 48(3):255–63.

Shepsle, Kenneth A. 1978. *The Giant Jigsaw Puzzle: Democratic Committee Assignments in the Modern House.* University of Chicago Press.

———. 1989. "The Changing Textbook Congress." In *Can the Government Govern?* edited by John E. Chubb and Paul E. Peterson, 238–66. Brookings.

Shepsle, Kenneth A., and Barry R. Weingast. 1987. "The Institutional Foundations of Committee Power." *American Political Science Review* 81 (March):85–104.

Skocpol, Theda. 1991. "Targeting within Universalism: Politically Viable Policies to Combat Poverty in the United States." In *The Urban Underclass,* edited by Christopher Jencks and Paul E. Peterson, 411–36. Brookings.

———. 1992. *Protecting Soldiers and Mothers: The Political Origins of Social Policy in the United States.* Belknap Press of Harvard University Press.

Smith, Steven S. 1989. *Call to Order: Floor Politics in the House and Senate.* Brookings.

Smith, Steven S., and Christopher J. Deering. 1984. *Committees in Congress.* Congressional Quarterly Press.

Sommers, Paul M., and Daniel B. Suits. 1973. "Analysis of Net Interstate Migration." *Southern Economic Journal* 40 (October):193–201.

Southwick, Lawrence, Jr. 1981. "Public Welfare Programs and Recipient Migration." *Growth and Change* 12 (October):22–32.

Stanfield, Rochelle L. 1985. "Playing Computer Politics with Local Aid Formulas." In *American Intergovernmental Relations,* edited by Laurence J. O'Toole, 172–77. Congressional Quarterly Press.

Stein, Robert M. 1981. "The Allocation of Federal Aid Monies: The Synthesis of Demand-Side and Supply-Side Explanations." *American Political Science Review* 75 (June):334–43.

———. 1990. *Urban Alternatives: Public and Private Markets in the Provision of Local Services.* University of Pittsburgh Press.

Stein, Robert M., and Kenneth N. Bickers. 1994. "Universalism and the Electoral Connection: A Test and Some Doubts." *Political Research Quarterly* 47 (June): 295–317.

Steiner, Gilbert Y. 1971. *The State of Welfare.* Brookings.

Stone, Clarence. 1989. *Regime Politics: Governing Atlanta, 1946–1988.* University Press of Kansas.

Sundquist, James. 1992. *Constitutional Reform and Effective Government,* 2d ed. Brookings.

Tate, Katherine. 1993. *From Protest to Politics: The New Black Voters in American Elections.* Harvard University Press.

Tax Foundation. 1969, 1973, 1983, 1992. *Facts and Figures on Government Finance*. Washington: Tax Foundation.

Teaford, Jon C. 1984. *The Unheralded Triumph: City Government in America, 1870–1900*. Johns Hopkins University Press.

Thomas, Clive S., and Ronald J. Hrebenar. 1992. "Changing Patterns of Interest Group Activity: A Regional Perspective." In *The Politics of Interests: Interest Groups Transformed*, edited by Mark P. Petracca, 150–74. Westview.

Thompson, Wilbur R. 1965. *A Preface to Urban Economics*. Johns Hopkins University Press.

Tiebout, Charles M. 1956. "A Pure Theory of Local Expenditures." *Journal of Political Economy* 64 (October):416–24.

Underwood, Julie K., and Deborah A. Verstegen, eds. 1990. *The Impacts of Litigation and Legislation on Public School Finance: Adequacy, Equity and Excellence*. New York: Ballinger.

U.S. Bureau of the Census. 1953. *U.S. Census of Population: 1950*. Vol. 2: *Characteristics of the Population*. Part 1: *United States Summary*.

———. 1961. *U.S. Census of Population: 1960*. Vol. 1: *Characteristics of the Population*. Part 1: *United States Summary*.

———. 1973. *U.S. Census of Population: 1970*. Vol. 1: *Characteristics of the Population*. Part 1: *United States Summary*. Section 2.

———. 1983. *U.S. Census of Population: 1980*. Vol. 1: *Characteristics of the Population*. Part 1: *United States Summary: General Social and Economic Characteristics*.

———. 1993a. *1990 Census of Population, Social and Economic Characteristics: United States*.

———. 1992, 1993b. *State Government Finances*. GF Series.

———. 1993c. "Poverty in the United States." *Current Population Reports*. Series P-60, no. 185.

U.S. House of Representatives. Committee on Ways and Means. 1981 and subsequent years. *Overview of Entitlement Programs: Background Material and Data on Programs within the Jurisdiction of the Committee on Ways and Means*. Committee Print. Government Printing Office.

Verba, Sidney, Kay Schlozman, and Henry Brady. 1995. *Voice and Equality: Civic Voluntarism in American Politics*. Harvard University Press.

Vogel, David. 1989. *Fluctuating Fortunes: The Political Power of Business in America*. Basic Books.

Walker, David B. 1995. *The Rebirth of Federalism: Slouching toward Washington*. Chatham, N.J.: Chatham House.

Weaver, R. Kent. 1986. "The Politics of Blame Avoidance." *Journal of Public Policy* 6 (October–December):371–98.

———. 1988. *Automatic Government: The Politics of Indexation*. Brookings.

Weingast, Barry R., and William Marshall. 1988. "The Industrial Organization of Congress." *Journal of Political Economy* 96 (February):132–63.

Wildavsky, Aaron B. 1964. *The Politics of the Budgetary Process*. Little, Brown.

Williams, Linda. 1987. "Black Political Progress in the 1980's: The Electoral Arena." In *The New Black Politics*, edited by M. Preston, L. Henderson, and P. Puryear, 97–136, 2d ed. New York: Longman Press.

Williams, Walter. 1980. *The Implementation Perspective: A Guide for Managing Social Service Delivery Programs.* University of California Press.

Wilson, William Julius. 1991. "Public Policy Research and the Truly Disadvantaged." In *The Urban Underclass,* edited by Christopher Jencks and Paul E. Peterson, 460–82. Brookings.

Winters, Richard F. 1976. "Party Control and Policy Change." *American Journal of Political Science* 20 (November):597–636.

Wiseman, Michael. 1993. "The New State Welfare Initiatives." Discussion Paper 1002–93. University of Wisconsin-Madison, Institute for Research on Poverty.

Wolfinger, Raymond E. 1974. *The Politics of Progress.* Prentice-Hall.

Wolfinger, Raymond E., and John Osgood Field. 1966. "Political Ethos and the Structure of City Government." *American Political Science Review* 60 (June):306–26.

Wong, Kenneth K. 1990. *City Choices: Education and Housing.* State University of New York Press.

Woodward, Bob. 1994. *The Agenda: Inside the Clinton White House.* Simon and Schuster.

Yin, Robert K. 1980. "Creeping Federalism: The Federal Impact on the Structure and Function of Local Government." In *The Urban Impacts of Federal Policies,* edited by Norman J. Glickman, 595–618. Johns Hopkins University Press.

Zeigler, Harmon. 1965. "Interest Groups in the States." In *Politics in the American States: A Comparative Analysis.* edited by Virginia Gray, Herbert Jacob, and Kenneth N. Vines, 101–47. 1st ed. Little, Brown.

Index